# DO I HAVE TO DRAW YOU A PICTURE?

Jack Ohman

Foreword by Steve Kelley

**PELICAN PUBLISHING COMPANY**
Gretna 1997

*To my wife, Jan, and our wonderful children, Eric, Julia, and Bobby*

---

*The word "Pelican" and the depiction of a pelican are trademarks
of Pelican Publishing Company, Inc., and are registered in the U.S. Patent and Trademark Office.*

---

**Library of Congress Cataloging-in-Publication Data**

Ohman, Jack.
    Do I have to draw you a picture? / Jack Ohman ; foreword by Steve
Kelley.
      p. cm.
    ISBN 1-56554-298-3 (pb)
    1. United States—Politics and government—1993- —Caricatures and
cartoons. 2. American wit and humor, Pictorial. 3. Editorial
cartoons—United States. I. Title.
    F.885.038 1997
    973.929'022'2—dc21                                 97-25641
                                                       CIP

Manufactured in the United States of America

Published by Pelican Publishing Company, Inc.
1101 Monroe Street, Gretna, Louisiana 70053

# Contents

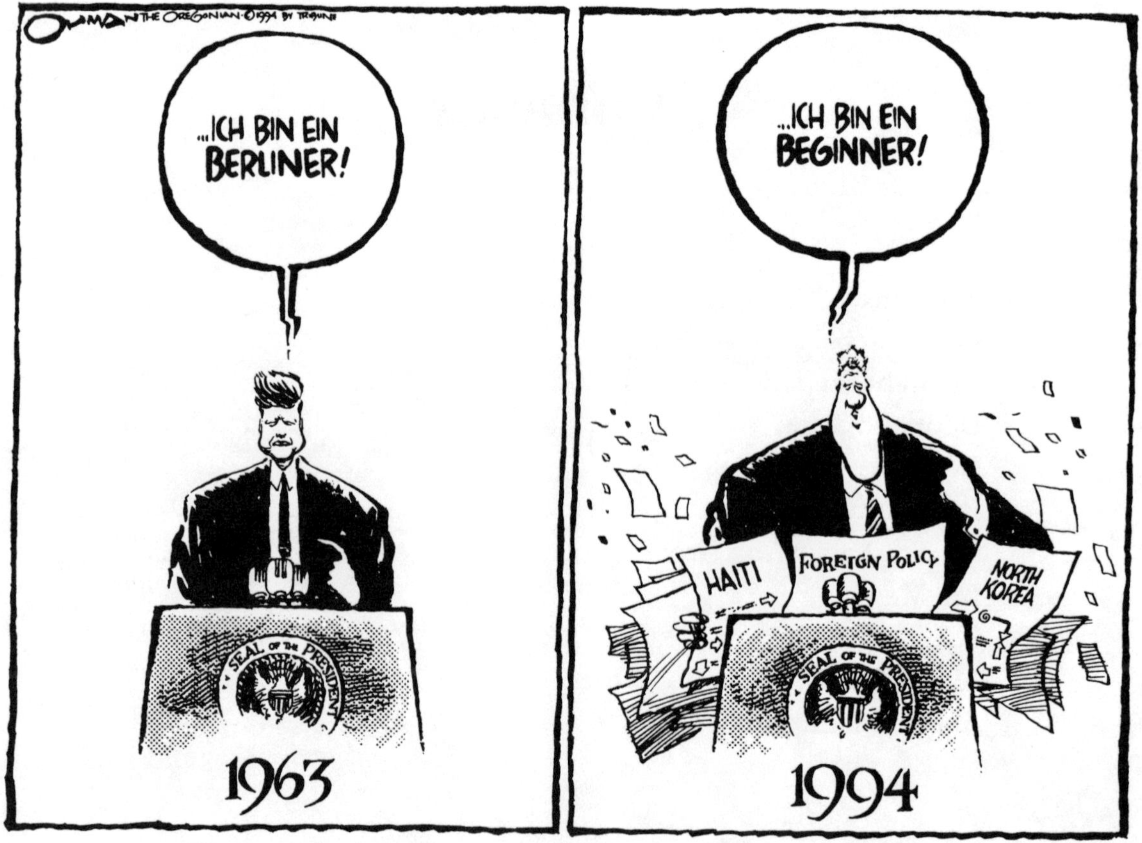
OHMAN THE OREGONIAN ©1994 BY TRIBUNE
...ICH BIN EIN BERLINER!
SEAL OF THE PRESIDENT
1963
...ICH BIN EIN BEGINNER!
HAITI
FOREIGN POLICY
NORTH KOREA
SEAL OF THE PRESIDENT
1994

# Foreword

My first clear recollection of Jack Ohman is that at a tender age he was disliked by virtually every political cartoonist in the country. More to the point, I suppose, it was because of his tender age.

In the early eighties, Jack's cartoons began turning up with alarming regularity in places ordinarily reserved for the masters of his profession. Many of the grizzled veterans of political cartooning whose work had been fashionable for decades found themselves being eclipsed by this whippersnapper savant from Minnesota who had yet to choose his major. *Time* and *Newsweek* were reprinting him weekly, often twice in a single issue. Ted Koppel started showcasing Ohman cartoons on "Nightline." *People* magazine ran a splashy story about journalism's new boy genius. Other cartoonists couldn't help noticing. And they didn't like it.

Not long after I realized who Jack Ohman was, I graduated from college and joined the ranks of those who envied him. I had struggled through my job drawing cartoons in San Diego for about two weeks when a slick marketing package arrived from the Chicago Tribune Syndicate with Jack, age twenty, on the cover. He was pictured full length, with perfect hair, in the midst of a purposeful stride. He wore a suit, tie, and wing tips, hands thrust into the pockets of a trench coat that was cinched tightly at the waist. I mean, a cartoonist in a trench coat? Please. Cartoonists are guys with three-day beards and ink stains on their pants. I thought Ohman looked like some preppy White House correspondent off to file his story in front of the West Wing.

That was my last thought about Jack for several years. I continued to see his cartoons everywhere, but he didn't attend the convention of editorial cartoonists where most of us venture once a year to get better acquainted (OK, drunk). People mentioned his work on occasion, but no one knew him. We just assumed that Trench Coat Boy was too busy depositing royalty checks to mix with the likes of us.

Then a visit to the home of a friend took me to Portland in 1984. On a lark, I telephoned Jack Ohman at the *Oregonian* to see if Mr. Big Shot might like to have lunch. To my complete surprise, he accepted.

His office was smaller than I anticipated and cluttered just enough to suggest too much work and too little time, an appearance coveted by journalists to keep visitors from staying too long ("Well, I can see you're busy so I won't take any more of your time . . ."). The only annoying element in the whole place was that damned trench coat, which hung rakishly on a hook by the door like a stage prop.

We walked to a restaurant near the paper. The sky was heavily overcast and foreboding, a meteorological phenomenon that on my visit was being referred to as "Friday." Jack ordered a hamburger for lunch and I had crab cakes, which I recommend if you like sticky bread crumbs with paprika on them. We exchanged the usual biographical data and played a few rounds of "Who's Got the Toughest Editor?" I think I won, but Jack clearly prevailed in the unacknowledged game of "Who's Got the Best Education?" Jack had apparently approached academia with more gusto than I. He had studied political science out of an intense intellectual curiosity about the subject. I had majored in English because, hey, I already spoke the language—how hard could it be?

I had always admired Jack's work for its technical and analytical precision. While other cartoonists routinely rely upon blunt clichés and lame one-liners, Jack's cartoons reflect a sharper command of the issues. There's an underlying sense that he is simply better informed than everyone else in the debate; that he has the goods. Rather than bashing public figures who step out of line, Jack Ohman's cartoons seem to prosecute them.

I've come to believe that the years preceding a guy's first forty years are meant for accomplishing things to ease the anxiety of his mid-life crisis. If that's the case, then Jack won't be buying any red Corvettes when he passes that milestone three years from now. His award-winning political cartoons are syndicated to more than 150 papers, and his comic strip, "Mixed Media," appears in 175. He has published nine books now, including two on fly-fishing and one on golf. He is married to free-lance writer Jan Ohman, and together the couple look as though they should be coanchoring a local news broadcast. They have three perfect children.

Although I didn't realize it as we left the restaurant in one of Oregon's torrential downpours, my lunch with Jack Ohman had begun a friendship that will no doubt last for life. It also taught me a couple of worthwhile lessons. First, never order crab cakes at that restaurant. And more importantly, if you're going outside in Portland, get yourself a really good trench coat.

STEVE KELLEY
Editorial Cartoonist
*The San Diego Union-Tribune*

# OVER THERE

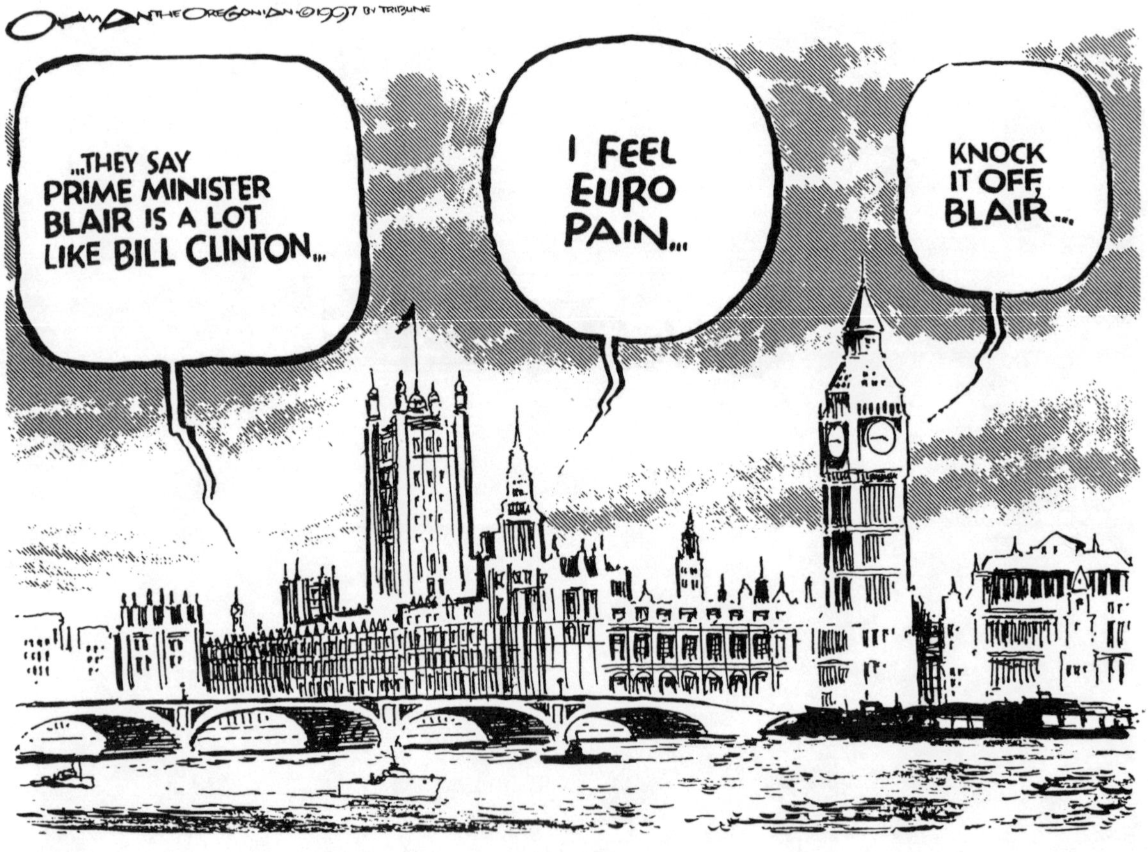
OLIPHANT THE OREGONIAN ©1997 BY TRIBUNE
...THEY SAY PRIME MINISTER BLAIR IS A LOT LIKE BILL CLINTON...
I FEEL EURO PAIN...
KNOCK IT OFF, BLAIR...

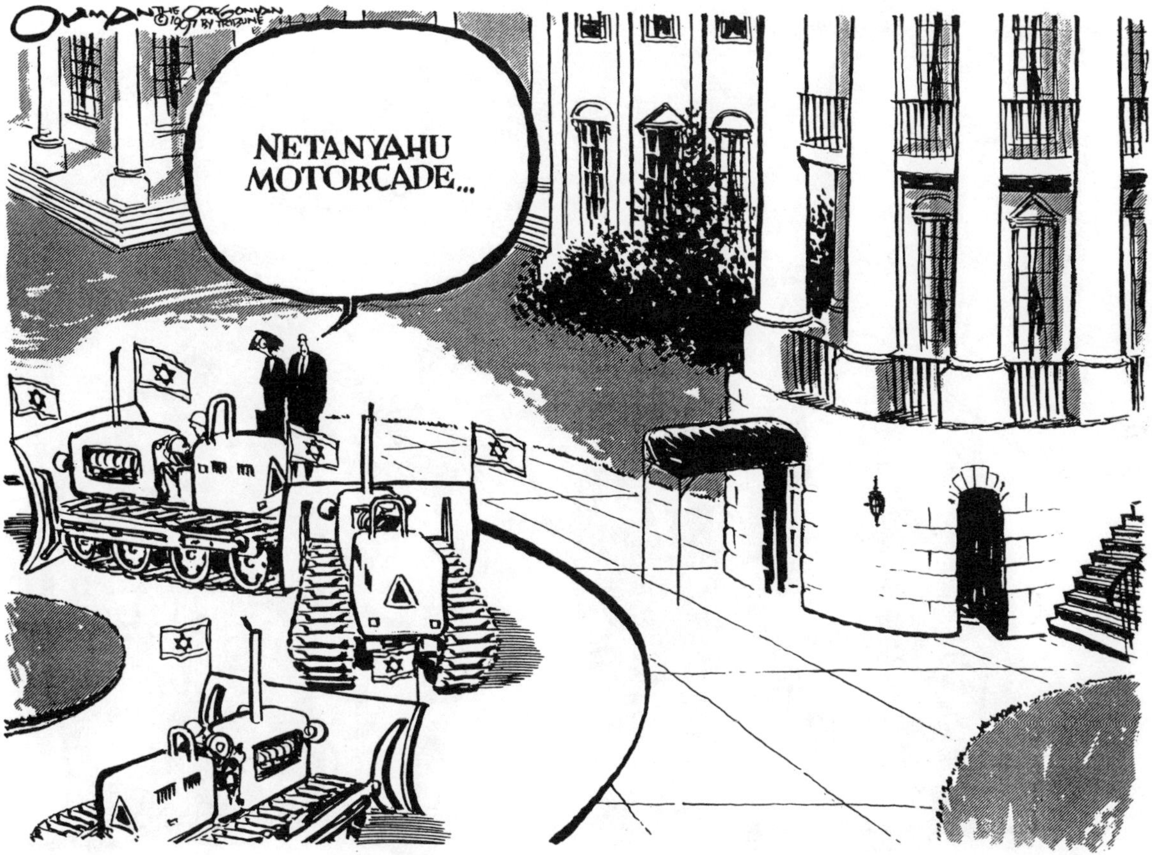
OHMAN THE OREGONIAN ©1997 BY TRIBUNE
NETANYAHU MOTORCADE...

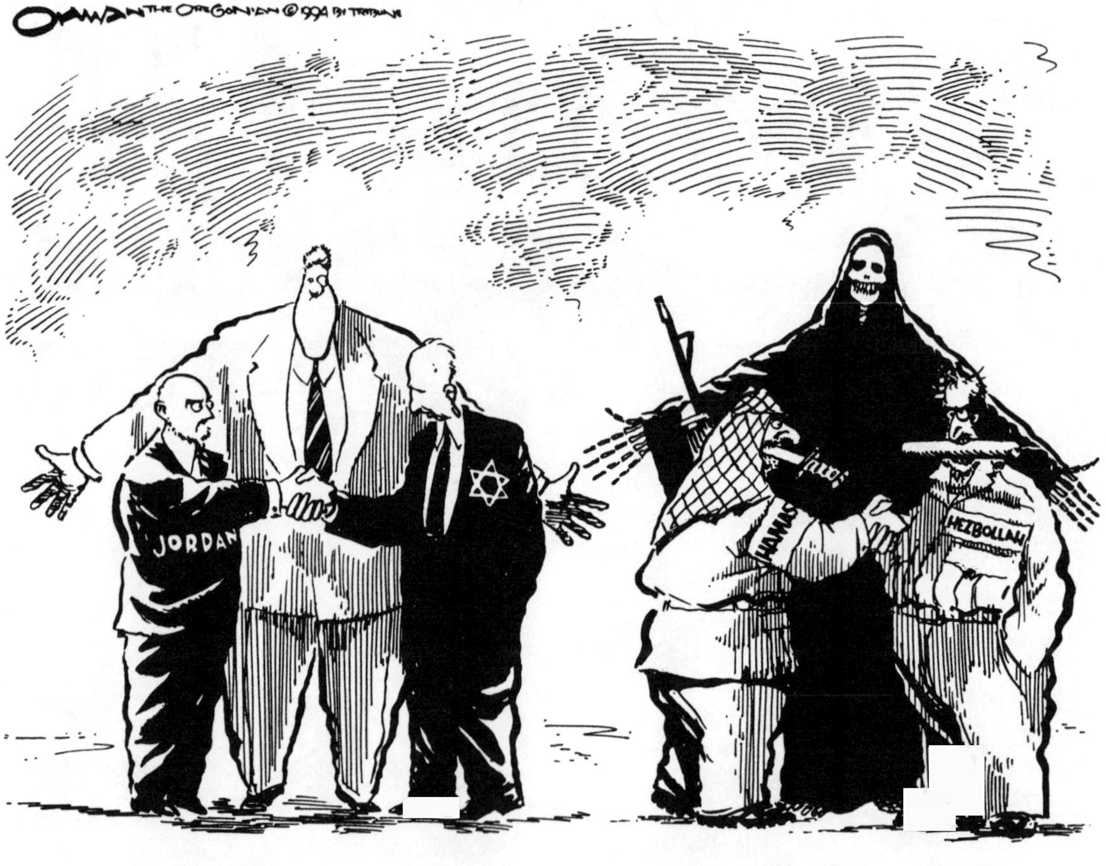
JORDAN
HAMAS
HEZBOLLAH

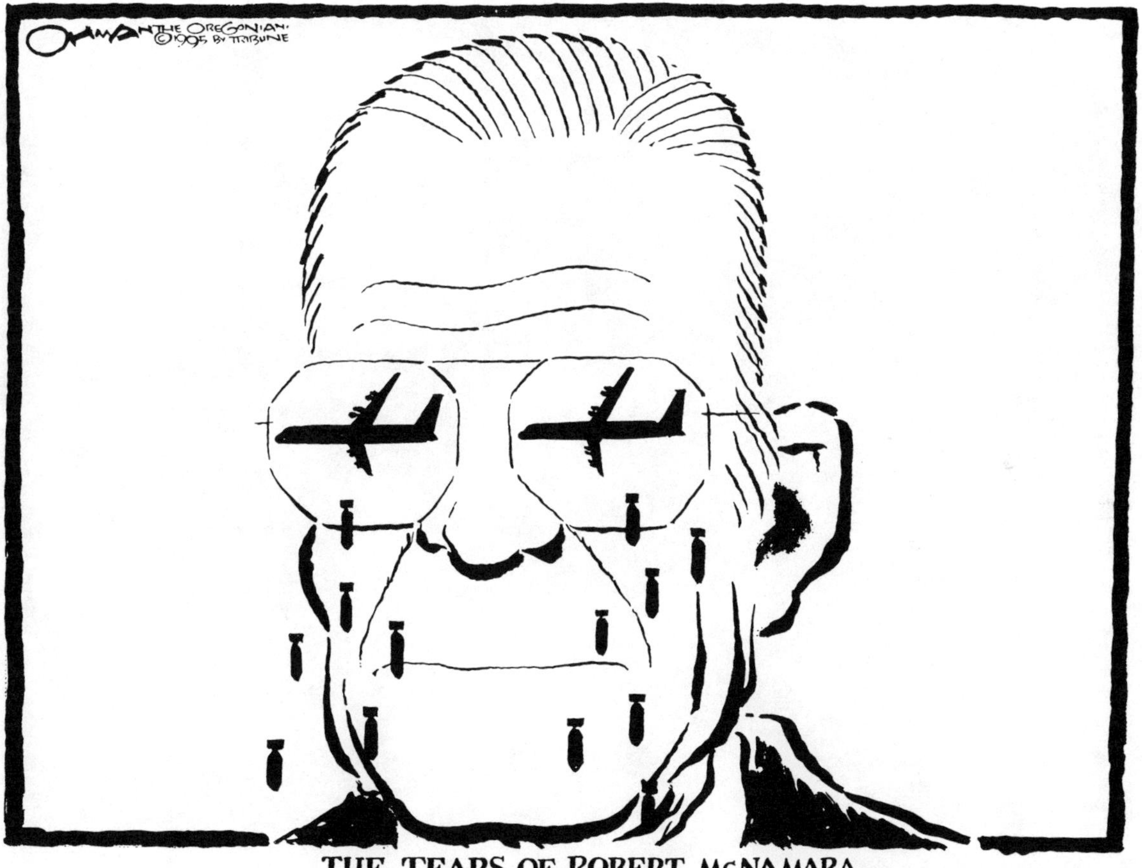
OHMAN THE OREGONIAN
©1995 BY TRIBUNE
THE TEARS OF ROBERT McNAMARA

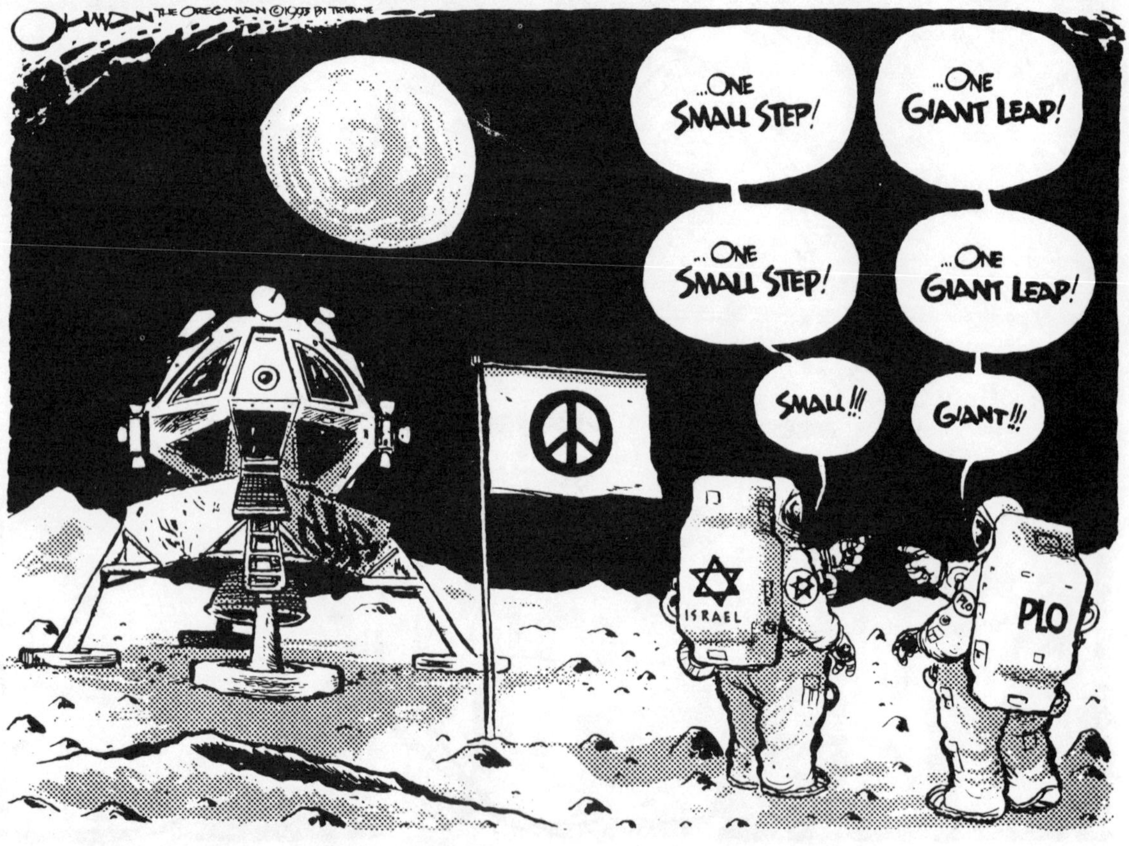
OLIPHANT THE OREGONIAN ©1993 BY TRIBUNE
...ONE SMALL STEP!
...ONE GIANT LEAP!
...ONE SMALL STEP!
...ONE GIANT LEAP!
SMALL!!!
GIANT!!!
ISRAEL
PLO
PLO

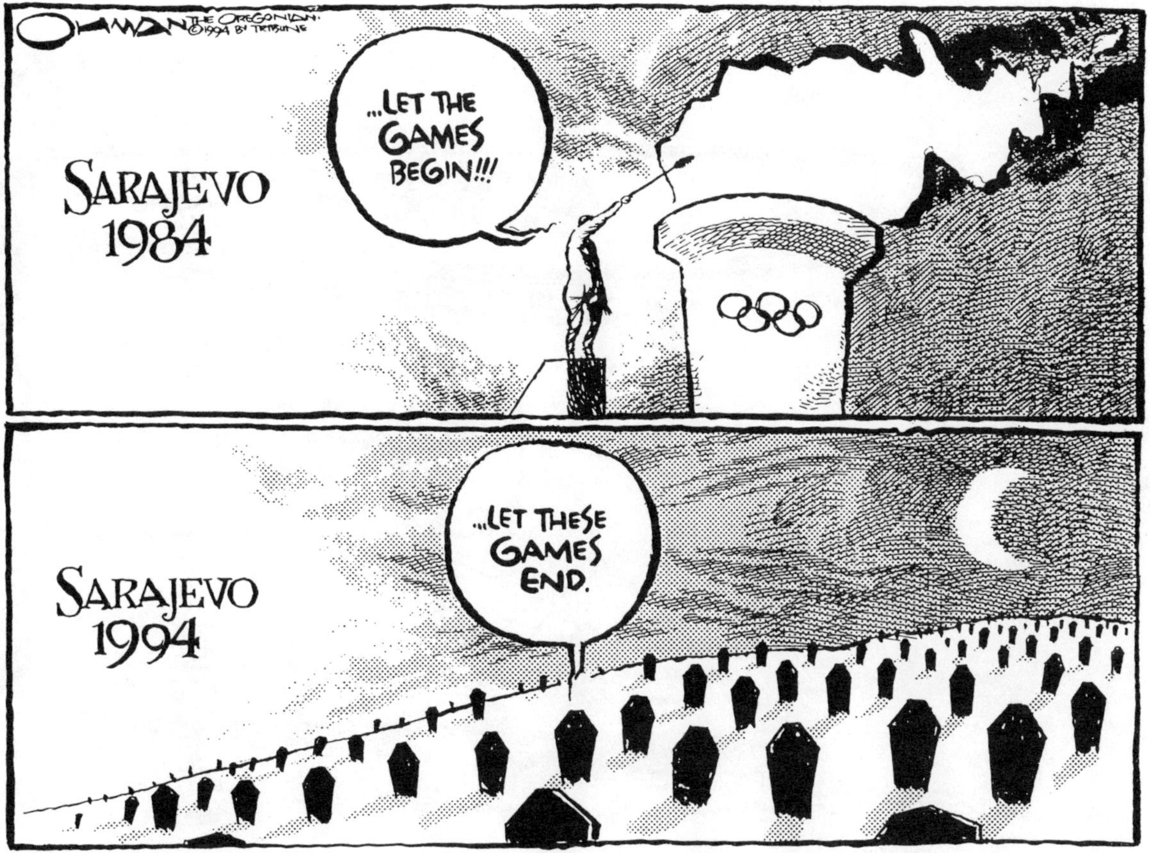
OHMAN THE OREGONIAN ©1994 BY TRIBUNE
SARAJEVO 1984
...LET THE GAMES BEGIN!!!
SARAJEVO 1994
...LET THESE GAMES END.

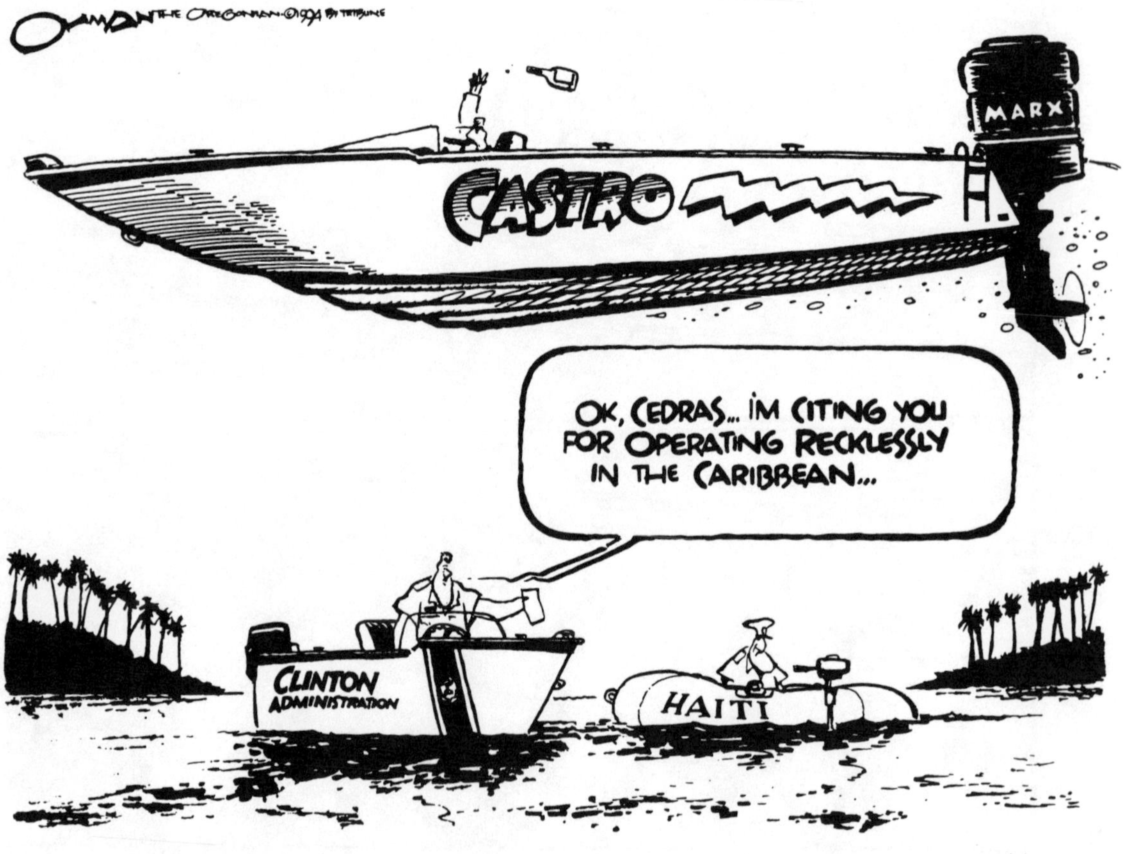
MARX
CASTRO
OK, CEDRAS... IM CITING YOU FOR OPERATING RECKLESSLY IN THE CARIBBEAN...
CLINTON ADMINISTRATION
HAITI

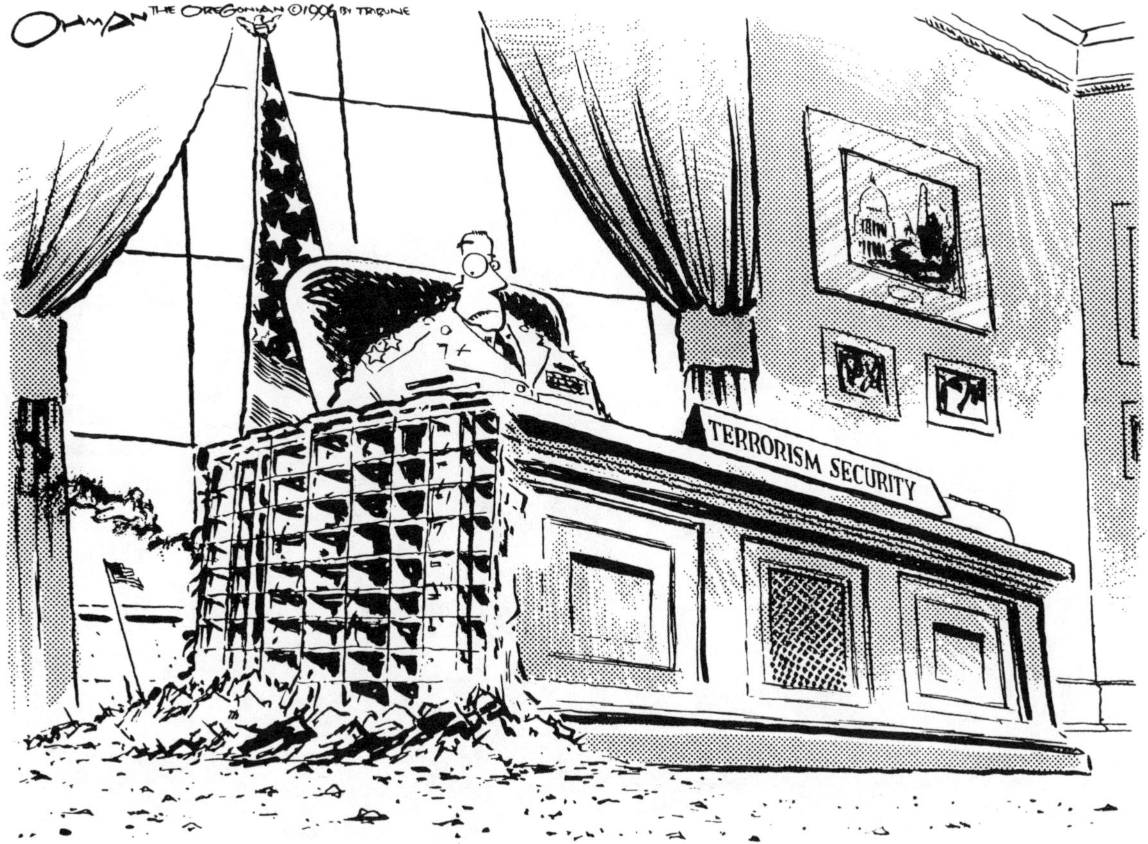
OHMAN THE OREGONIAN ©1996 BY TRIBUNE
TERRORISM SECURITY

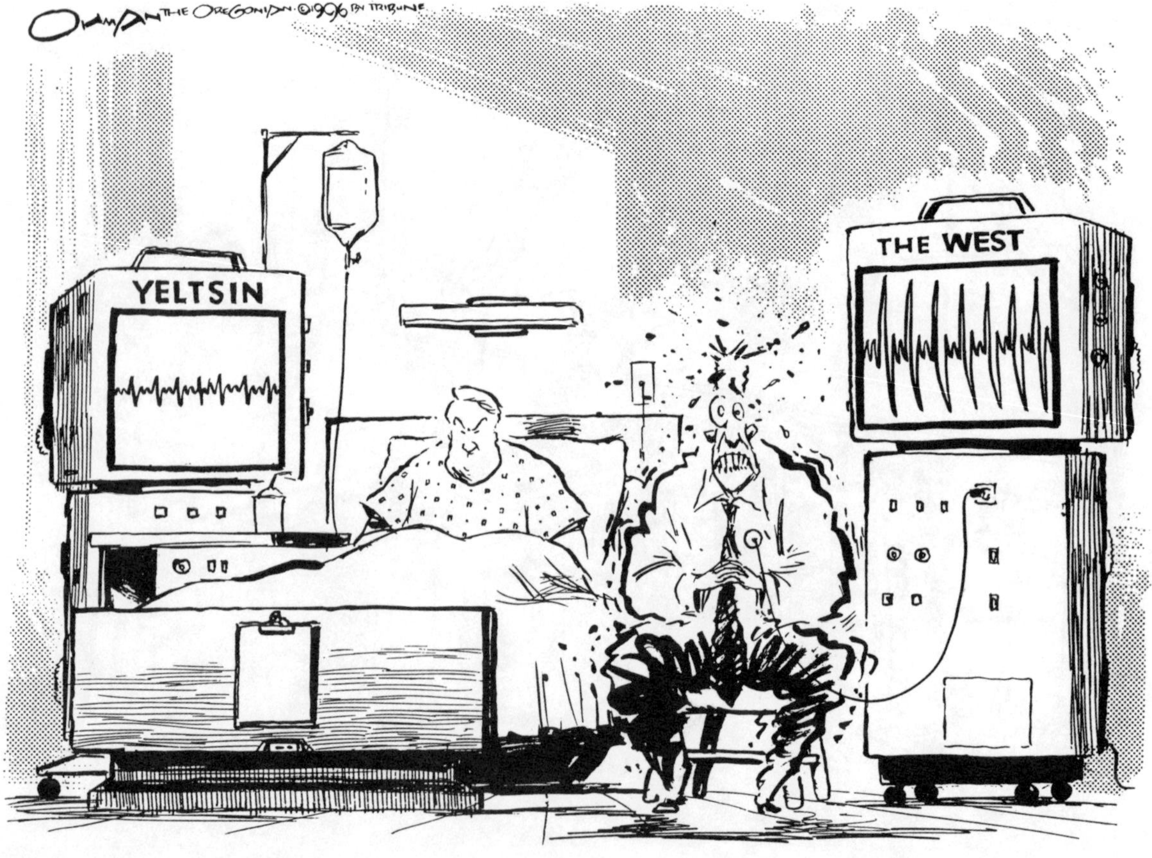

OHMAN THE OREGONIAN ©1996 BY TRIBUNE
YELTSIN
THE WEST

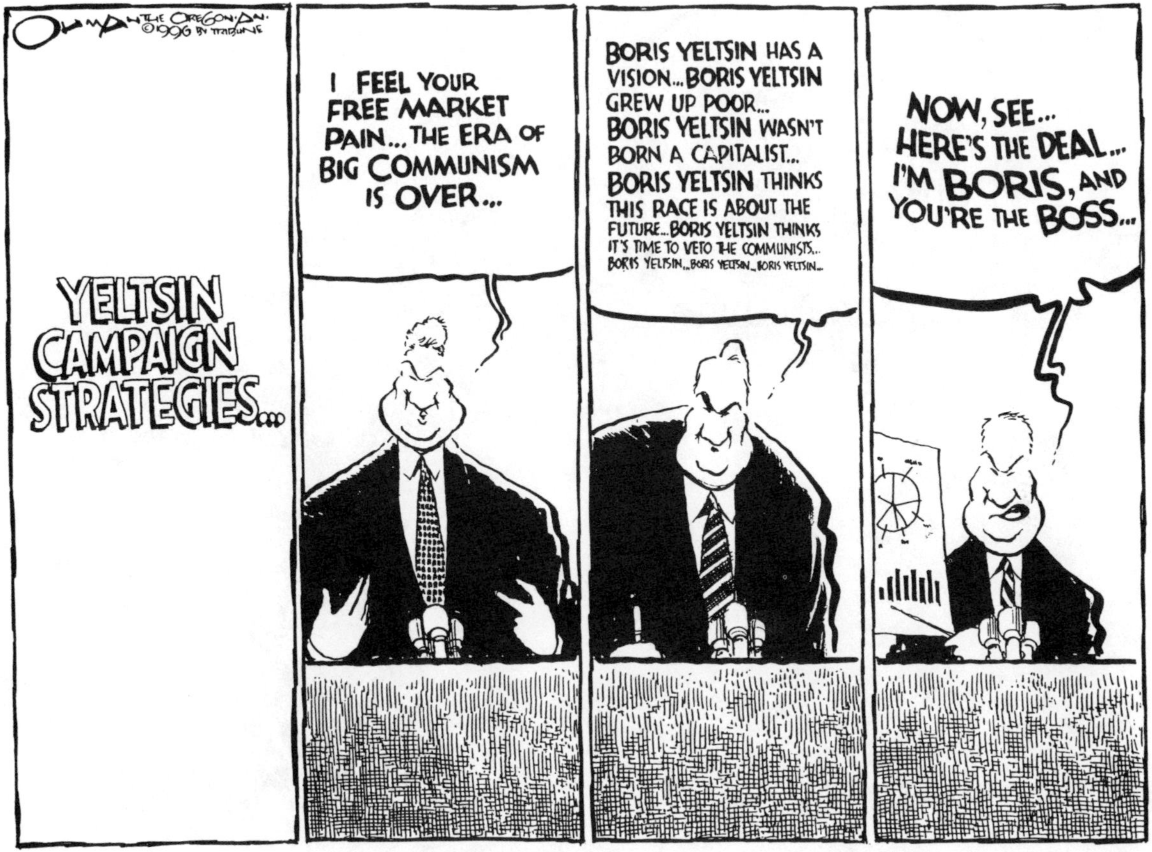
OHMAN THE OREGONIAN ©1996 BY TRIBUNE
YELTSIN CAMPAIGN STRATEGIES...
I FEEL YOUR FREE MARKET PAIN... THE ERA OF BIG COMMUNISM IS OVER...
BORIS YELTSIN HAS A VISION... BORIS YELTSIN GREW UP POOR... BORIS YELTSIN WASN'T BORN A CAPITALIST... BORIS YELTSIN THINKS THIS RACE IS ABOUT THE FUTURE... BORIS YELTSIN THINKS IT'S TIME TO VETO THE COMMUNISTS... BORIS YELTSIN... BORIS YELTSIN... BORIS YELTSIN...
NOW, SEE... HERE'S THE DEAL... I'M BORIS, AND YOU'RE THE BOSS...

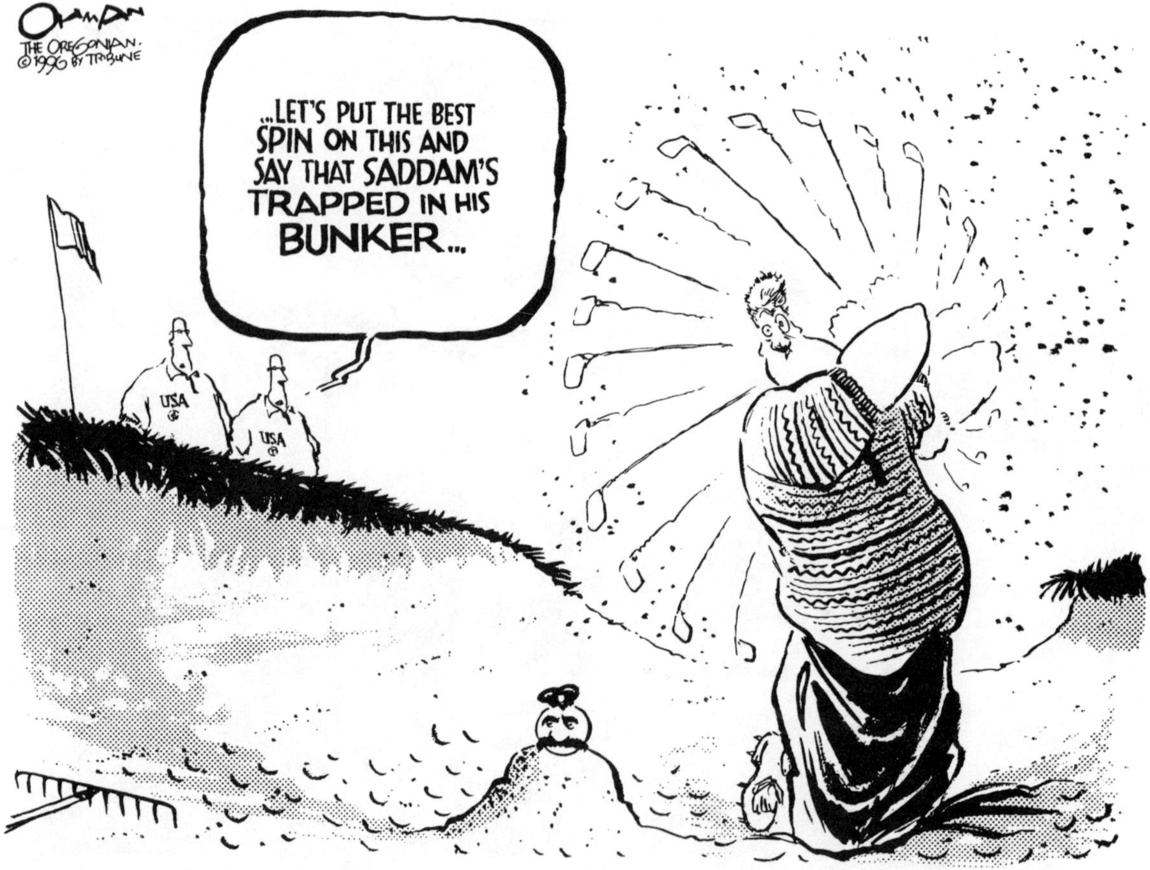
OHMAN
THE OREGONIAN.
©1996 BY TRIBUNE
...LET'S PUT THE BEST SPIN ON THIS AND SAY THAT SADDAM'S TRAPPED IN HIS BUNKER...
USA
USA

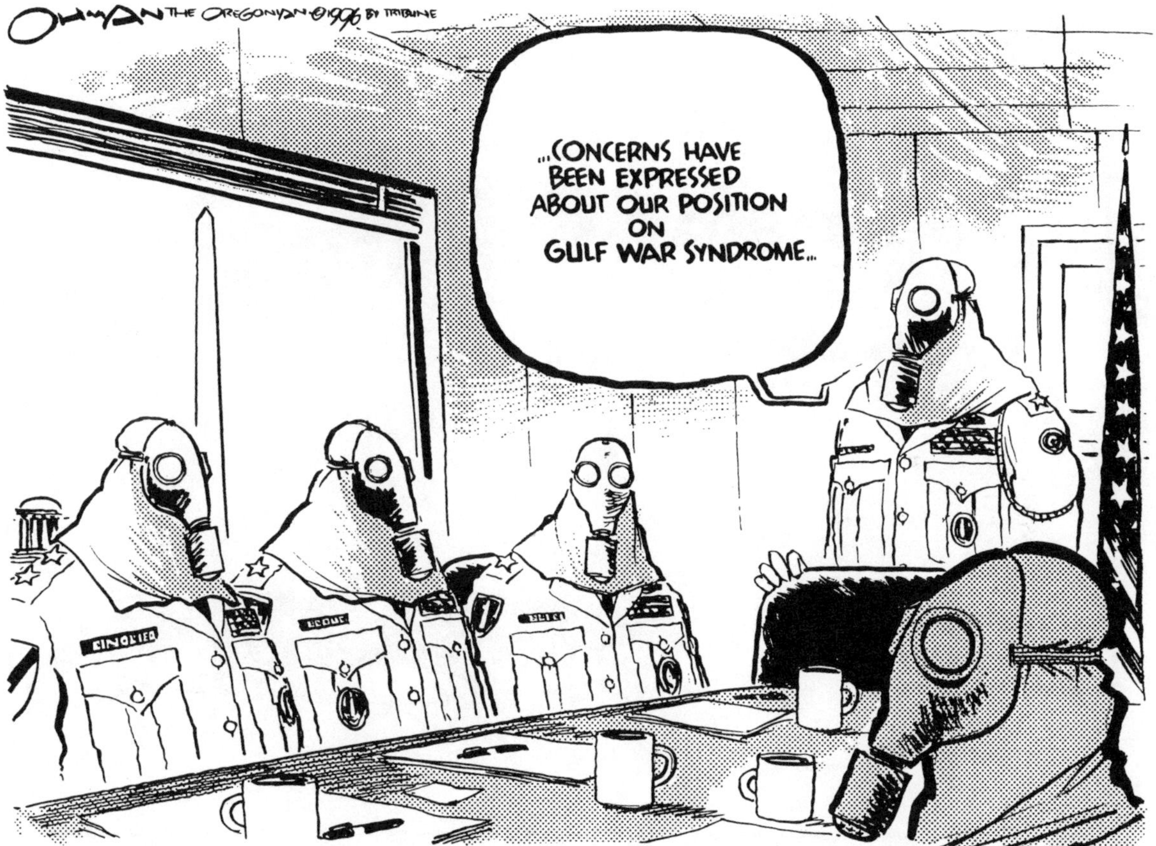
OHMAN THE OREGONIAN ©1996 BY TRIBUNE
...CONCERNS HAVE BEEN EXPRESSED ABOUT OUR POSITION ON GULF WAR SYNDROME...

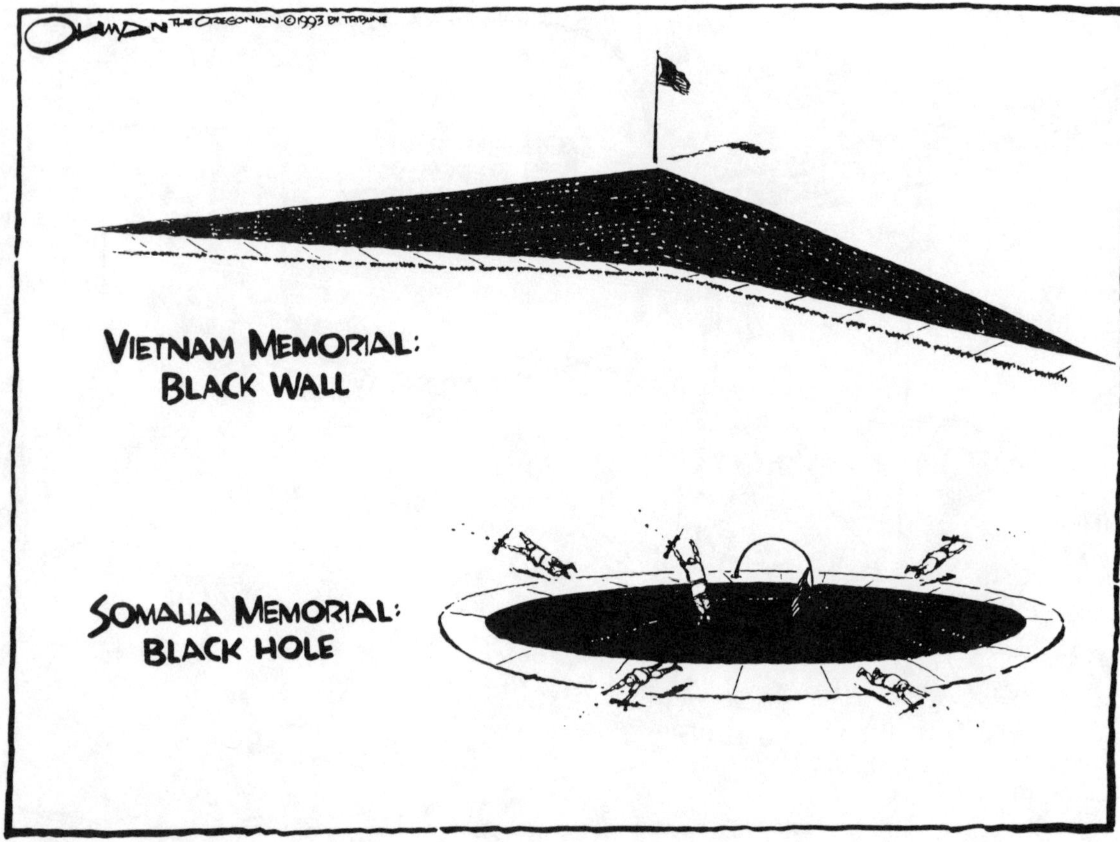

THE OREGONIAN ©1993 BY TRIBUNE
VIETNAM MEMORIAL:
BLACK WALL
SOMALIA MEMORIAL:
BLACK HOLE

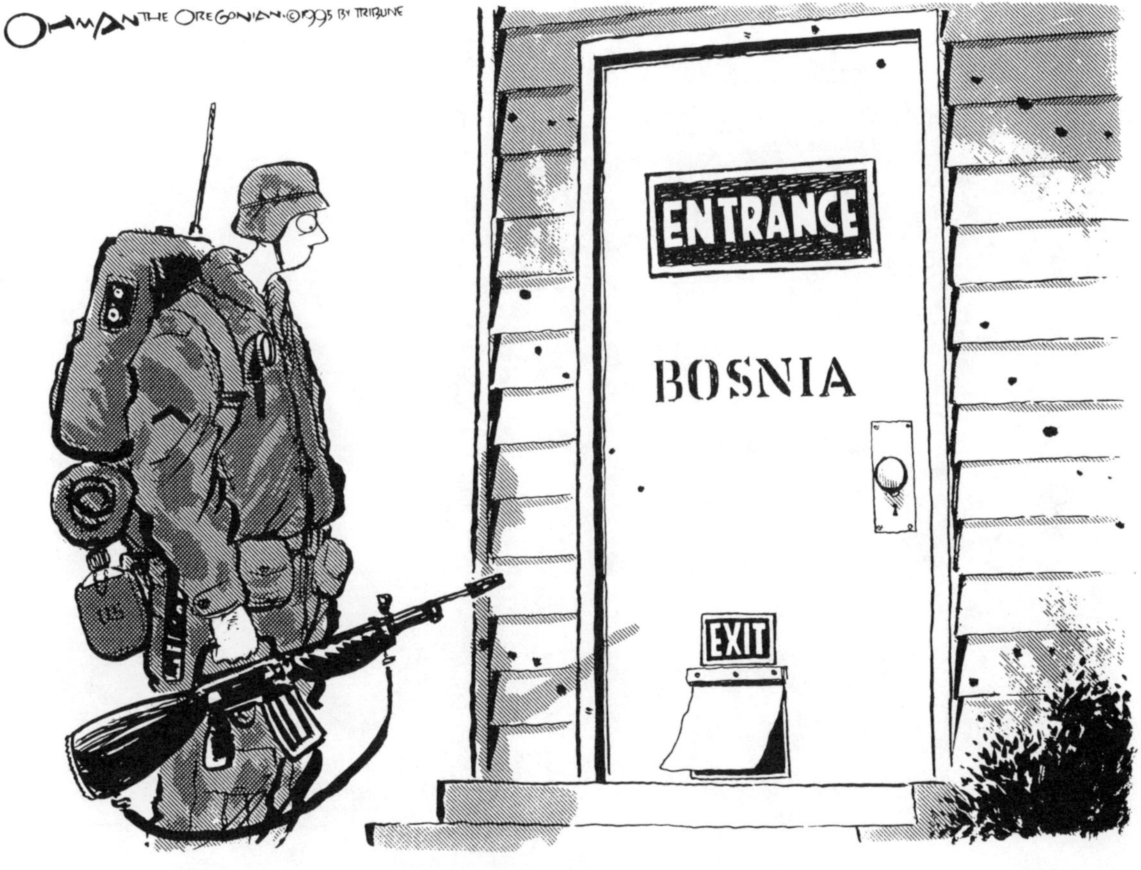
OHMAN THE OREGONIAN ©1995 BY TRIBUNE
ENTRANCE
BOSNIA
EXIT
U.S.

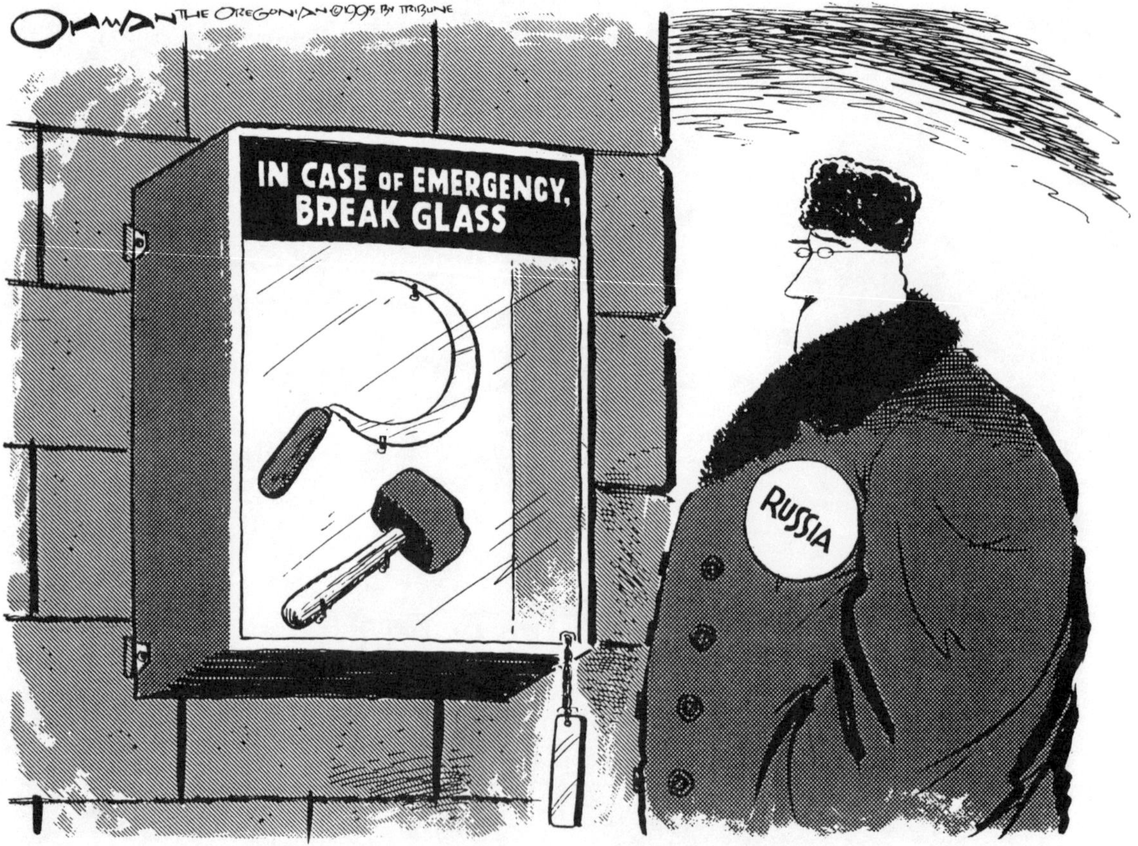
OHMAN THE OREGONIAN ©1995 BY TRIBUNE
IN CASE OF EMERGENCY,
BREAK GLASS
RUSSIA

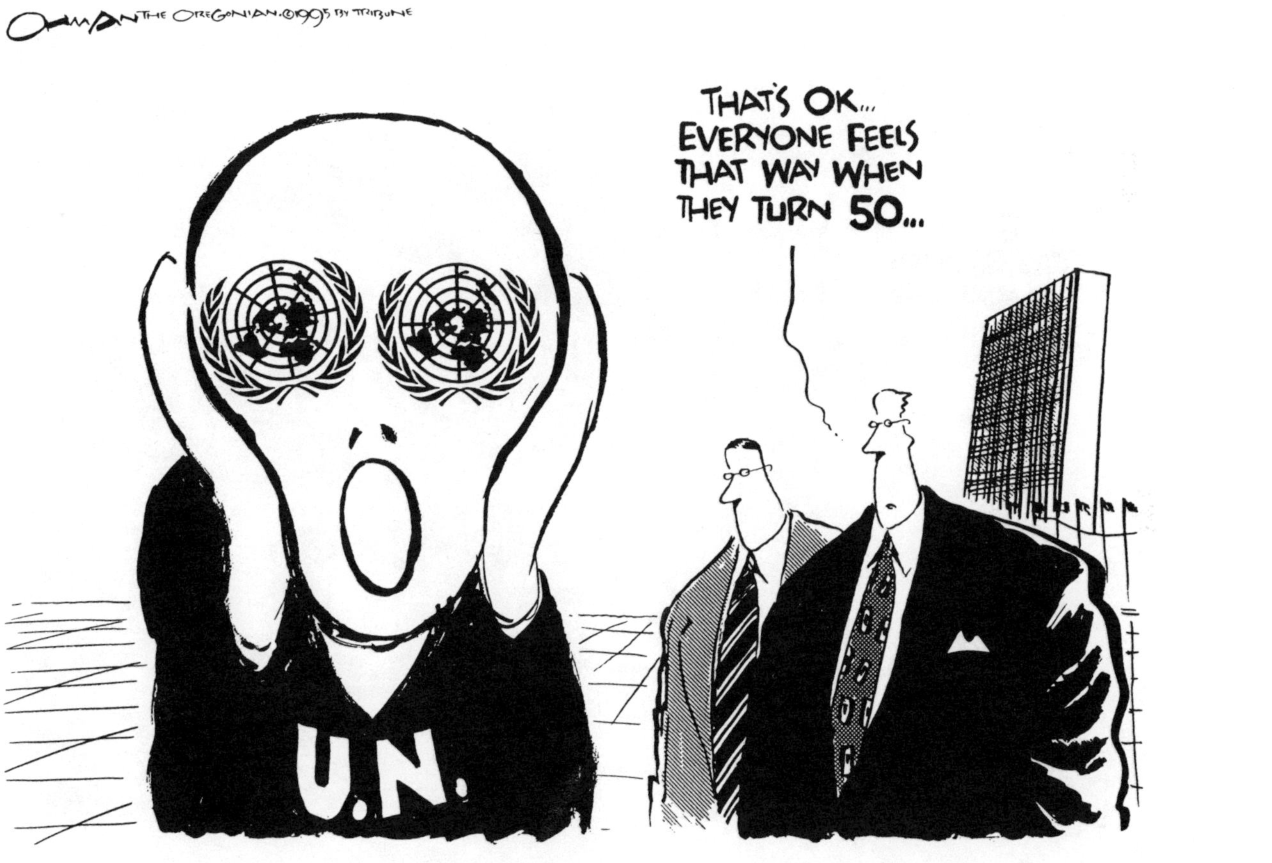
OHMAN THE OREGONIAN ©1995 BY TRIBUNE
THAT'S OK... EVERYONE FEELS THAT WAY WHEN THEY TURN 50...
U.N.

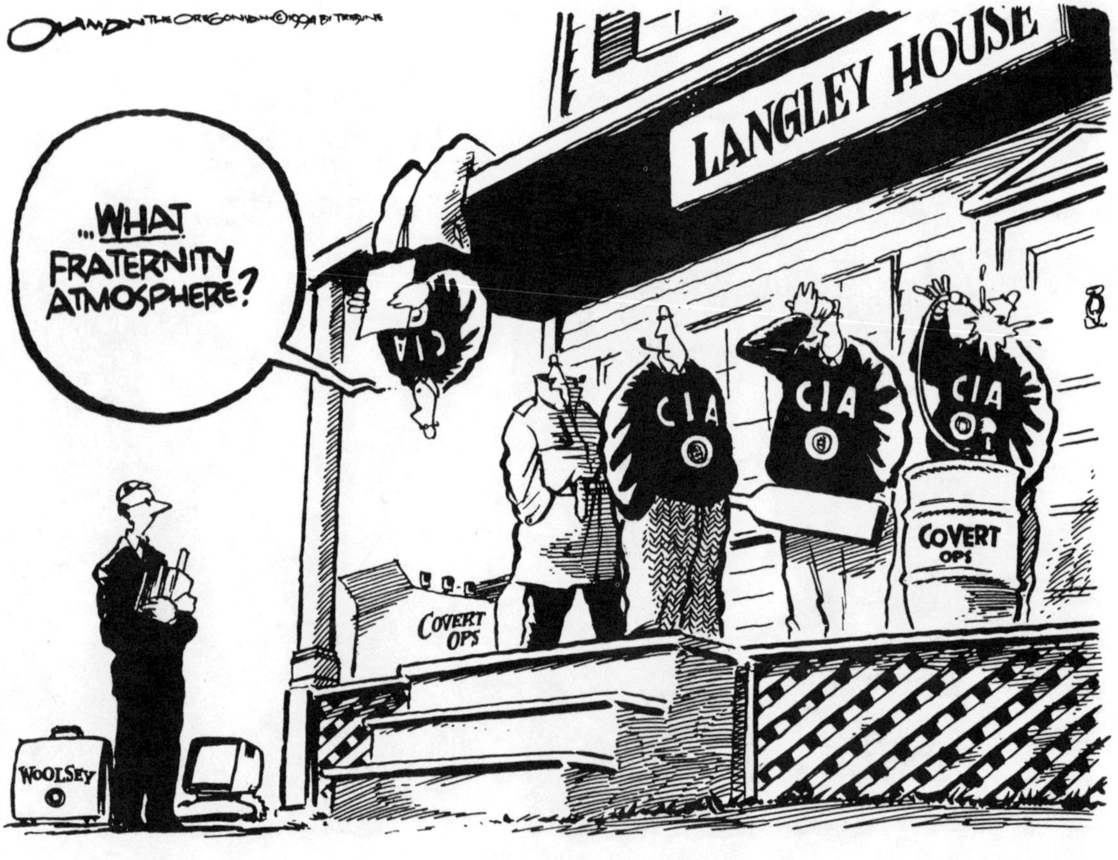

LANGLEY HOUSE
...WHAT FRATERNITY ATMOSPHERE?
CIA
CIA
CIA
CIA
COVERT OPS
COVERT OPS
WOOLSEY

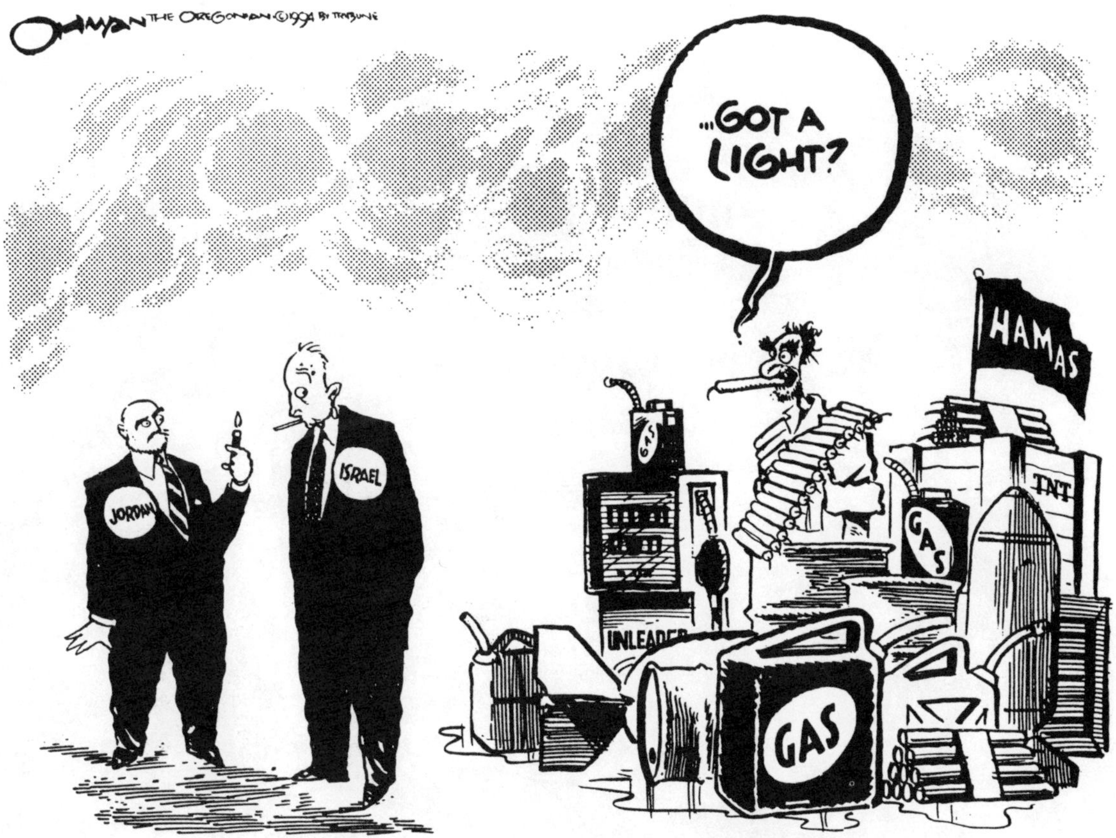
OHMAN THE OREGONIAN ©1994 BY TRIBUNE
...GOT A LIGHT?
HAMAS
JORDAN
ISRAEL
GAS
TNT
GAS
GAS

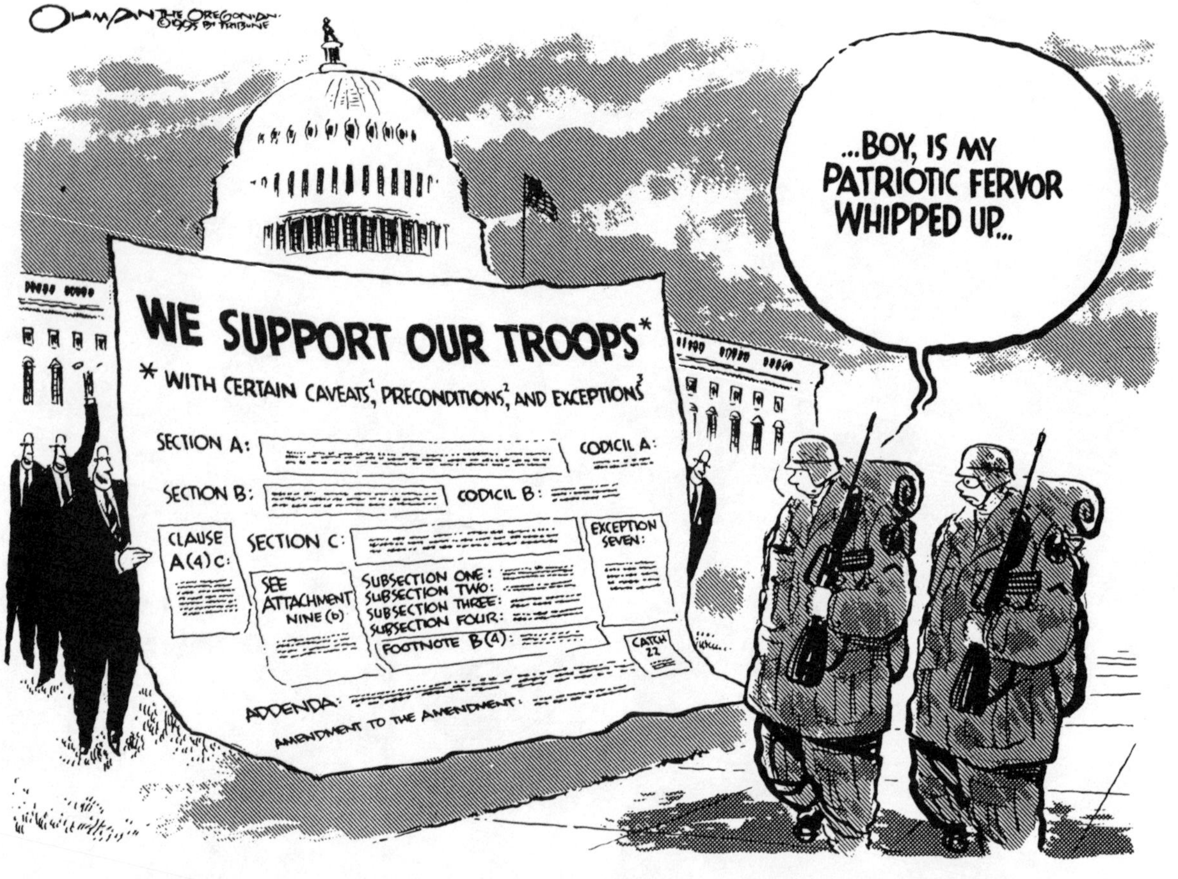
OHMAN THE OREGONIAN ©1995 BY TRIBUNE
WE SUPPORT OUR TROOPS*
* WITH CERTAIN CAVEATS,1 PRECONDITIONS,2 AND EXCEPTIONS3
SECTION A:
CODICIL A:
SECTION B:
CODICIL B:
CLAUSE A(4)C:
SECTION C:
EXCEPTION SEVEN:
SEE ATTACHMENT NINE (b)
SUBSECTION ONE:
SUBSECTION TWO:
SUBSECTION THREE:
SUBSECTION FOUR:
FOOTNOTE B(4):
CATCH 22
ADDENDA:
AMENDMENT TO THE AMENDMENT:
...BOY, IS MY PATRIOTIC FERVOR WHIPPED UP...

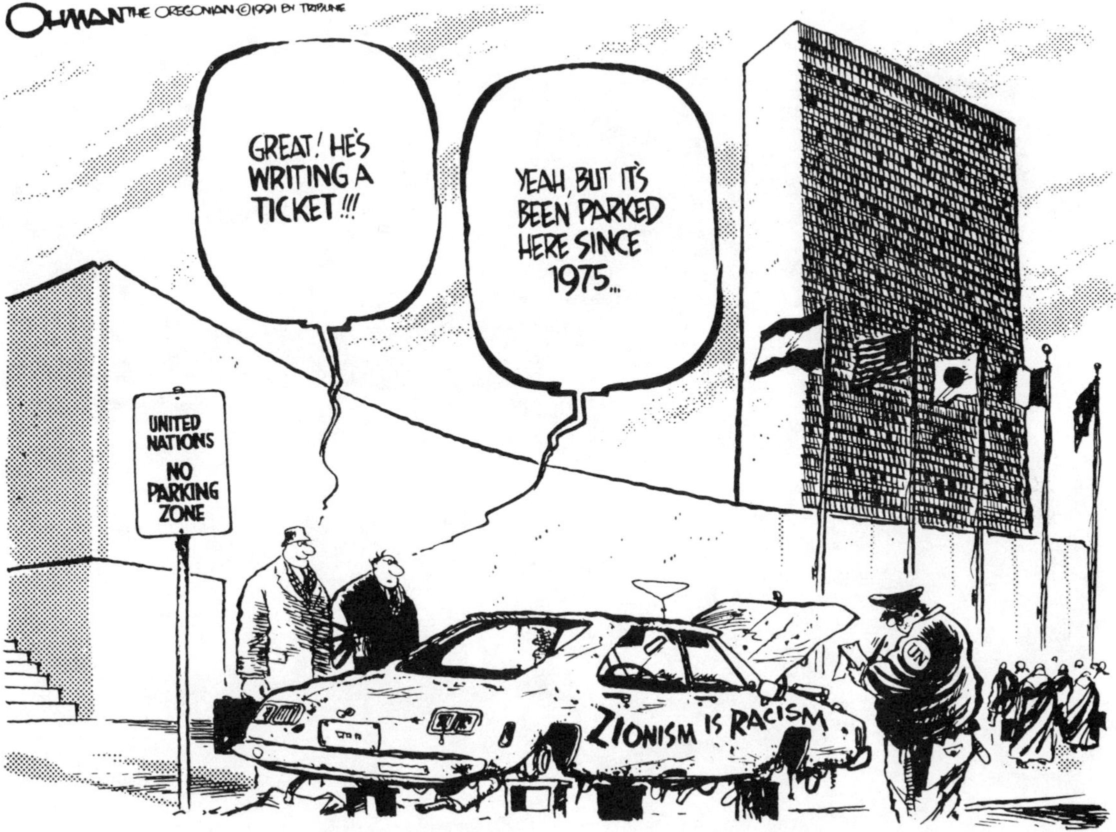

OHMAN THE OREGONIAN ©1991 BY TRIBUNE
GREAT! HE'S WRITING A TICKET!!!
YEAH, BUT IT'S BEEN PARKED HERE SINCE 1975...
UNITED NATIONS NO PARKING ZONE
ZIONISM IS RACISM
UN

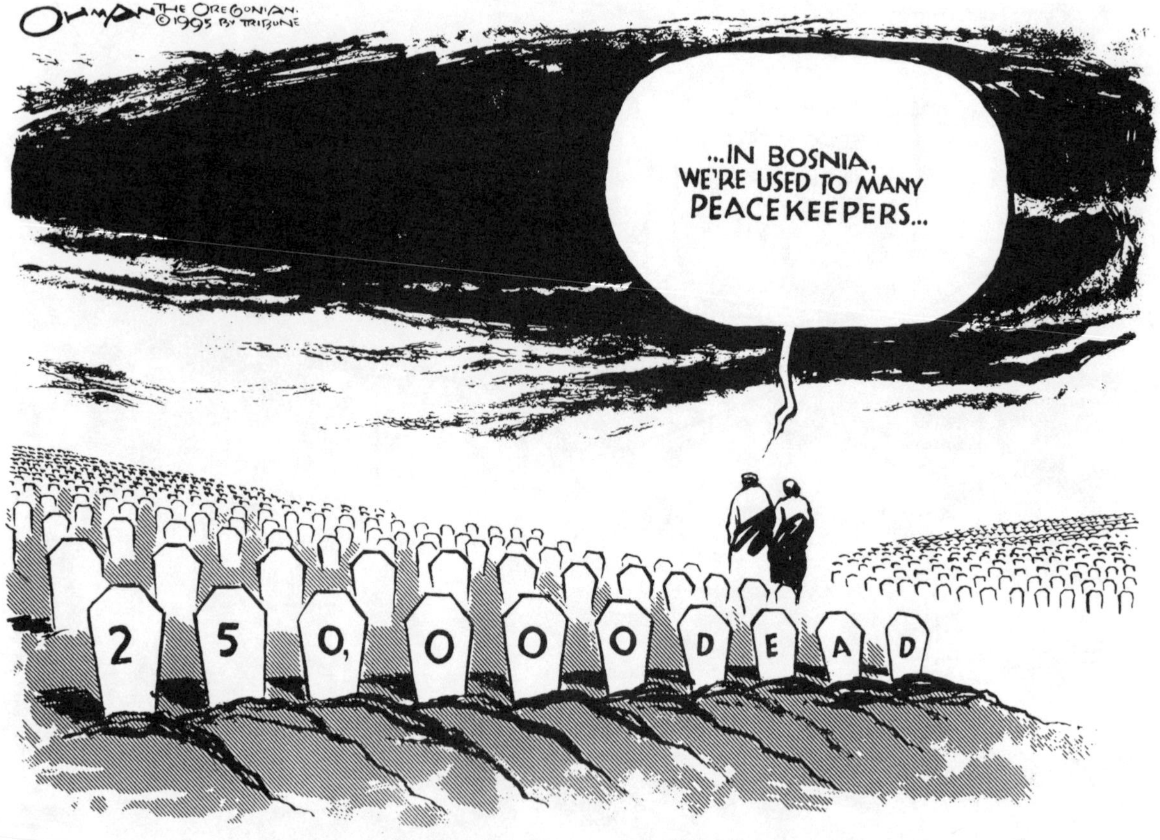
OHMAN THE OREGONIAN ©1995 BY TRIBUNE
...IN BOSNIA, WE'RE USED TO MANY PEACEKEEPERS...
250,000 DEAD

I FOUGHT THE LAW
AND THE
LAW WON

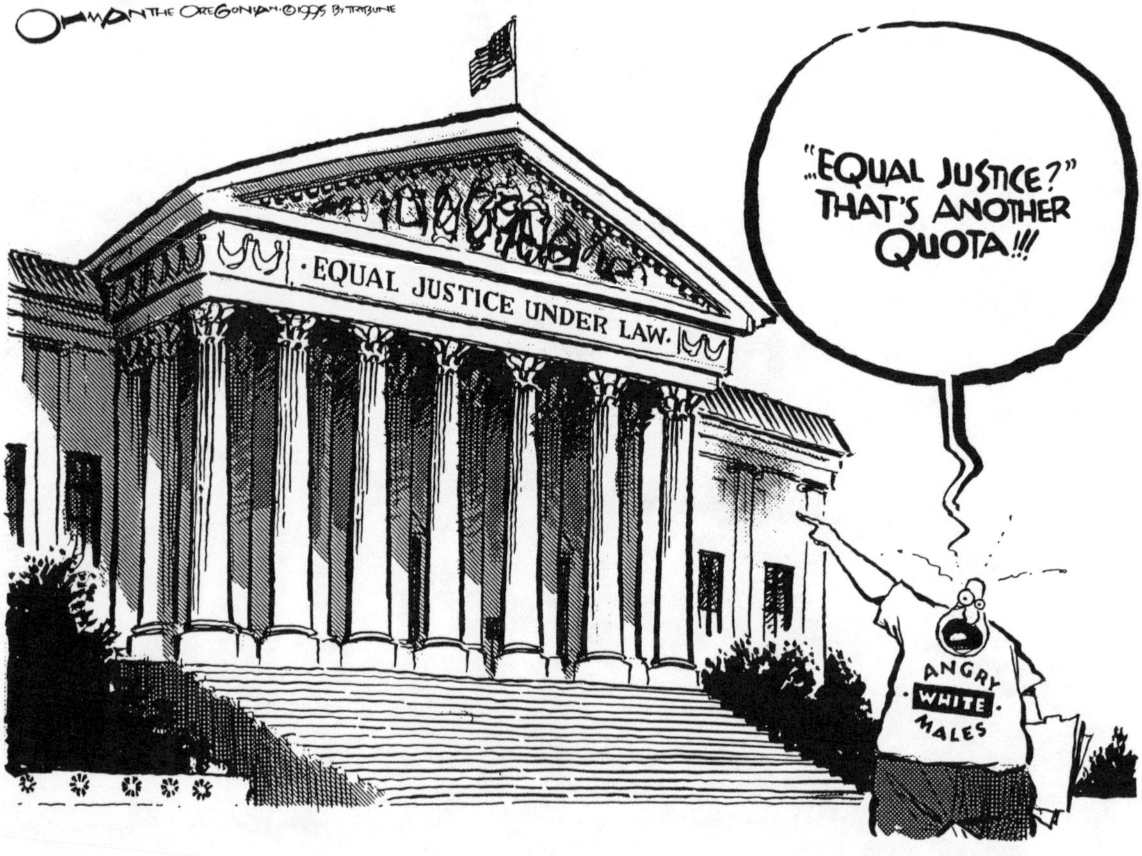
OHMAN THE OREGONIAN ©1995 BY TRIBUNE
· EQUAL JUSTICE UNDER LAW ·
"...EQUAL JUSTICE?" THAT'S ANOTHER QUOTA!!!
ANGRY WHITE MALES

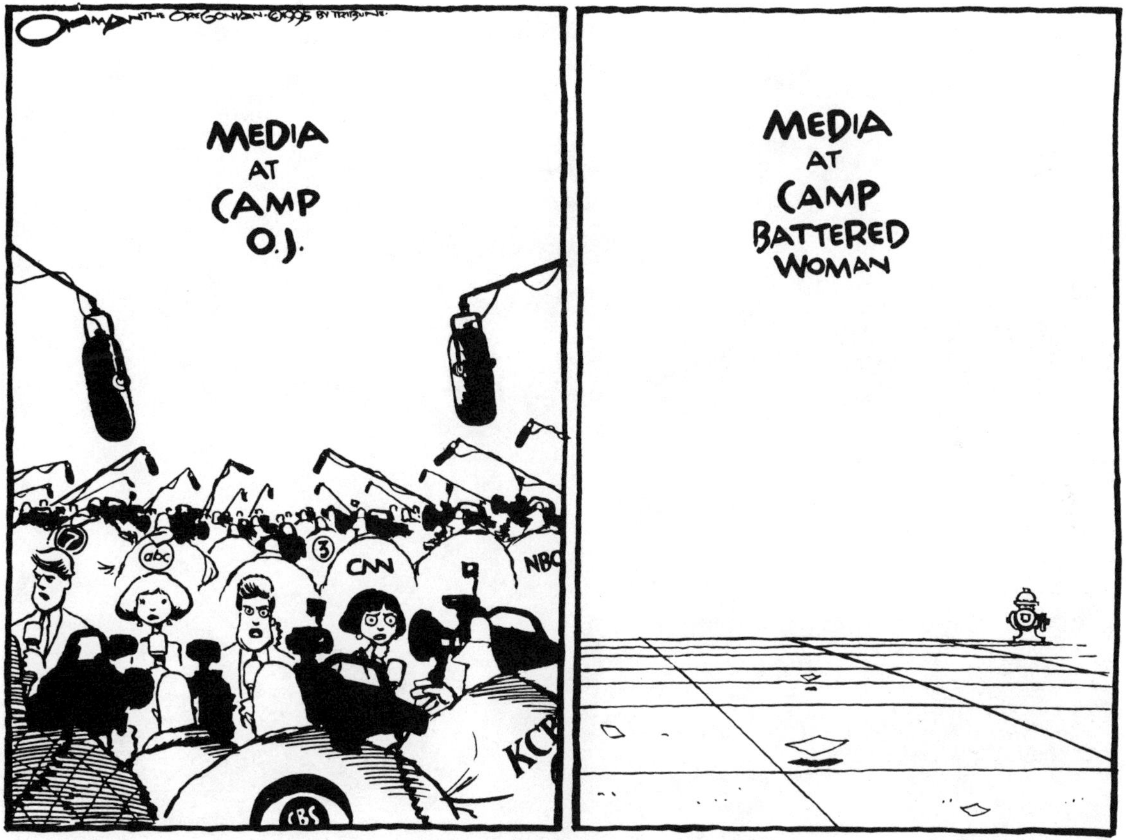
OHMAN THE OREGONIAN ©1995 BY TRIBUNE
MEDIA AT CAMP O.J.
7
abc
3
CNN
NBC
KCB
CBS
MEDIA AT CAMP BATTERED WOMAN

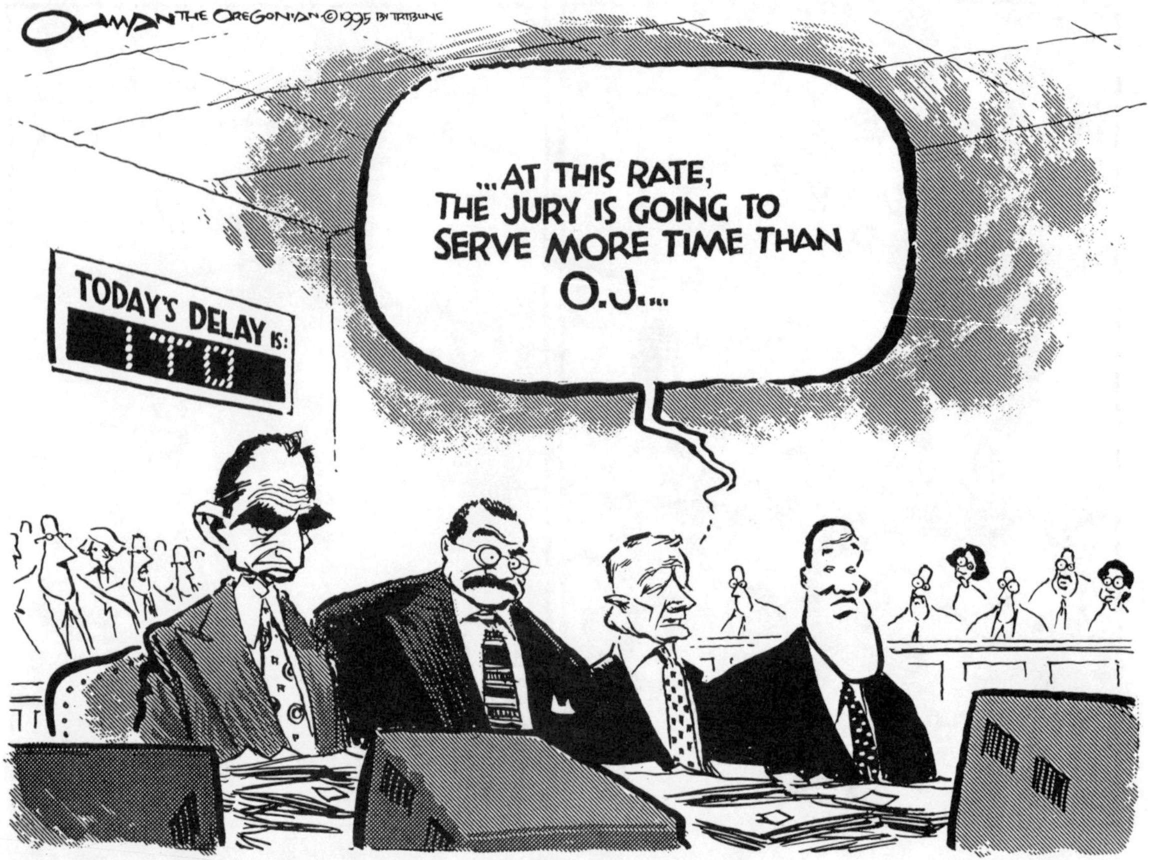
OHMAN THE OREGONIAN ©1995 BY TRIBUNE
TODAY'S DELAY IS:
ITO
...AT THIS RATE, THE JURY IS GOING TO SERVE MORE TIME THAN O.J....

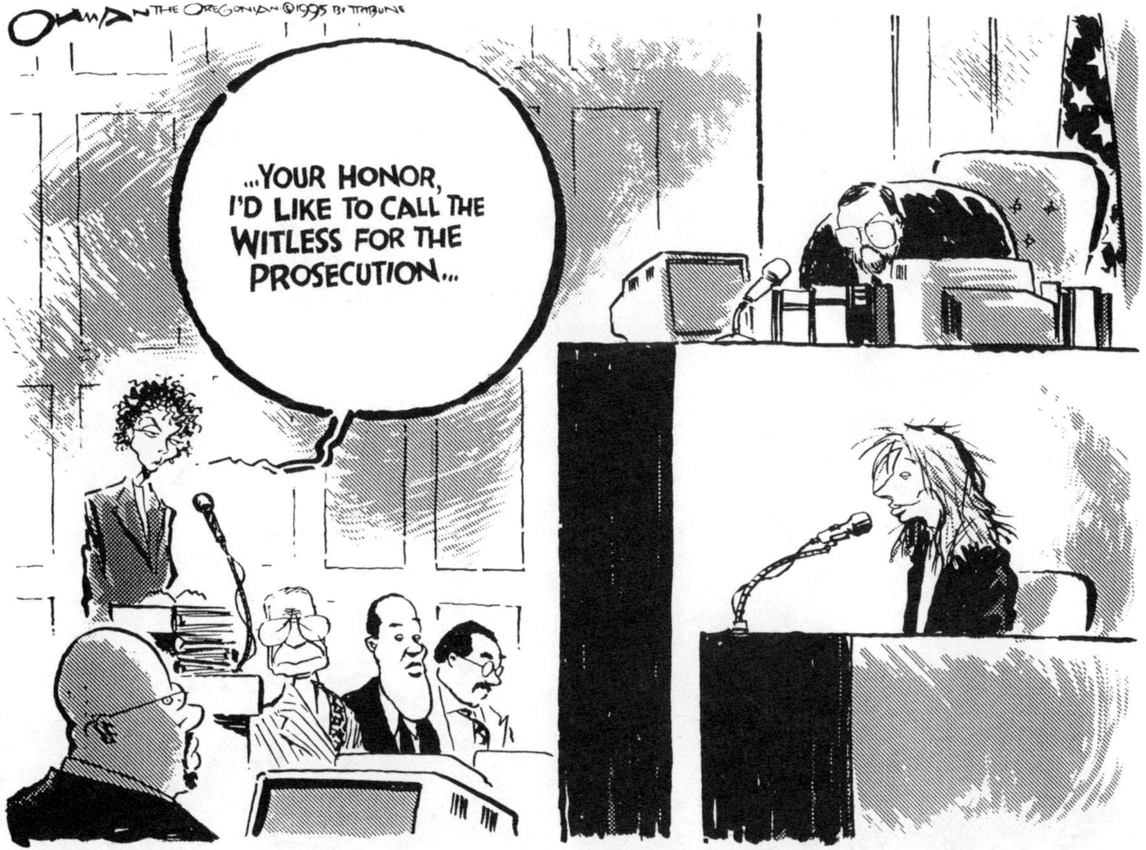
OHMAN THE OREGONIAN ©1995 BY TRIBUNE
...YOUR HONOR, I'D LIKE TO CALL THE WITLESS FOR THE PROSECUTION...

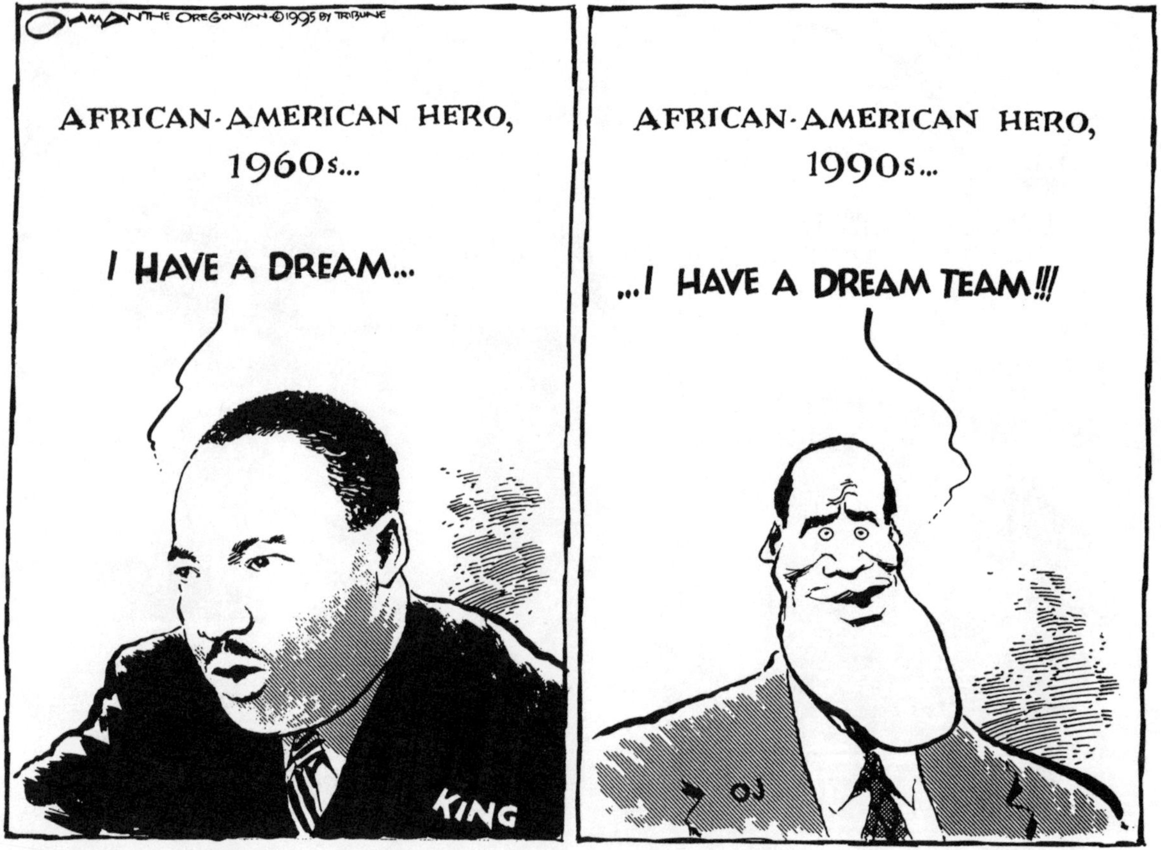
OHMAN THE OREGONIAN ©1995 BY TRIBUNE
AFRICAN-AMERICAN HERO, 1960s...
I HAVE A DREAM...
KING
AFRICAN-AMERICAN HERO, 1990s...
...I HAVE A DREAM TEAM!!!
OJ

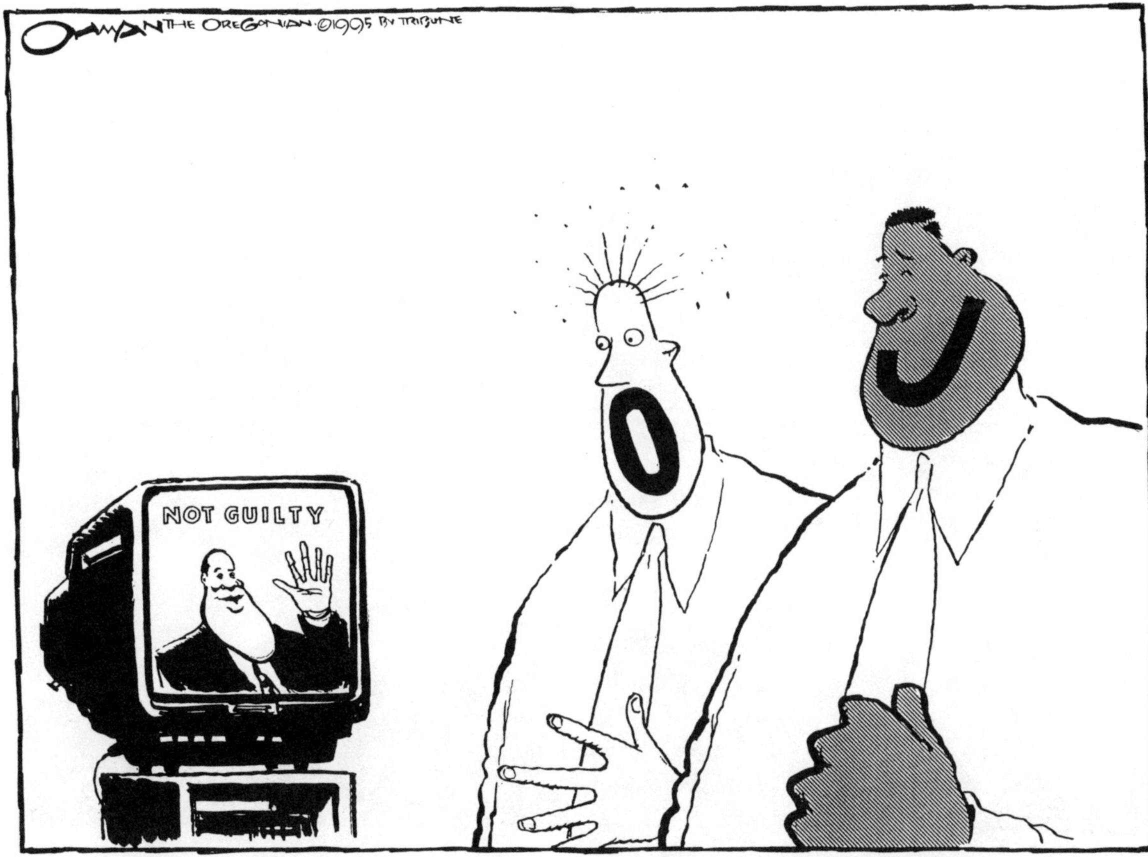
OHMAN THE OREGONIAN ©1995 BY TRIBUNE
NOT GUILTY

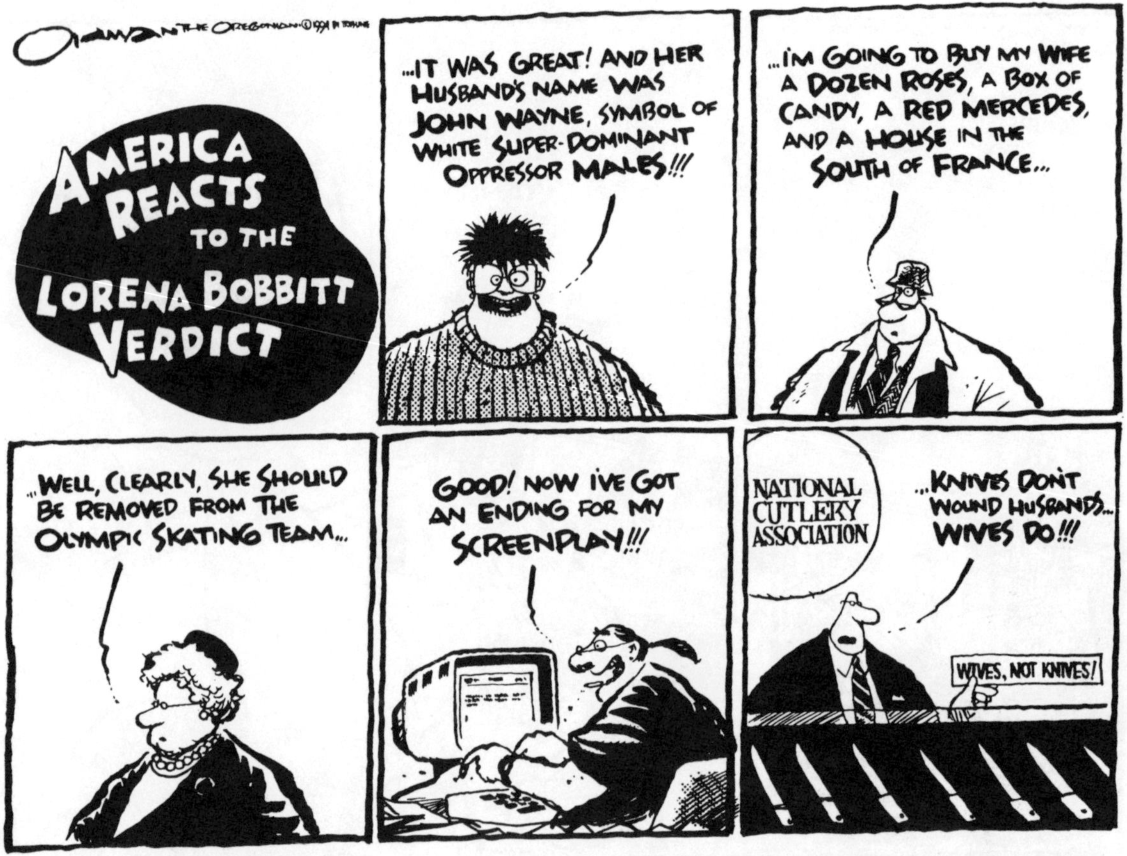
AMERICA REACTS TO THE LORENA BOBBITT VERDICT
...IT WAS GREAT! AND HER HUSBAND'S NAME WAS JOHN WAYNE, SYMBOL OF WHITE SUPER-DOMINANT OPPRESSOR MALES!!!
...I'M GOING TO BUY MY WIFE A DOZEN ROSES, A BOX OF CANDY, A RED MERCEDES, AND A HOUSE IN THE SOUTH OF FRANCE...
...WELL, CLEARLY, SHE SHOULD BE REMOVED FROM THE OLYMPIC SKATING TEAM...
GOOD! NOW I'VE GOT AN ENDING FOR MY SCREENPLAY!!!
NATIONAL CUTLERY ASSOCIATION
...KNIVES DON'T WOUND HUSBANDS... WIVES DO!!!
WIVES, NOT KNIVES!

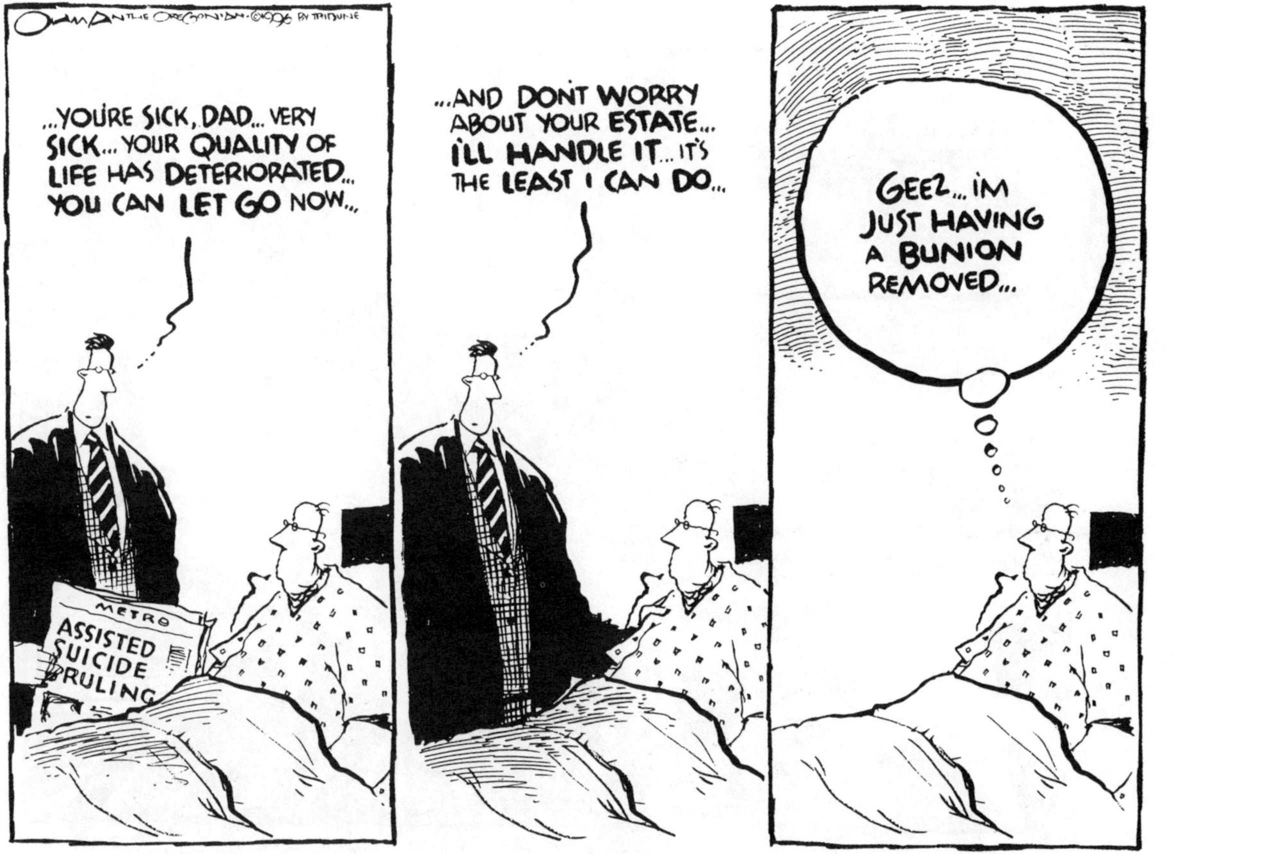

OHMAN THE OREGONIAN ©1996 BY TRIBUNE
...YOU'RE SICK, DAD... VERY SICK... YOUR QUALITY OF LIFE HAS DETERIORATED... YOU CAN LET GO NOW...
METRO
ASSISTED SUICIDE RULING
...AND DON'T WORRY ABOUT YOUR ESTATE... I'LL HANDLE IT... IT'S THE LEAST I CAN DO...
GEEZ... I'M JUST HAVING A BUNION REMOVED...

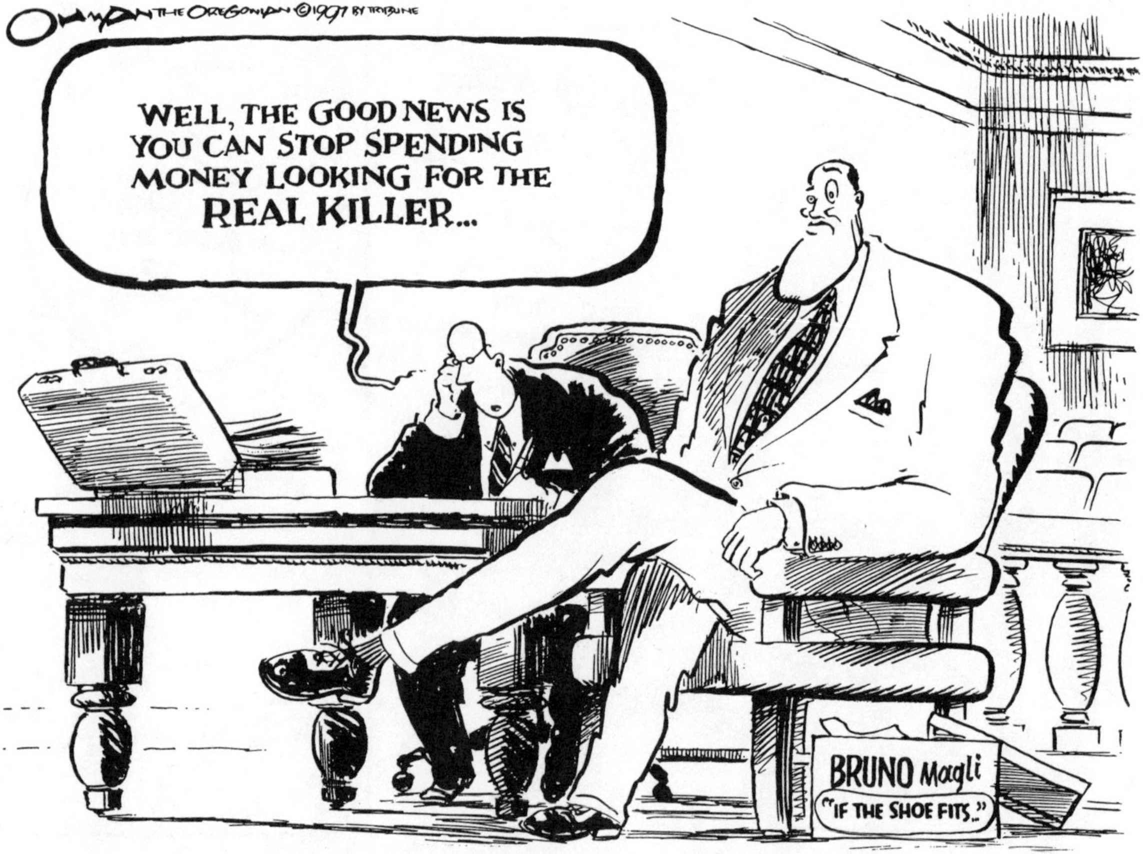
THE OREGONIAN ©1997 BY TRIBUNE
WELL, THE GOOD NEWS IS YOU CAN STOP SPENDING MONEY LOOKING FOR THE REAL KILLER...
BRUNO Magli
"IF THE SHOE FITS."

# DEBT AND TAXES

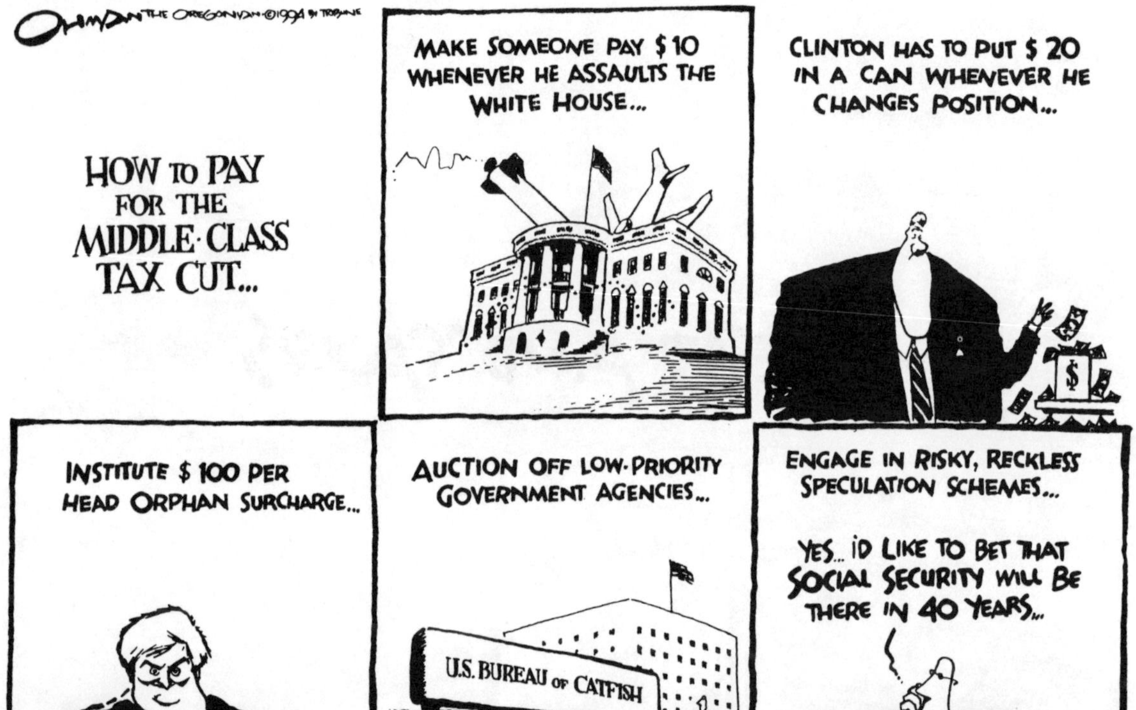

OHMAN THE OREGONIAN ©1994 BY TRIBUNE
HOW TO PAY FOR THE MIDDLE-CLASS TAX CUT...
MAKE SOMEONE PAY $10 WHENEVER HE ASSAULTS THE WHITE HOUSE...
CLINTON HAS TO PUT $20 IN A CAN WHENEVER HE CHANGES POSITION...
$
INSTITUTE $100 PER HEAD ORPHAN SURCHARGE...
AUCTION OFF LOW-PRIORITY GOVERNMENT AGENCIES...
U.S. BUREAU OF CATFISH
ENGAGE IN RISKY, RECKLESS SPECULATION SCHEMES...
YES... I'D LIKE TO BET THAT SOCIAL SECURITY WILL BE THERE IN 40 YEARS...

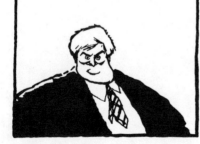

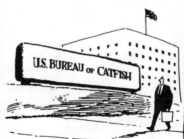

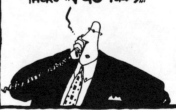

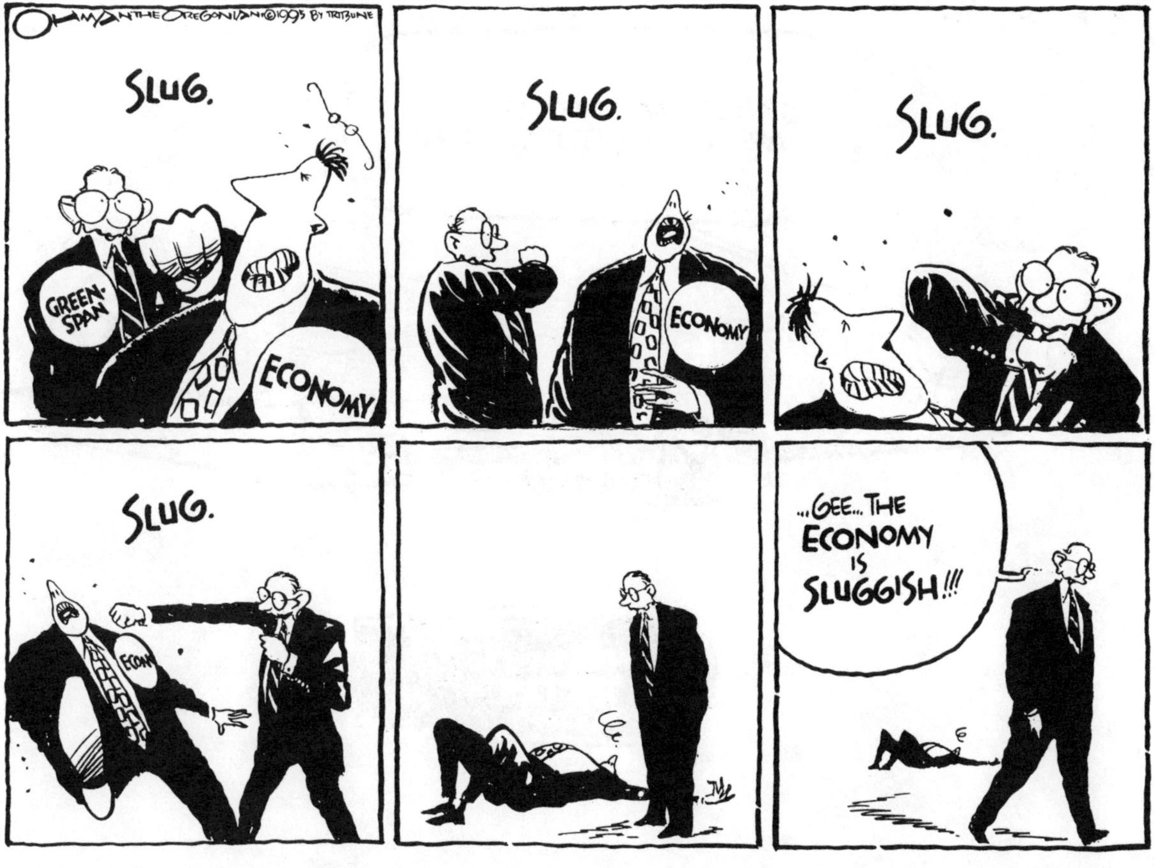
OHMAN THE OREGONIAN ©1993 BY TRIBUNE
SLUG.
GREEN-SPAN
ECONOMY
SLUG.
ECONOMY
SLUG.
SLUG.
ECON
...GEE... THE ECONOMY IS SLUGGISH!!!

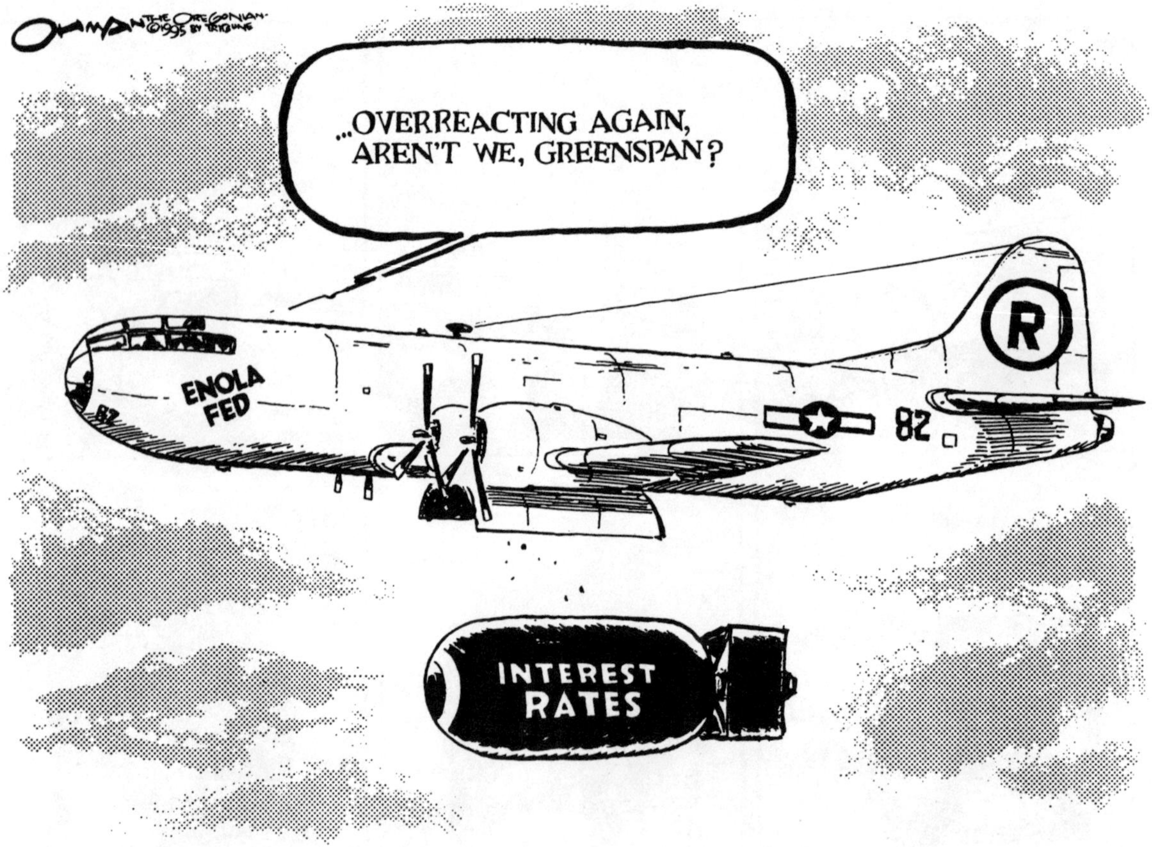
OHMAN THE OREGONIAN ©1995 BY TRIBUNE
...OVERREACTING AGAIN, AREN'T WE, GREENSPAN?
ENOLA FED
82
R
82
INTEREST RATES

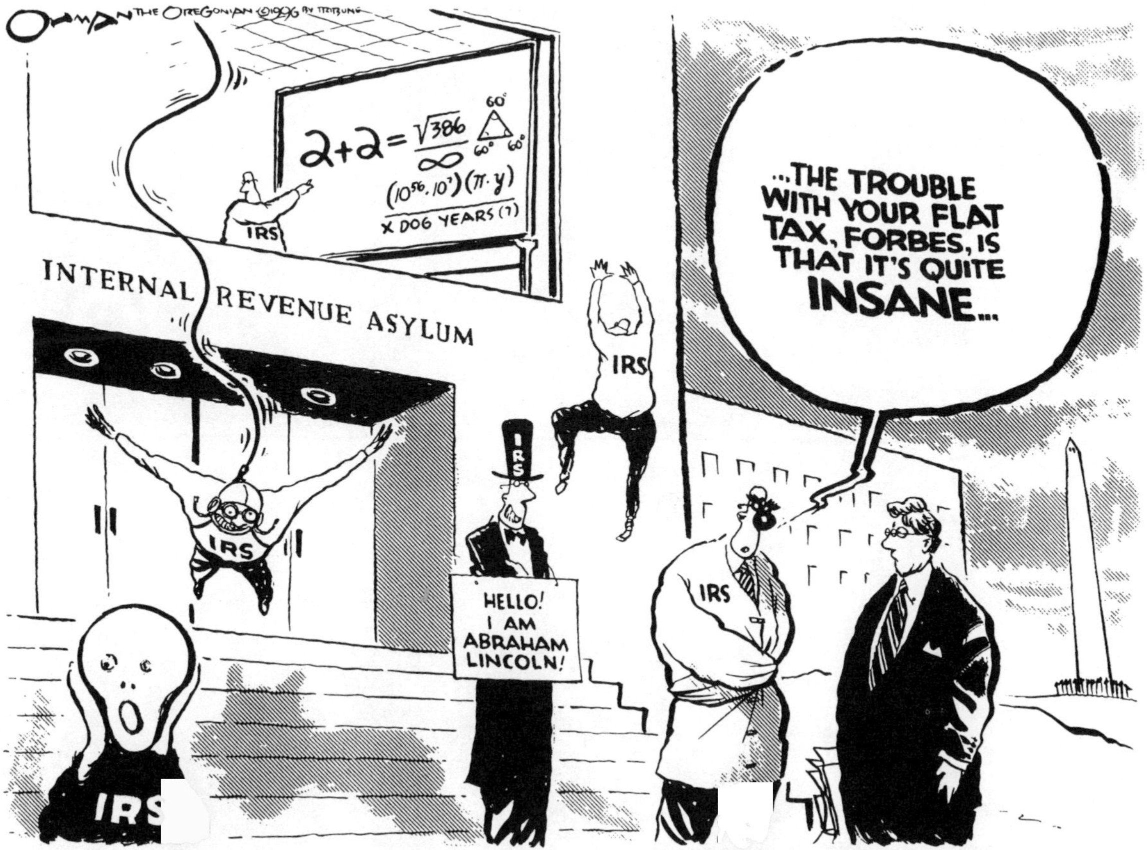
OHMAN THE OREGONIAN ©1996 BY TRIBUNE
2+2 = √386 / ∞
60° 60° 60°
(10⁵⁶·10⁷)(π·y)
X DOG YEARS (7)
IRS
INTERNAL REVENUE ASYLUM
IRS
IRS
IRS
HELLO! I AM ABRAHAM LINCOLN!
IRS
IRS
...THE TROUBLE WITH YOUR FLAT TAX, FORBES, IS THAT IT'S QUITE INSANE...
IRS

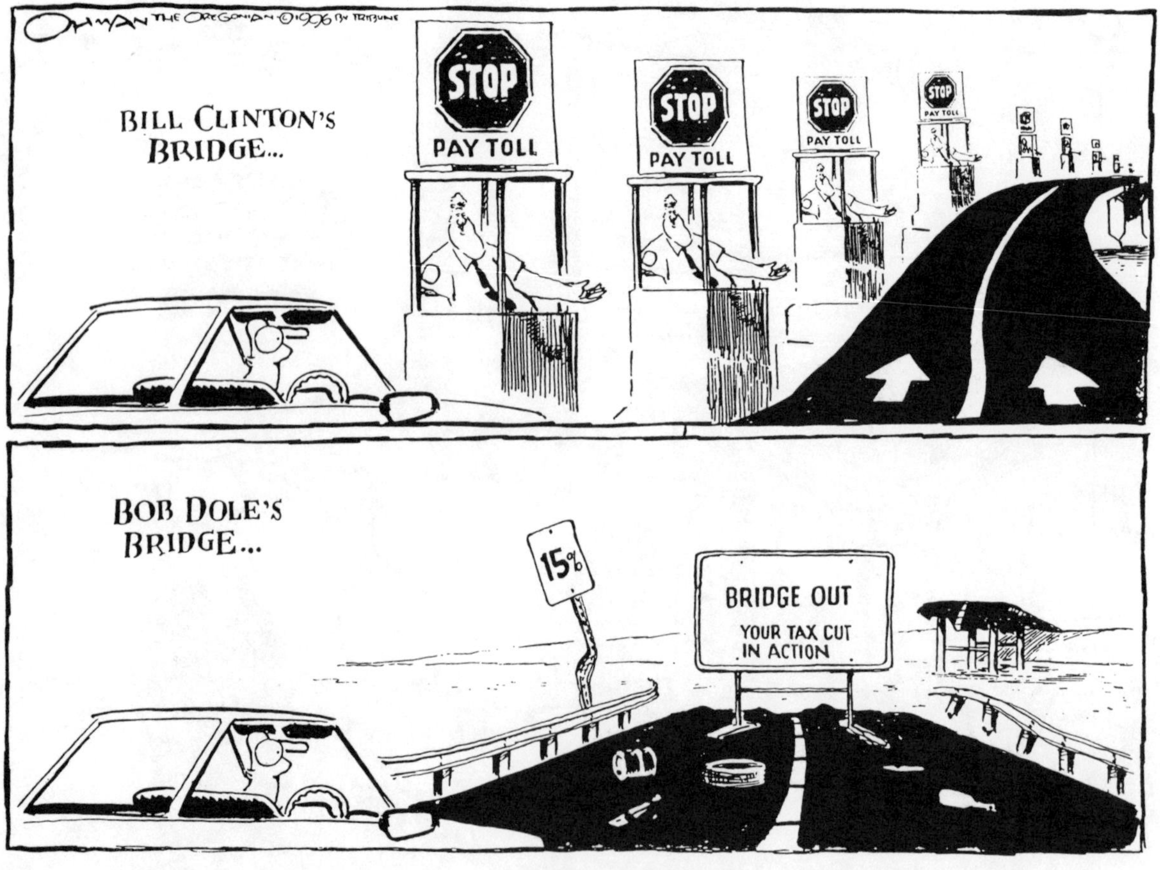
OHMAN THE OREGONIAN ©1996 BY TRIBUNE
BILL CLINTON'S BRIDGE...
STOP
PAY TOLL
STOP
PAY TOLL
STOP
PAY TOLL
STOP
PAY TOLL
BOB DOLE'S BRIDGE...
15%
BRIDGE OUT
YOUR TAX CUT IN ACTION

# CONGRESSIONAL OVERSIGHTS

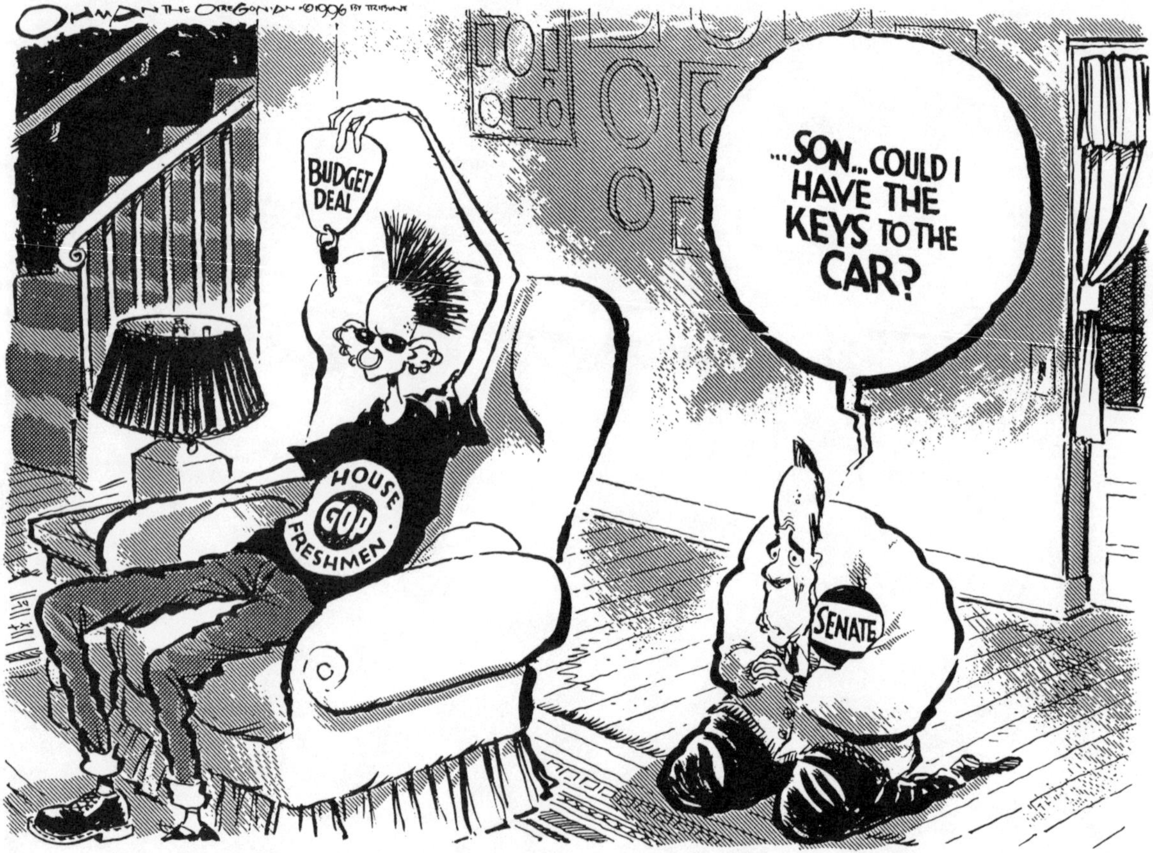
OHMAN THE OREGONIAN ©1996 BY TRIBUNE
BUDGET DEAL
HOUSE GOP FRESHMEN
...SON...COULD I HAVE THE KEYS TO THE CAR?
SENATE

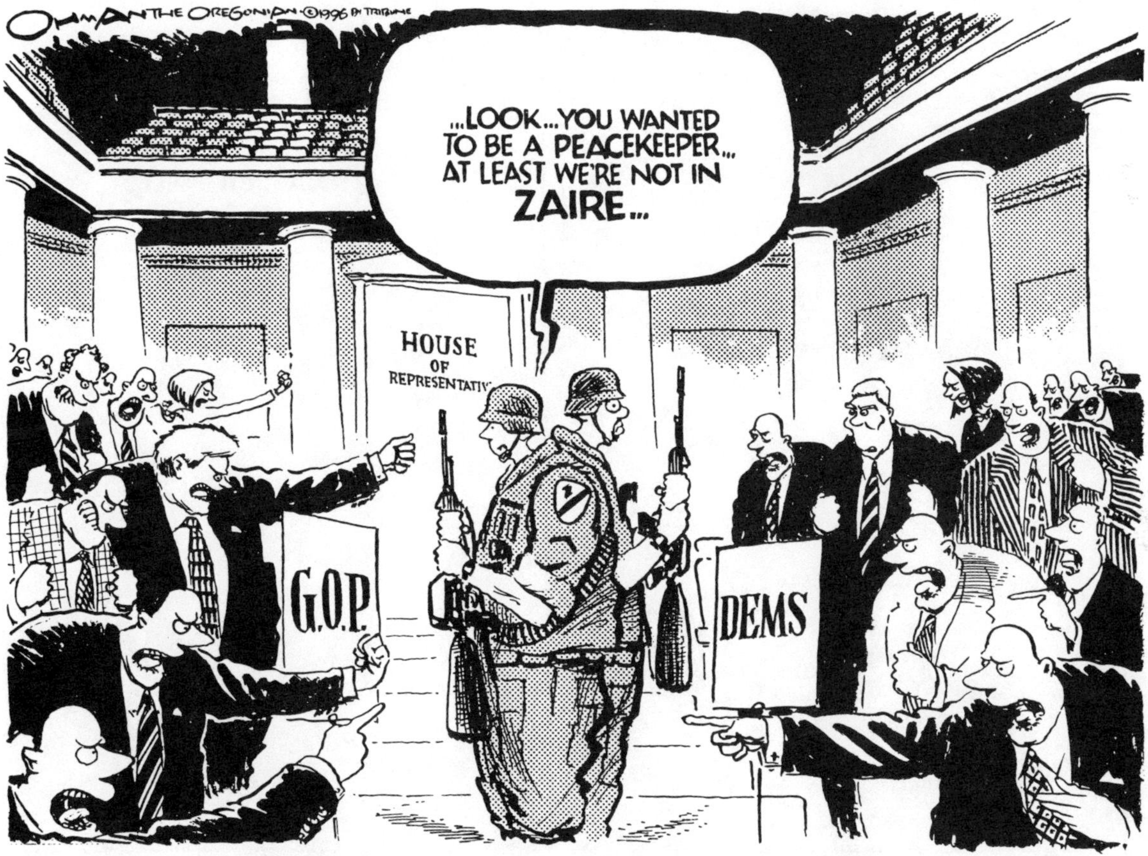
OHMAN THE OREGONIAN ©1996 BY TRIBUNE
...LOOK...YOU WANTED TO BE A PEACEKEEPER... AT LEAST WE'RE NOT IN ZAIRE...
HOUSE OF REPRESENTATIV
G.O.P.
DEMS

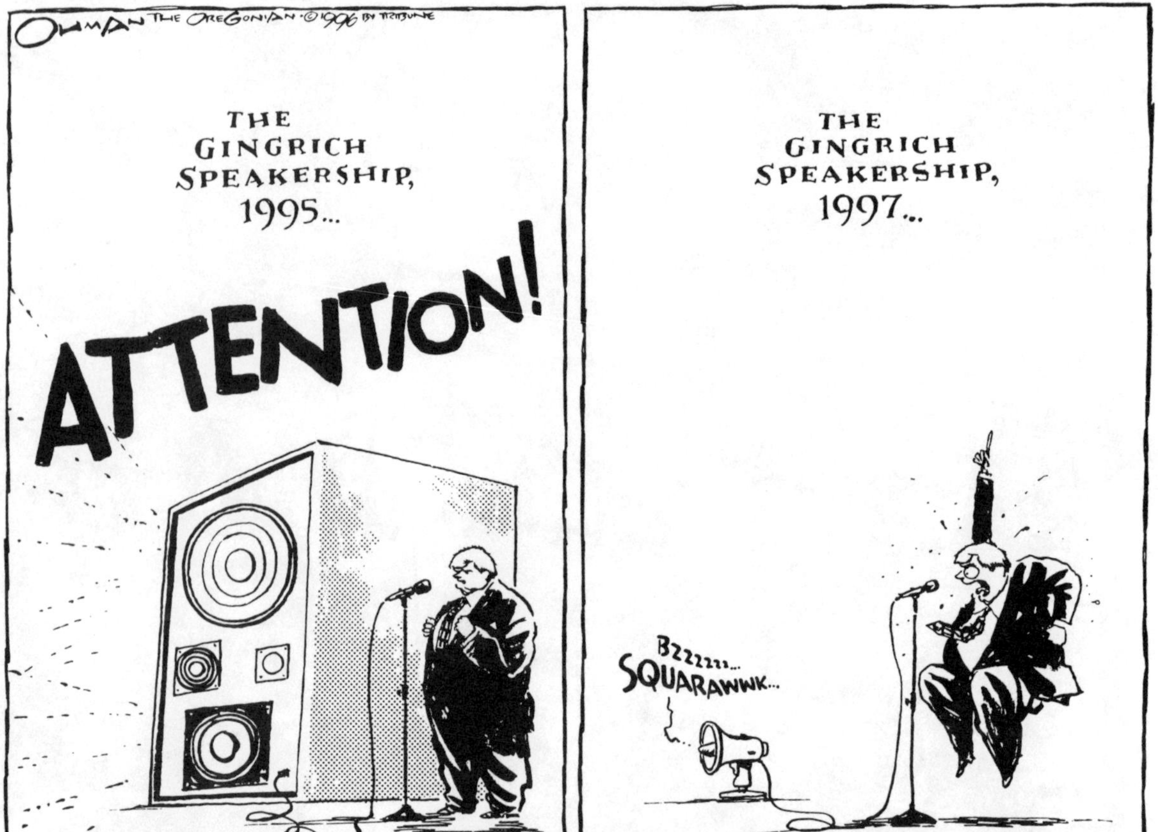
OHMAN THE OREGONIAN ©1996 BY TRIBUNE
THE GINGRICH SPEAKERSHIP, 1995...
ATTENTION!
THE GINGRICH SPEAKERSHIP, 1997...
BZZZZZZ...
SQUARAWWK...

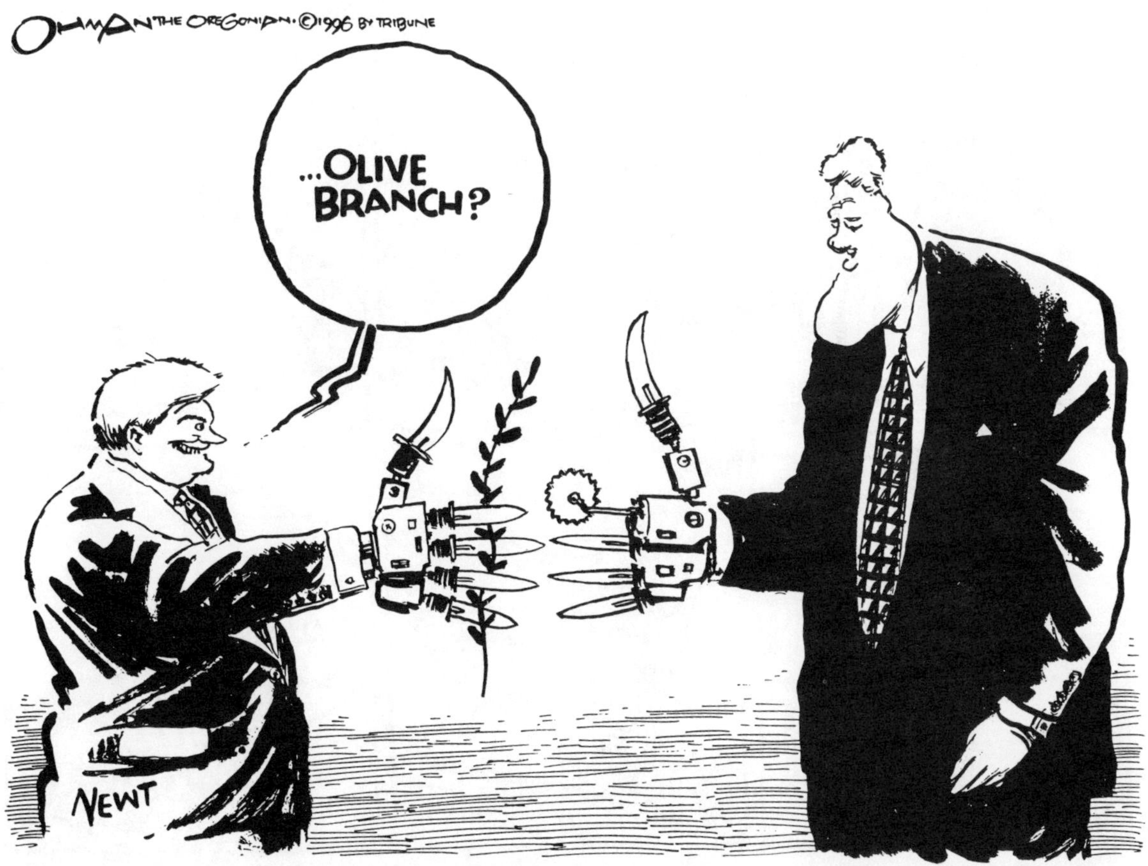
OHMAN THE OREGONIAN ©1996 BY TRIBUNE
...OLIVE BRANCH?
NEWT

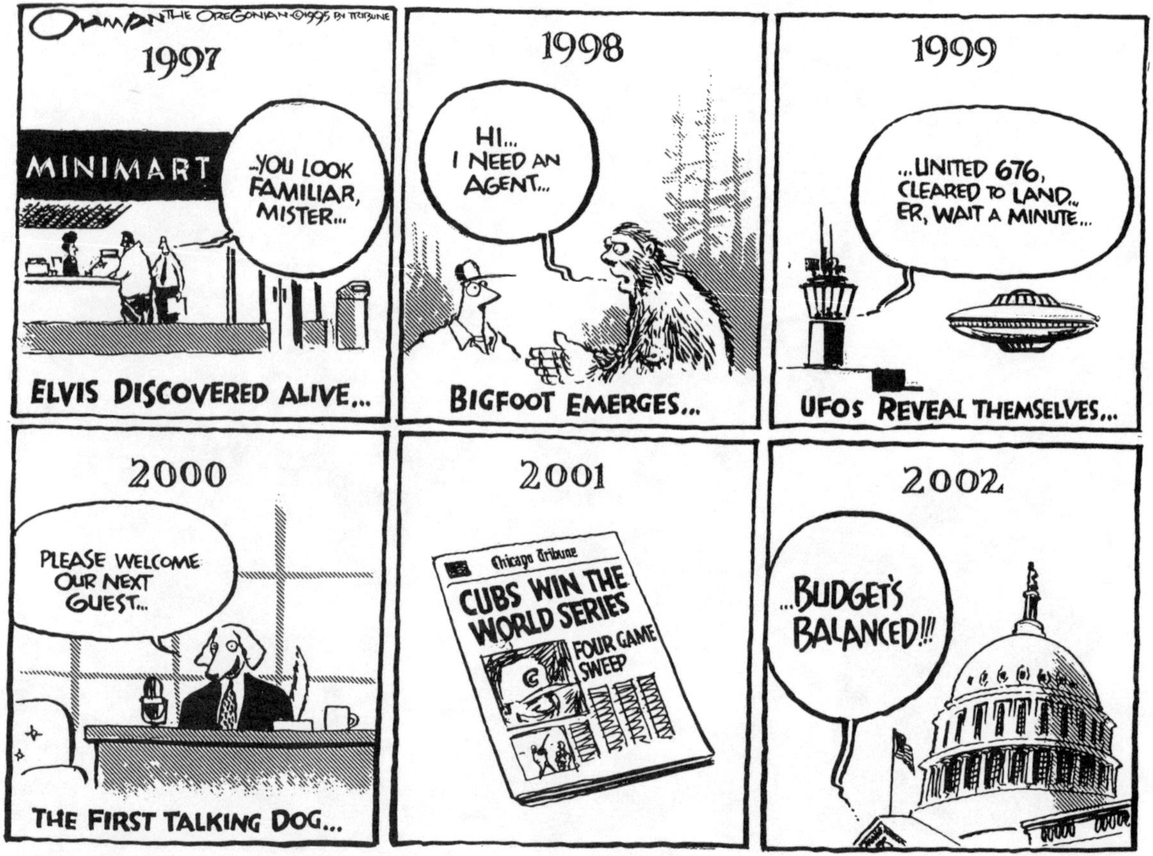
OHMAN THE OREGONIAN ©1995 BY TRIBUNE
1997
MINIMART
...YOU LOOK FAMILIAR, MISTER...
ELVIS DISCOVERED ALIVE...
1998
HI... I NEED AN AGENT...
BIGFOOT EMERGES...
1999
...UNITED 676, CLEARED TO LAND... ER, WAIT A MINUTE...
UFOs REVEAL THEMSELVES...
2000
PLEASE WELCOME OUR NEXT GUEST...
THE FIRST TALKING DOG...
2001
Chicago Tribune
CUBS WIN THE WORLD SERIES
FOUR GAME SWEEP
2002
...BUDGET'S BALANCED!!!

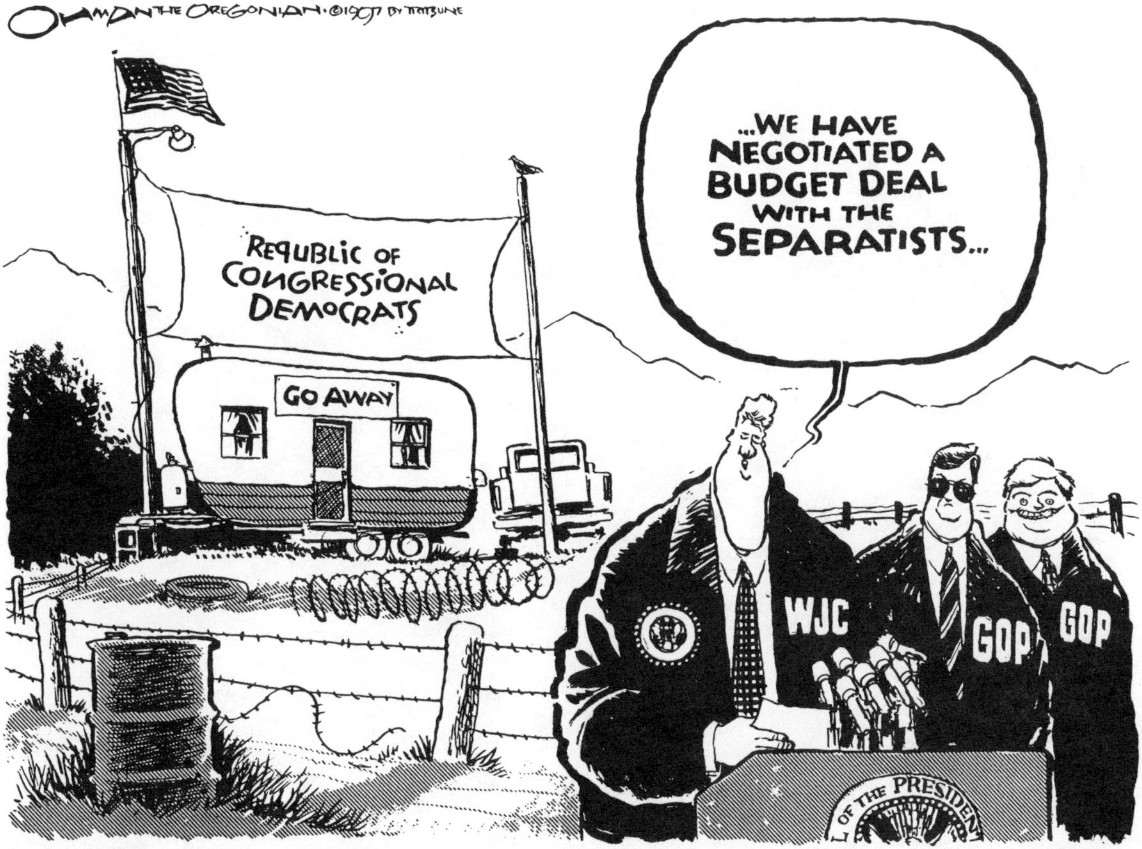
REPUBLIC OF CONGRESSIONAL DEMOCRATS
GO AWAY
...WE HAVE NEGOTIATED A BUDGET DEAL WITH THE SEPARATISTS...
WJC
GOP
GOP
SEAL OF THE PRESIDENT

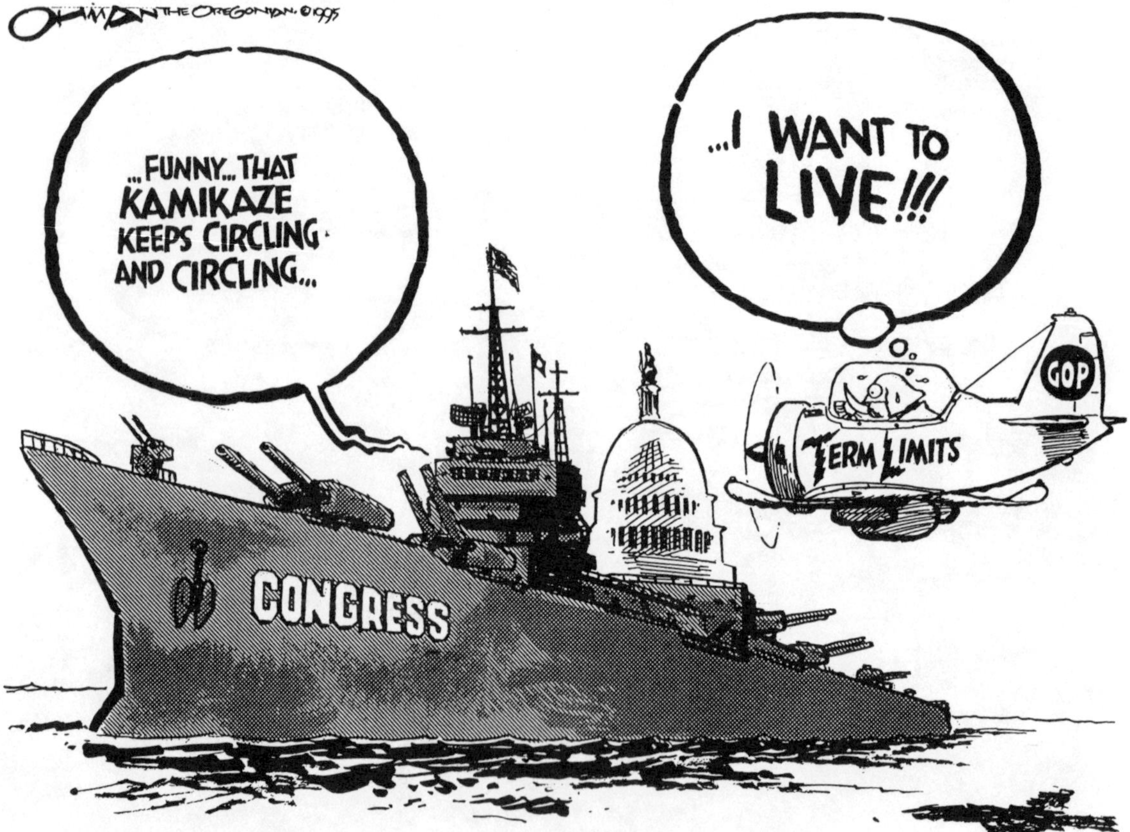

OHMAN THE OREGONIAN ©1995
...FUNNY...THAT KAMIKAZE KEEPS CIRCLING AND CIRCLING...
...I WANT TO LIVE!!!
GOP
TERM LIMITS
CONGRESS

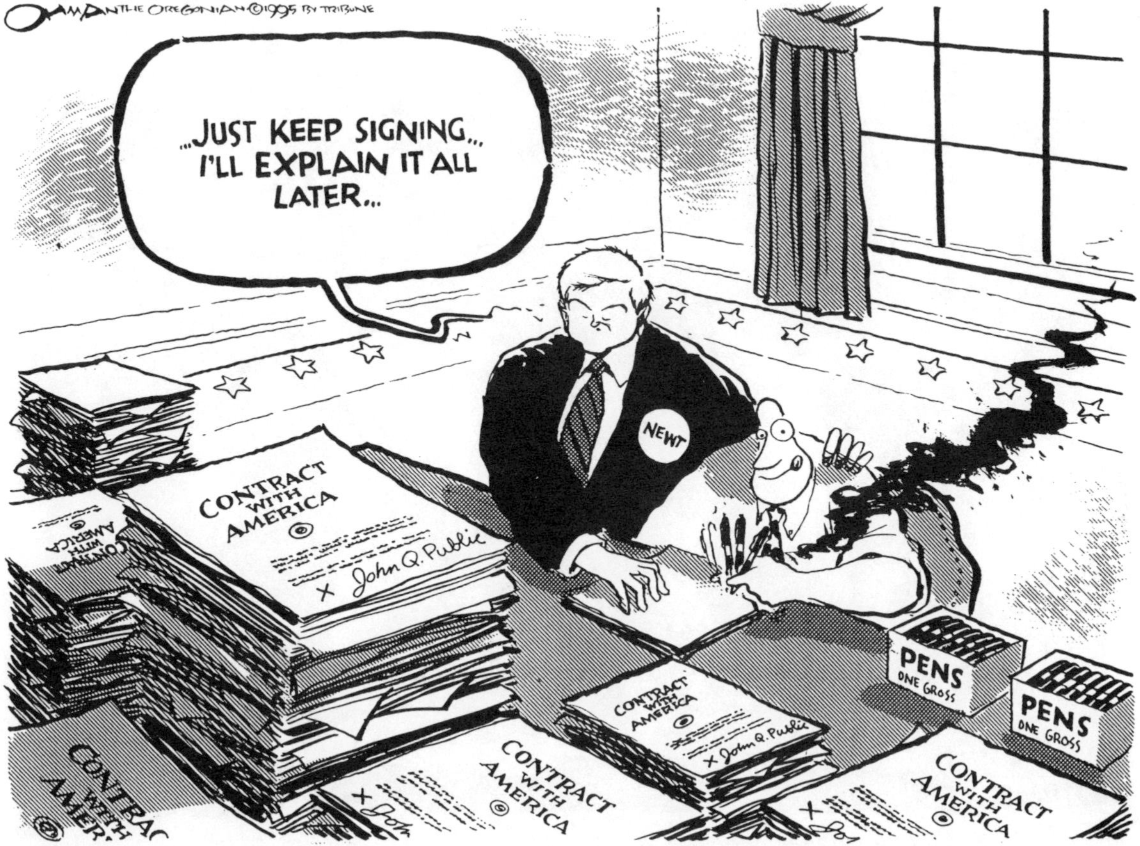
OHMAN THE OREGONIAN ©1995 BY TRIBUNE
...JUST KEEP SIGNING... I'LL EXPLAIN IT ALL LATER...
NEWT
CONTRACT WITH AMERICA
X John Q. Public
PENS ONE GROSS
PENS ONE GROSS
CONTRACT WITH AMERICA
X John Q. Public
CONTRACT WITH AMERICA
CONTRACT WITH AMERICA

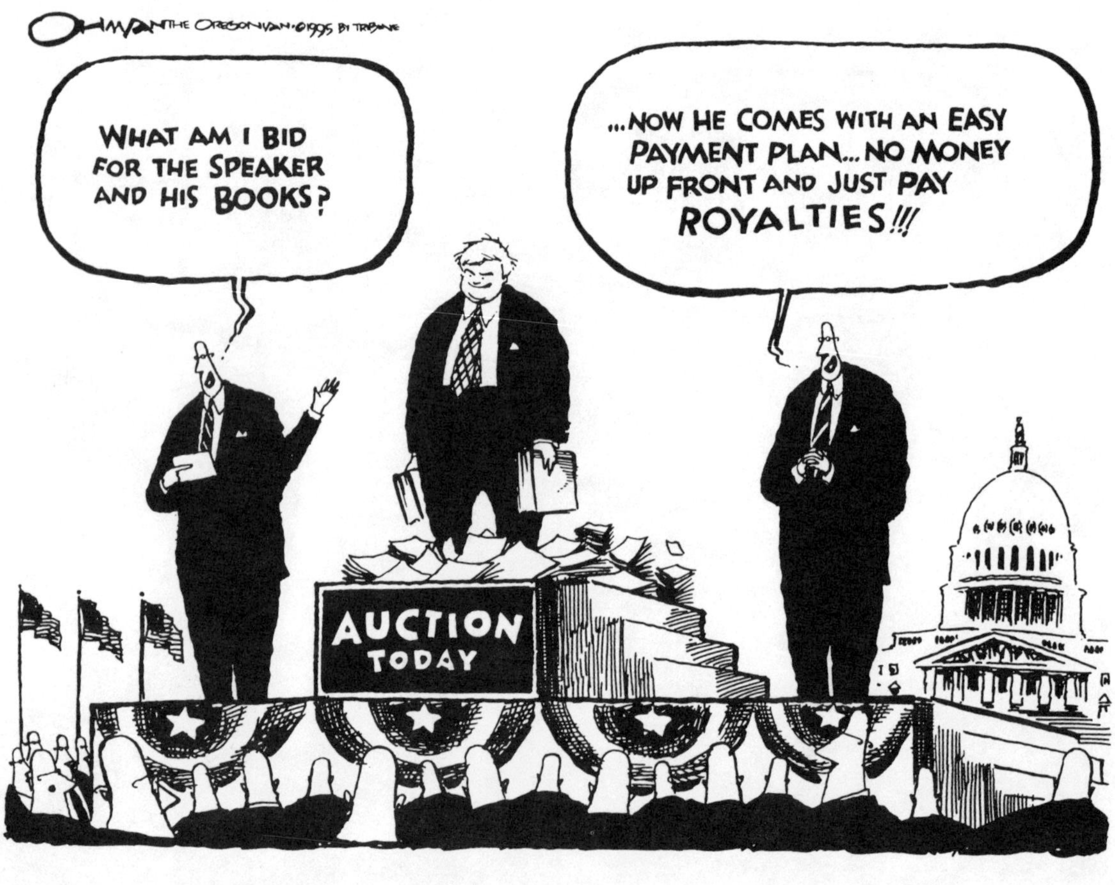
OHMAN THE OREGONIAN ©1995 BY TRIBUNE
WHAT AM I BID FOR THE SPEAKER AND HIS BOOKS?
AUCTION TODAY
...NOW HE COMES WITH AN EASY PAYMENT PLAN... NO MONEY UP FRONT AND JUST PAY ROYALTIES!!!

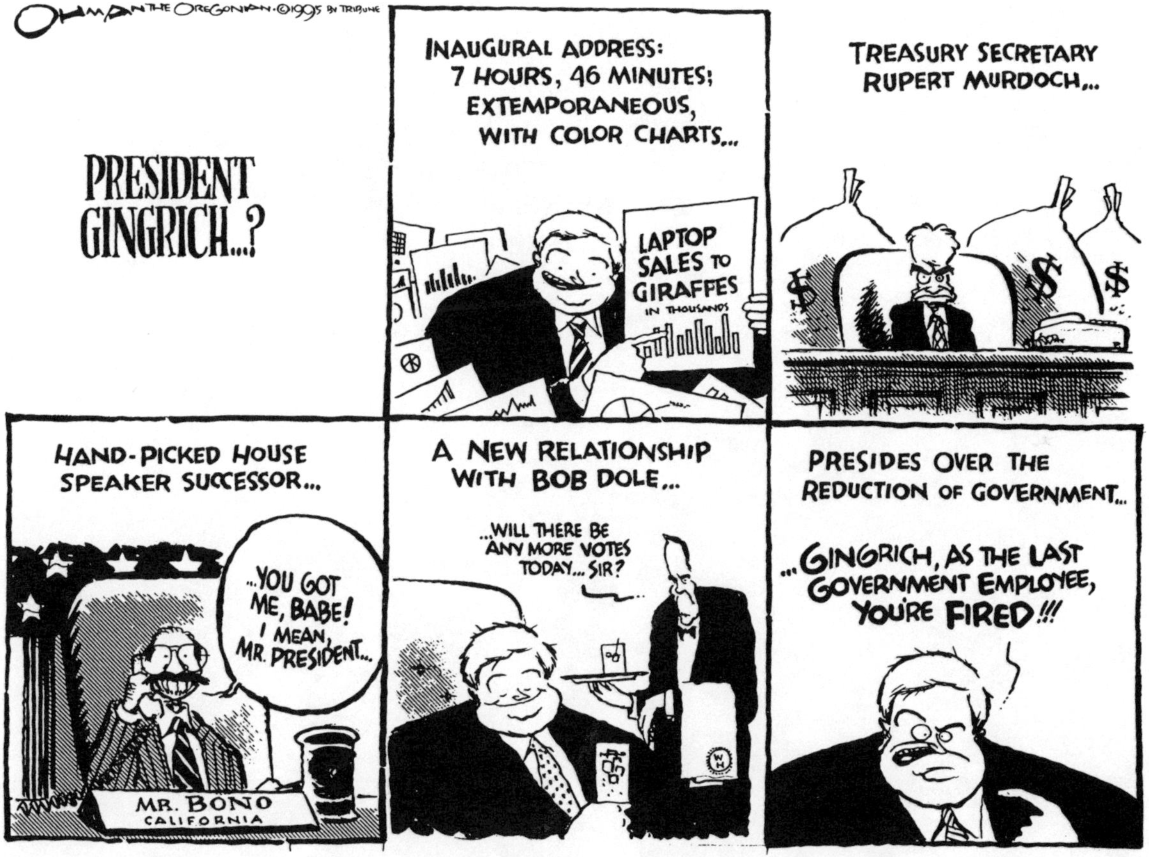
OHMAN THE OREGONIAN ©1995 BY TRIBUNE
PRESIDENT GINGRICH...?
INAUGURAL ADDRESS: 7 HOURS, 46 MINUTES; EXTEMPORANEOUS, WITH COLOR CHARTS...
LAPTOP SALES TO GIRAFFES
IN THOUSANDS
TREASURY SECRETARY RUPERT MURDOCH...
HAND-PICKED HOUSE SPEAKER SUCCESSOR...
...YOU GOT ME, BABE! I MEAN, MR. PRESIDENT...
MR. BONO
CALIFORNIA
A NEW RELATIONSHIP WITH BOB DOLE...
...WILL THERE BE ANY MORE VOTES TODAY... SIR?
PRESIDES OVER THE REDUCTION OF GOVERNMENT...
...GINGRICH, AS THE LAST GOVERNMENT EMPLOYEE, YOU'RE FIRED!!!

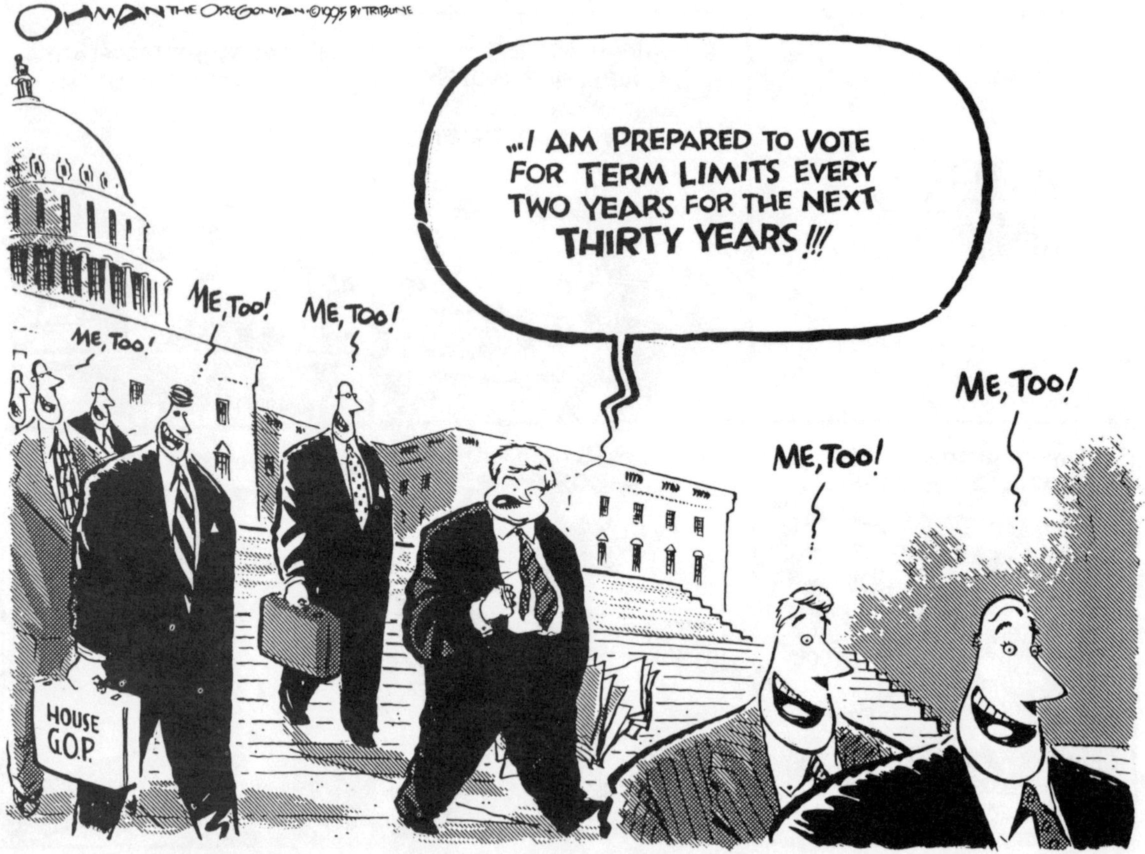
OHMAN THE OREGONIAN ©1995 BY TRIBUNE
...I AM PREPARED TO VOTE FOR TERM LIMITS EVERY TWO YEARS FOR THE NEXT THIRTY YEARS!!!
ME, TOO!
ME, TOO!
ME, TOO!
ME, TOO!
ME, TOO!
HOUSE G.O.P.

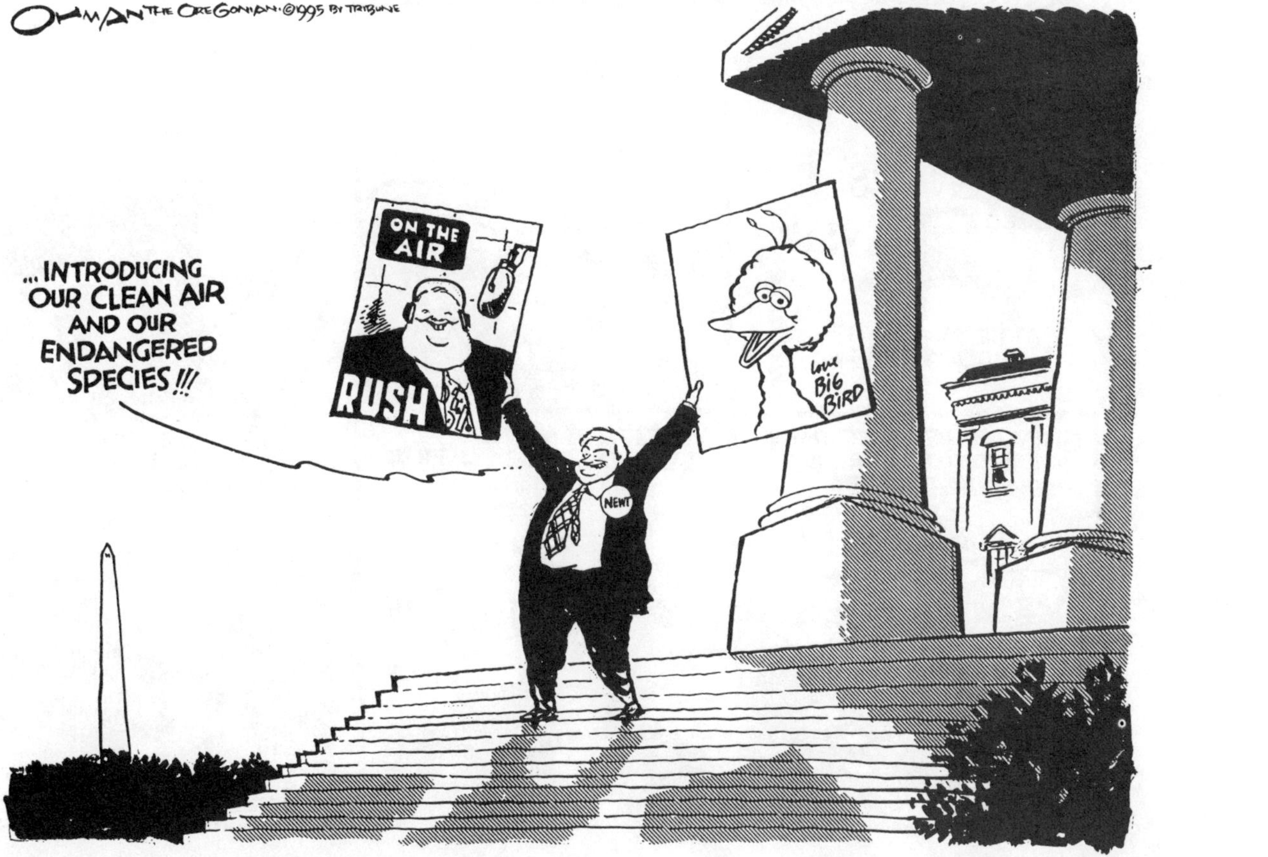
OHMAN THE OREGONIAN ©1995 BY TRIBUNE
...INTRODUCING OUR CLEAN AIR AND OUR ENDANGERED SPECIES!!!
ON THE AIR
RUSH
Love BIG BIRD
NEWT

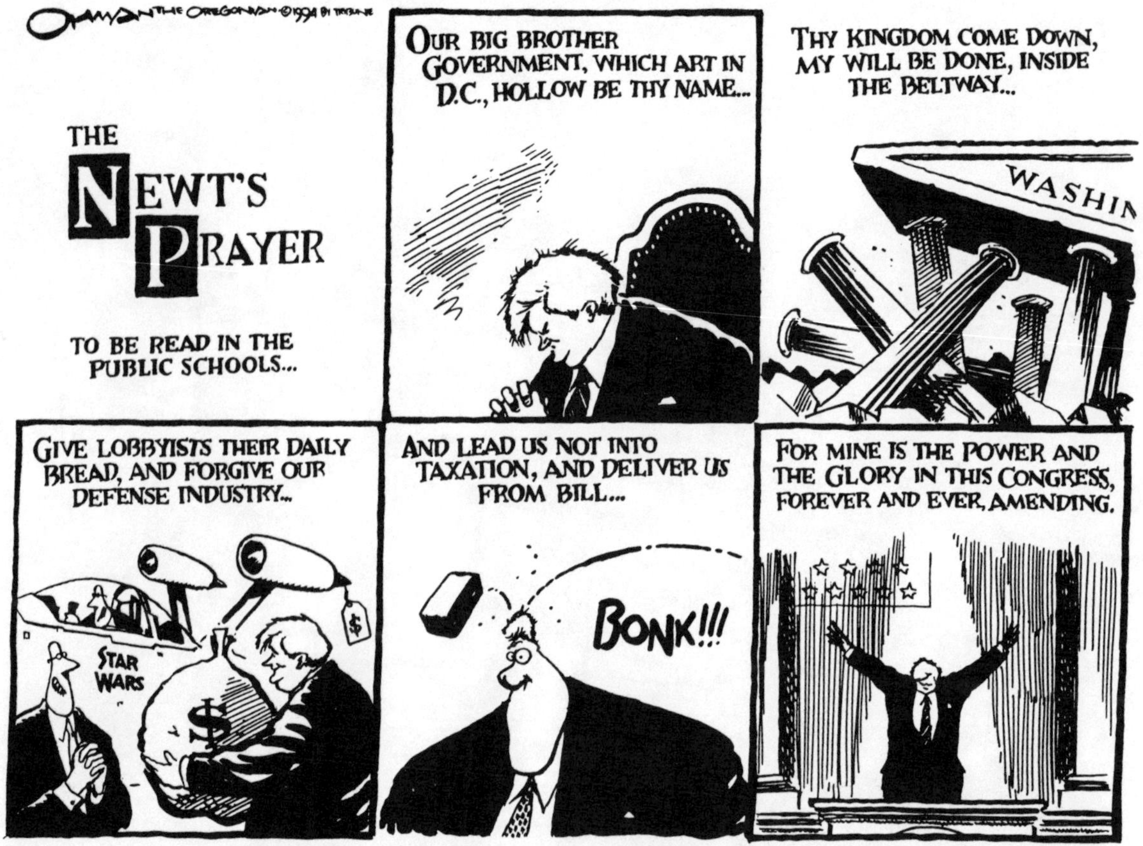
OHMAN THE OREGONIAN ©1994 BY TRIBUNE
THE NEWT'S PRAYER
TO BE READ IN THE PUBLIC SCHOOLS...
OUR BIG BROTHER GOVERNMENT, WHICH ART IN D.C., HOLLOW BE THY NAME...
THY KINGDOM COME DOWN, MY WILL BE DONE, INSIDE THE BELTWAY...
WASHIN
GIVE LOBBYISTS THEIR DAILY BREAD, AND FORGIVE OUR DEFENSE INDUSTRY...
STAR WARS
$
$
AND LEAD US NOT INTO TAXATION, AND DELIVER US FROM BILL...
BONK!!!
FOR MINE IS THE POWER AND THE GLORY IN THIS CONGRESS, FOREVER AND EVER, AMENDING.

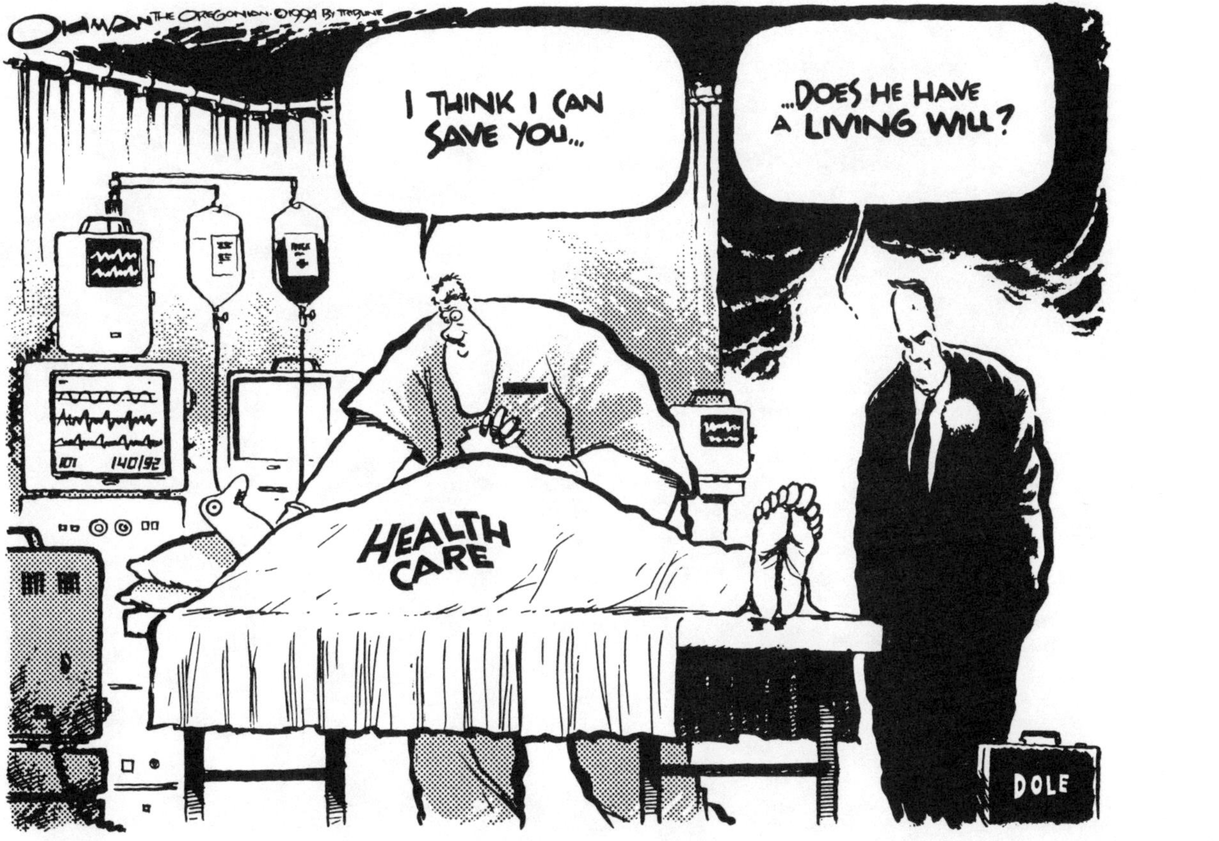
OHMAN THE OREGONIAN ©1994 BY TRIBUNE
I THINK I CAN SAVE YOU...
...DOES HE HAVE A LIVING WILL?
101 140/92
HEALTH CARE
DOLE

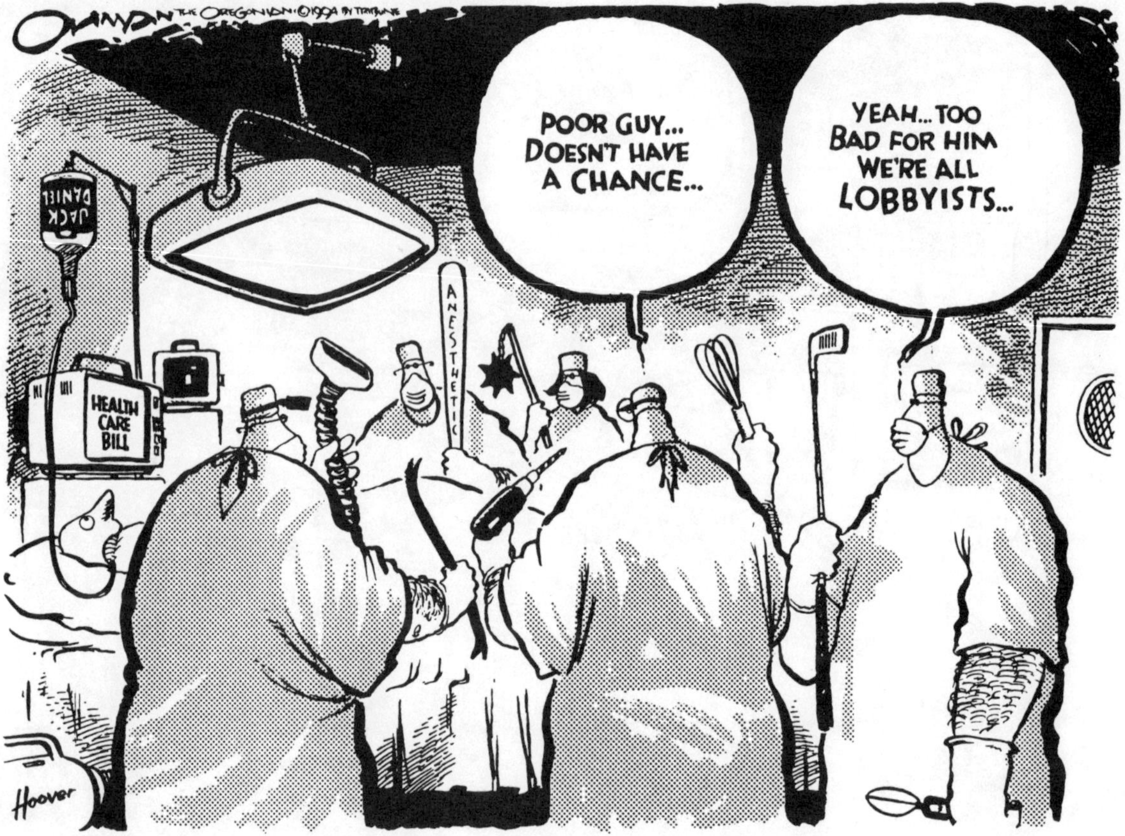

OLIPHANT THE OREGONIAN ©1994 BY TRIBUNE
JACK DANIEL
HEALTH CARE BILL
ANESTHETIC
POOR GUY... DOESN'T HAVE A CHANCE...
YEAH... TOO BAD FOR HIM WE'RE ALL LOBBYISTS...
Hoover

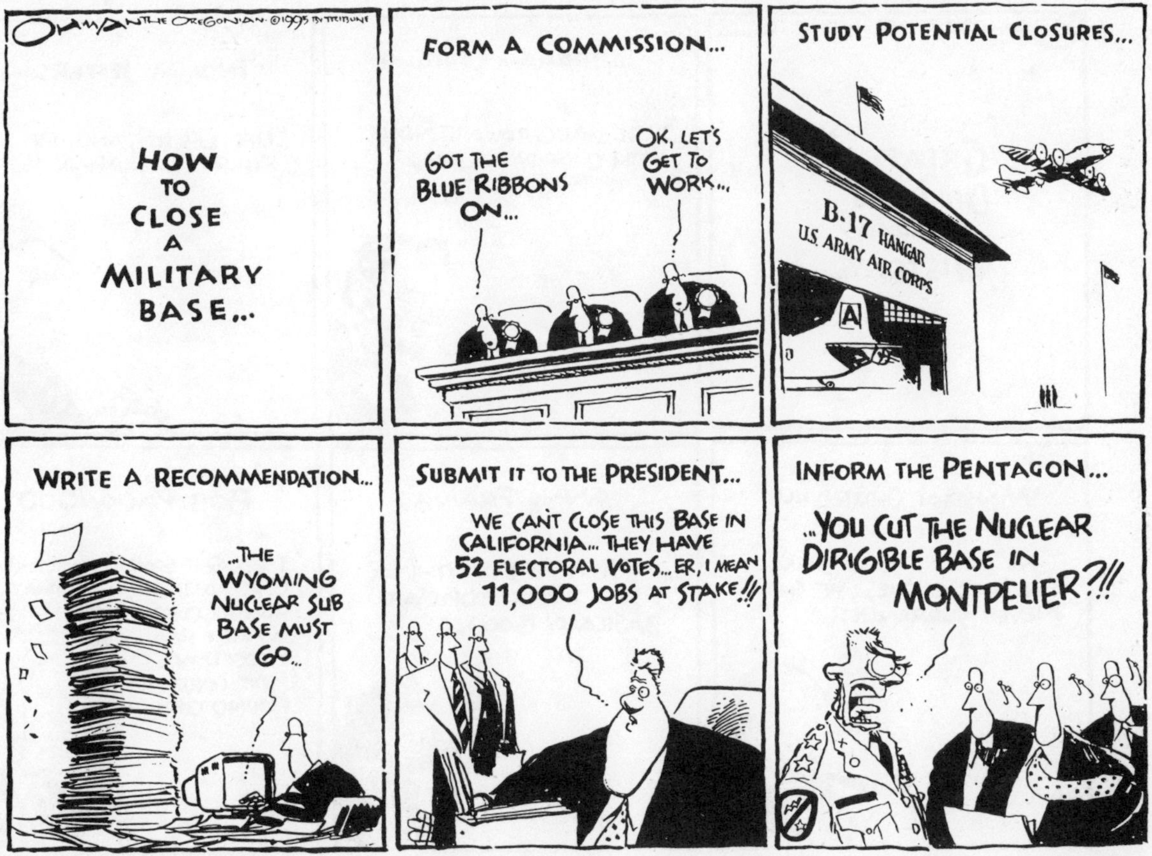
OHMAN THE OREGONIAN ©1995 BY TRIBUNE
HOW TO CLOSE A MILITARY BASE...
FORM A COMMISSION...
GOT THE BLUE RIBBONS ON...
OK, LET'S GET TO WORK...
STUDY POTENTIAL CLOSURES...
B-17 HANGAR
U.S. ARMY AIR CORPS
A
WRITE A RECOMMENDATION...
...THE WYOMING NUCLEAR SUB BASE MUST GO...
SUBMIT IT TO THE PRESIDENT...
WE CAN'T CLOSE THIS BASE IN CALIFORNIA... THEY HAVE 52 ELECTORAL VOTES... ER, I MEAN 11,000 JOBS AT STAKE!!!
INFORM THE PENTAGON...
...YOU CUT THE NUCLEAR DIRIGIBLE BASE IN MONTPELIER?!!

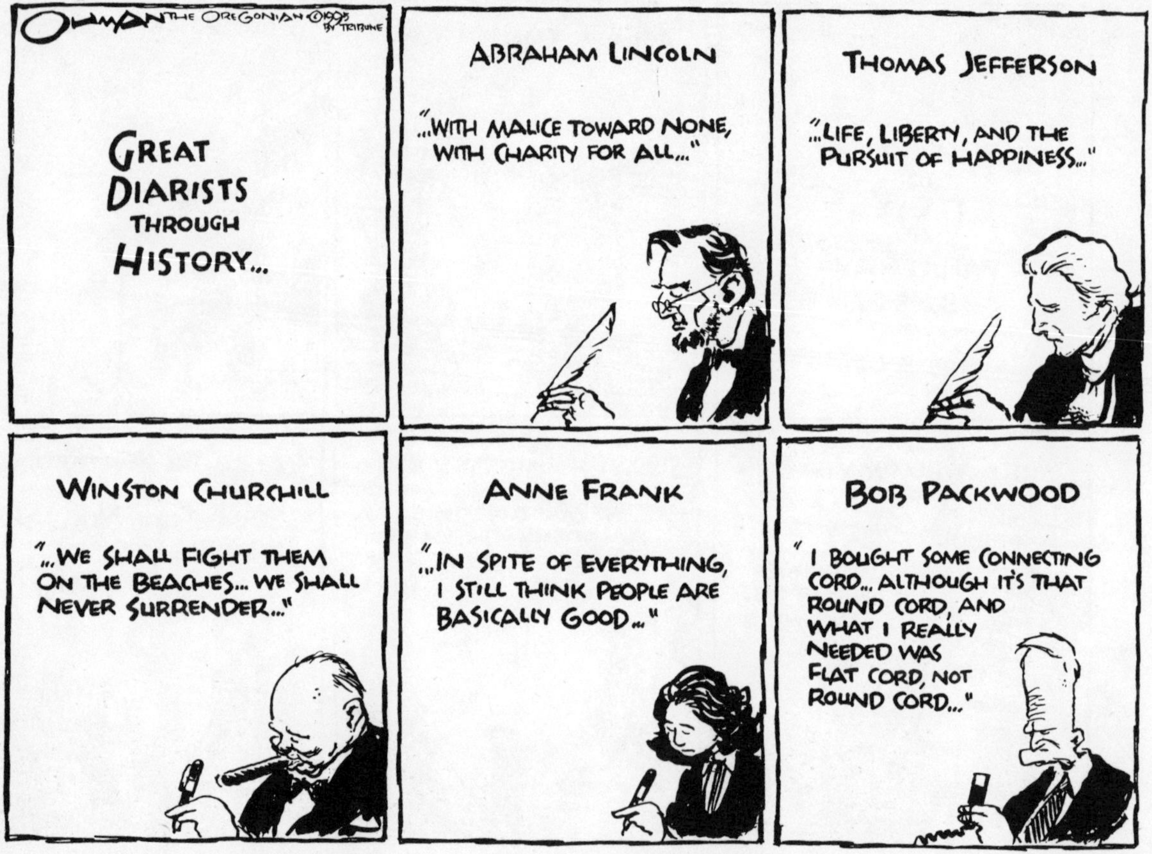
OHMAN THE OREGONIAN ©1995 BY TRIBUNE
GREAT DIARISTS THROUGH HISTORY...
ABRAHAM LINCOLN
"...WITH MALICE TOWARD NONE, WITH CHARITY FOR ALL..."
THOMAS JEFFERSON
"...LIFE, LIBERTY, AND THE PURSUIT OF HAPPINESS..."
WINSTON CHURCHILL
"...WE SHALL FIGHT THEM ON THE BEACHES... WE SHALL NEVER SURRENDER..."
ANNE FRANK
"...IN SPITE OF EVERYTHING, I STILL THINK PEOPLE ARE BASICALLY GOOD..."
BOB PACKWOOD
"I BOUGHT SOME CONNECTING CORD... ALTHOUGH IT'S THAT ROUND CORD, AND WHAT I REALLY NEEDED WAS FLAT CORD, NOT ROUND CORD..."

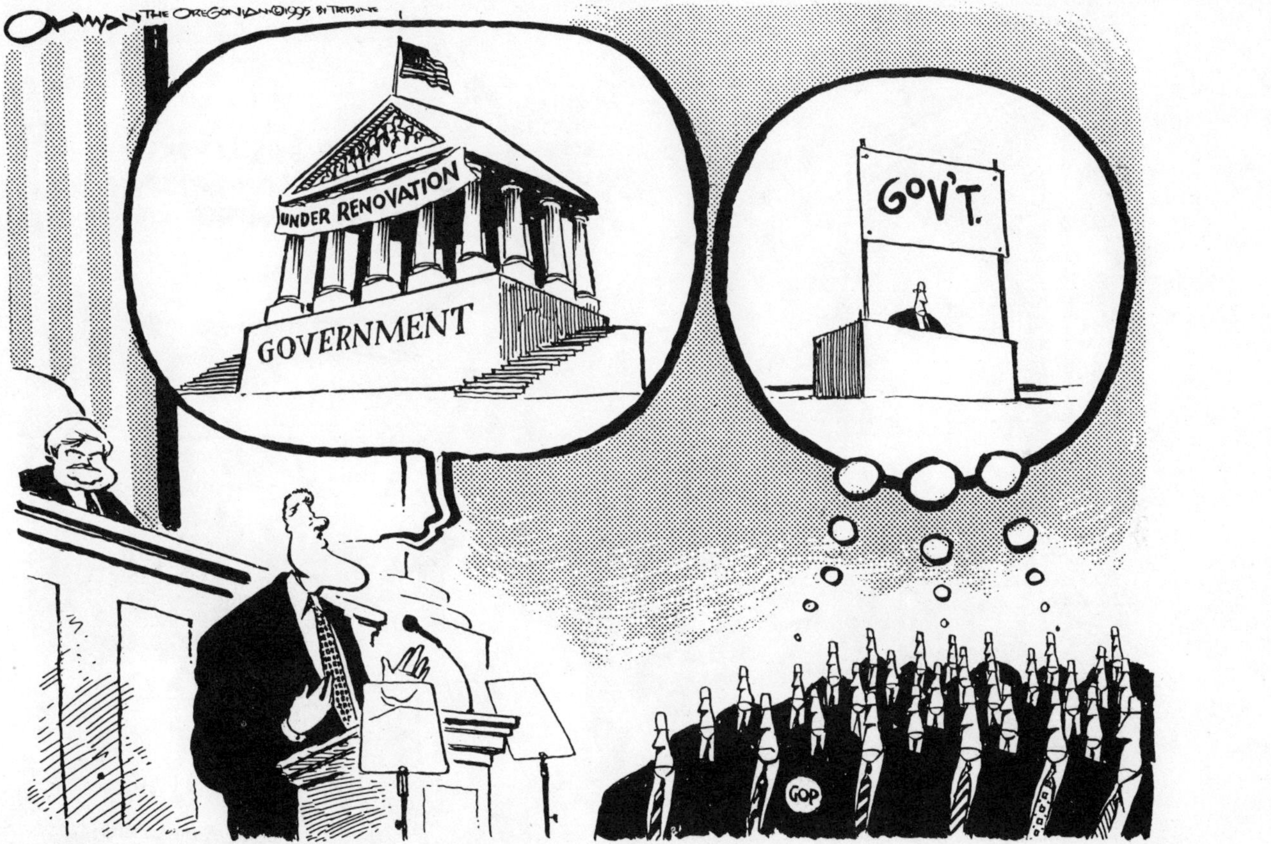
OHMAN THE OREGONIAN ©1995 BY TRIBUNE
UNDER RENOVATION
GOVERNMENT
GOV'T.
GOP

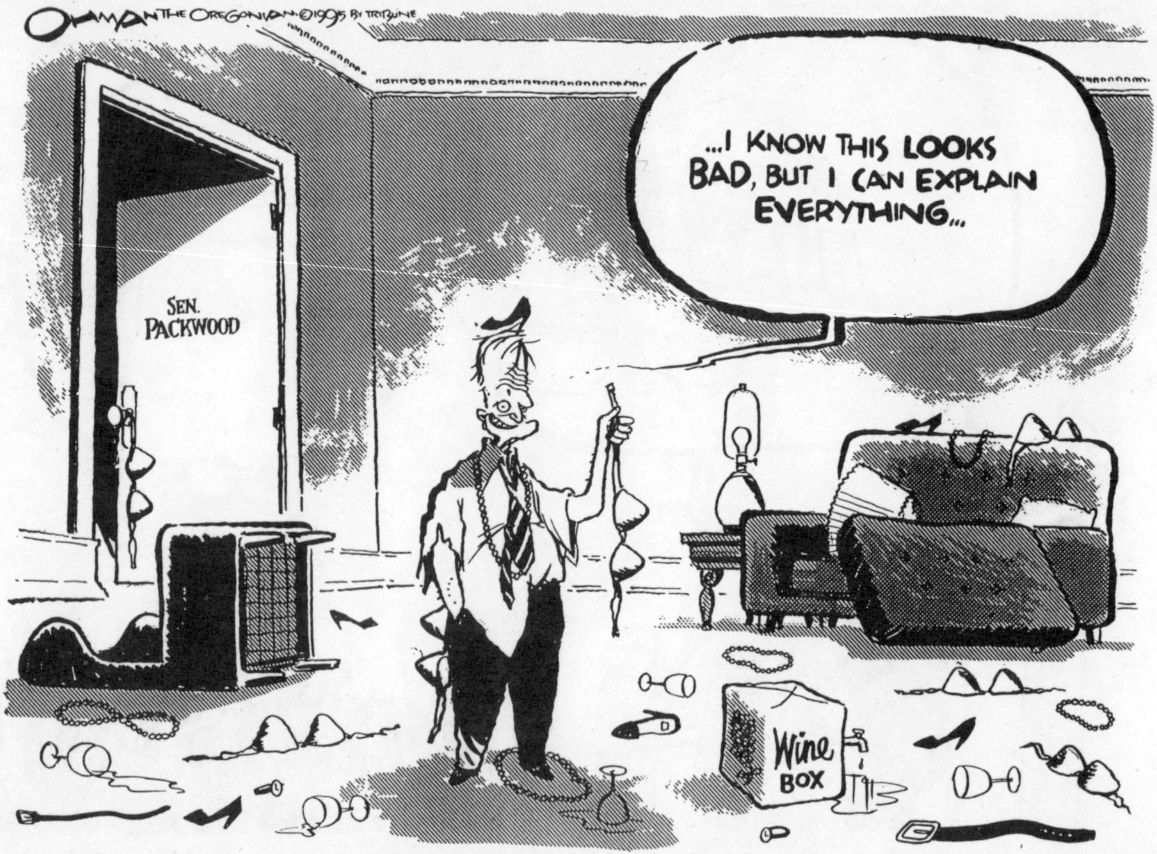
OHMAN THE OREGONIAN ©1995 BY TRIBUNE
SEN. PACKWOOD
...I KNOW THIS LOOKS BAD, BUT I CAN EXPLAIN EVERYTHING...
WINE BOX

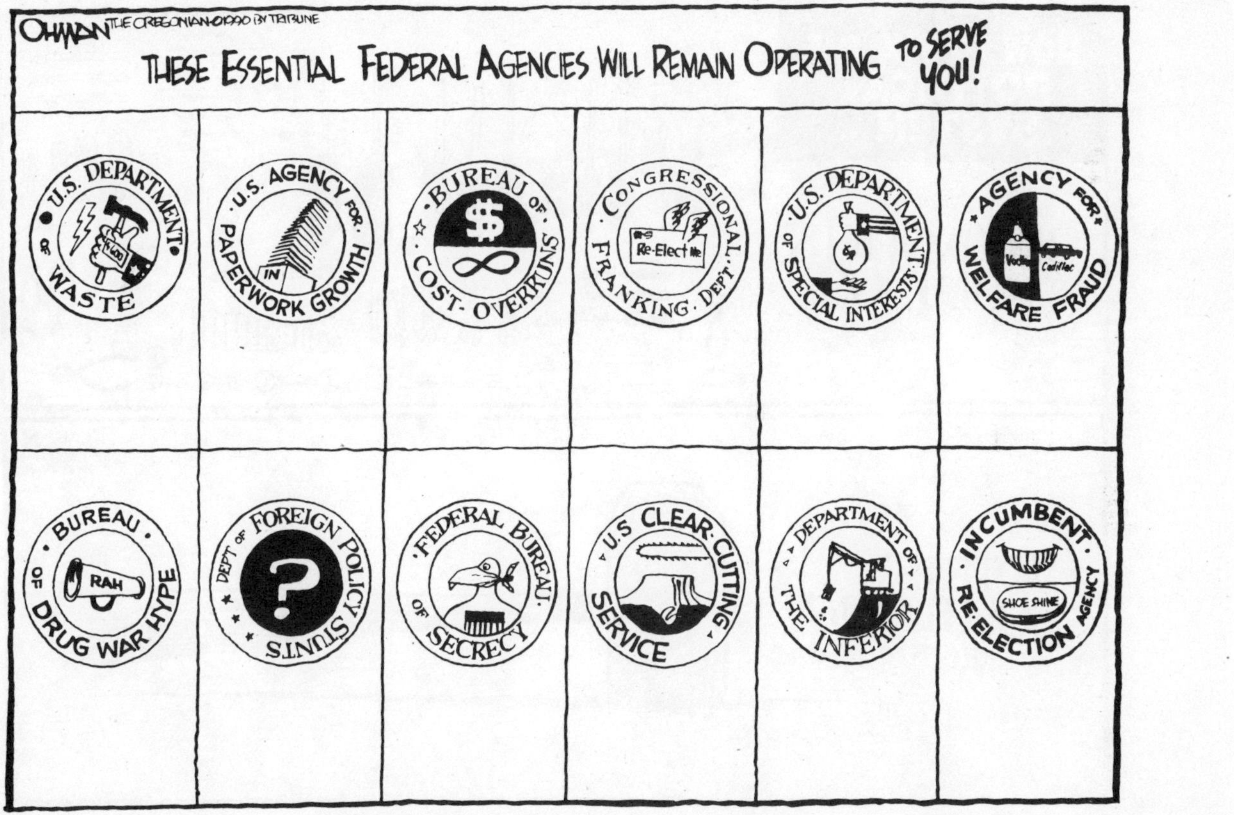
OHMAN THE OREGONIAN ©1990 BY TRIBUNE
THESE ESSENTIAL FEDERAL AGENCIES WILL REMAIN OPERATING TO SERVE YOU!
U.S. DEPARTMENT OF WASTE
$400
U.S. AGENCY FOR PAPERWORK GROWTH
IN
BUREAU OF COST-OVERRUNS
$
CONGRESSIONAL FRANKING DEPT.
Re-Elect Me
U.S. DEPARTMENT OF SPECIAL INTERESTS
AGENCY FOR WELFARE FRAUD
Cadillac
BUREAU OF DRUG WAR HYPE
RAH
DEPT OF FOREIGN POLICY STUNTS
?
FEDERAL BUREAU OF SECRECY
U.S CLEAR-CUTTING SERVICE
DEPARTMENT OF THE INFERIOR
INCUMBENT RE-ELECTION AGENCY
SHOE SHINE

HOW TO FIX THE POLITICAL SYSTEM...
INCUMBENTS' SOLUTION:
VOTERS' SOLUTION:
OHMAN
THE OREGONIAN
©1991 BY TRIBUNE

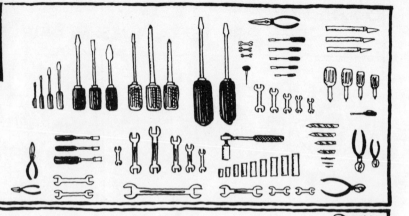

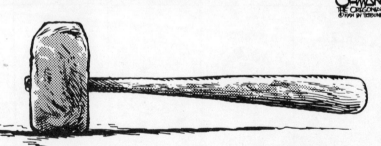

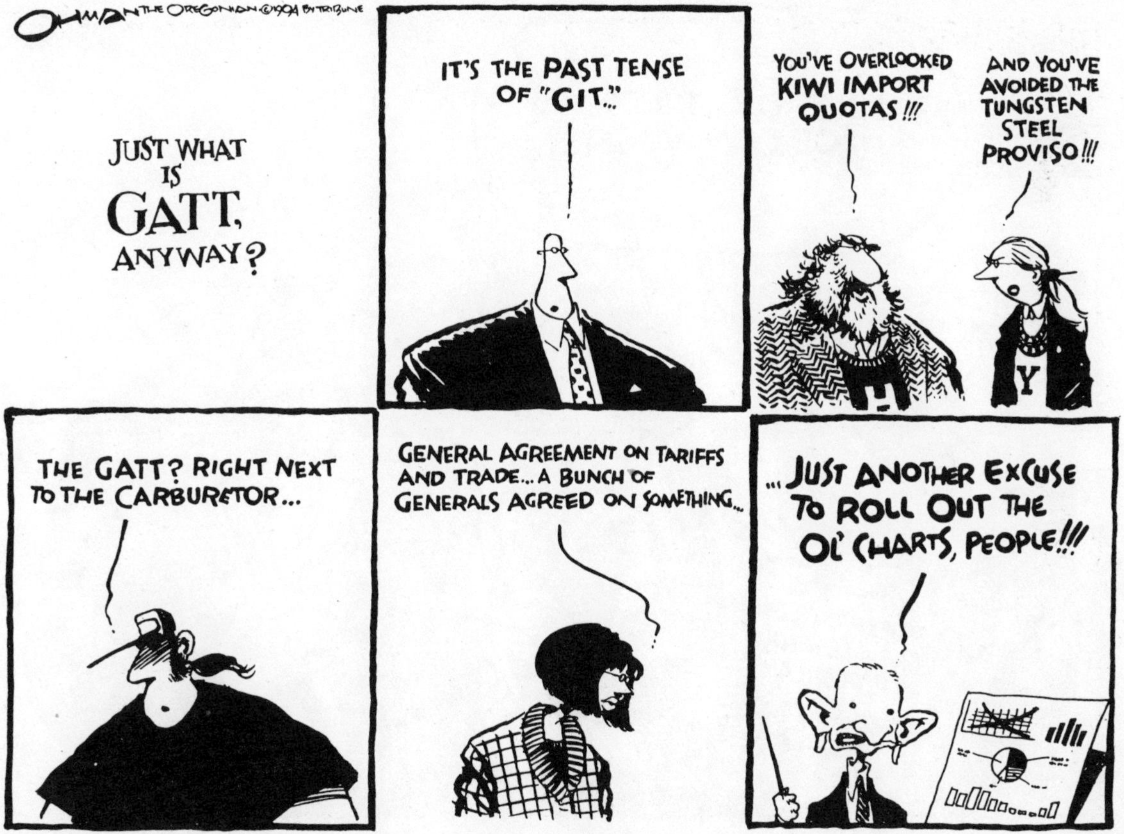
OHMAN THE OREGONIAN ©1994 BY TRIBUNE
JUST WHAT IS GATT, ANYWAY?
IT'S THE PAST TENSE OF "GIT."
YOU'VE OVERLOOKED KIWI IMPORT QUOTAS!!!
AND YOU'VE AVOIDED THE TUNGSTEN STEEL PROVISO!!!
THE GATT? RIGHT NEXT TO THE CARBURETOR...
GENERAL AGREEMENT ON TARIFFS AND TRADE... A BUNCH OF GENERALS AGREED ON SOMETHING...
...JUST ANOTHER EXCUSE TO ROLL OUT THE OL' CHARTS, PEOPLE!!!

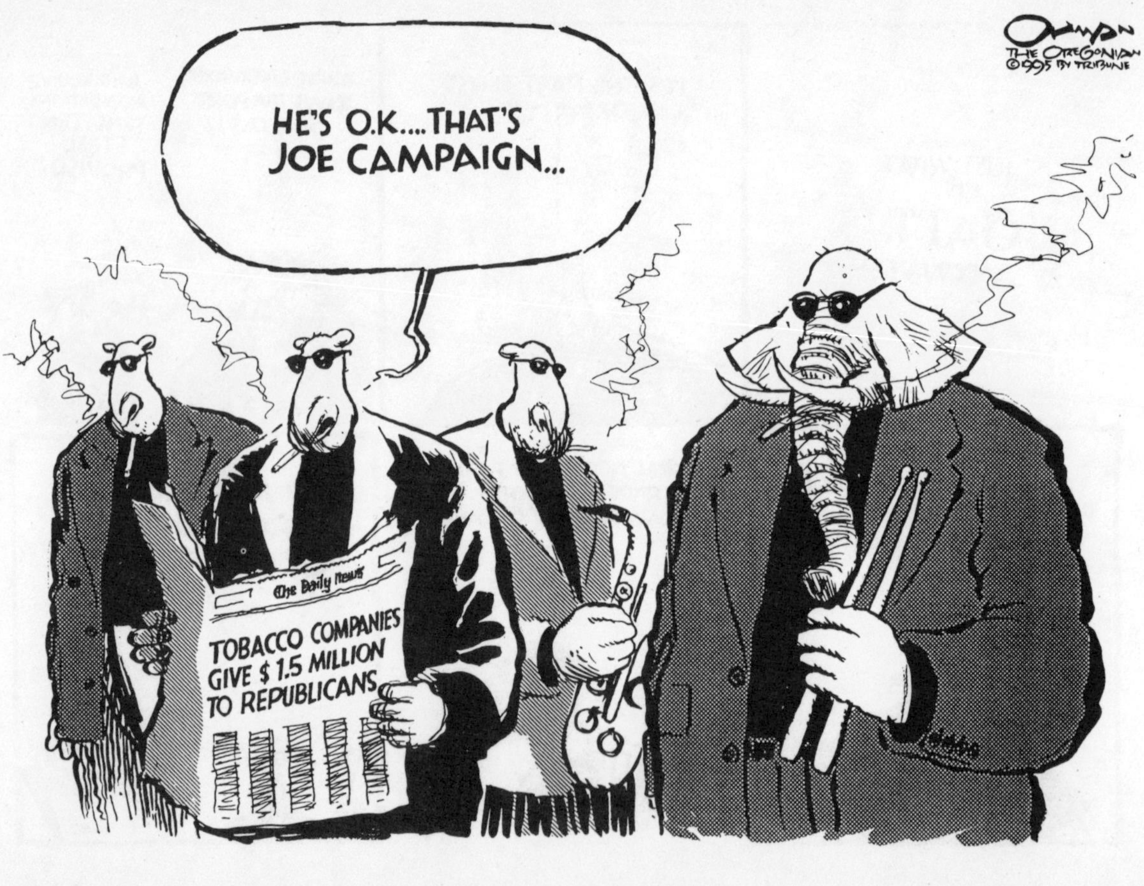
HE'S O.K.....THAT'S JOE CAMPAIGN...
The Daily News
TOBACCO COMPANIES GIVE $ 1.5 MILLION TO REPUBLICANS
THE OREGONIAN
©1995 BY TRIBUNE

# POPPED CULTURE

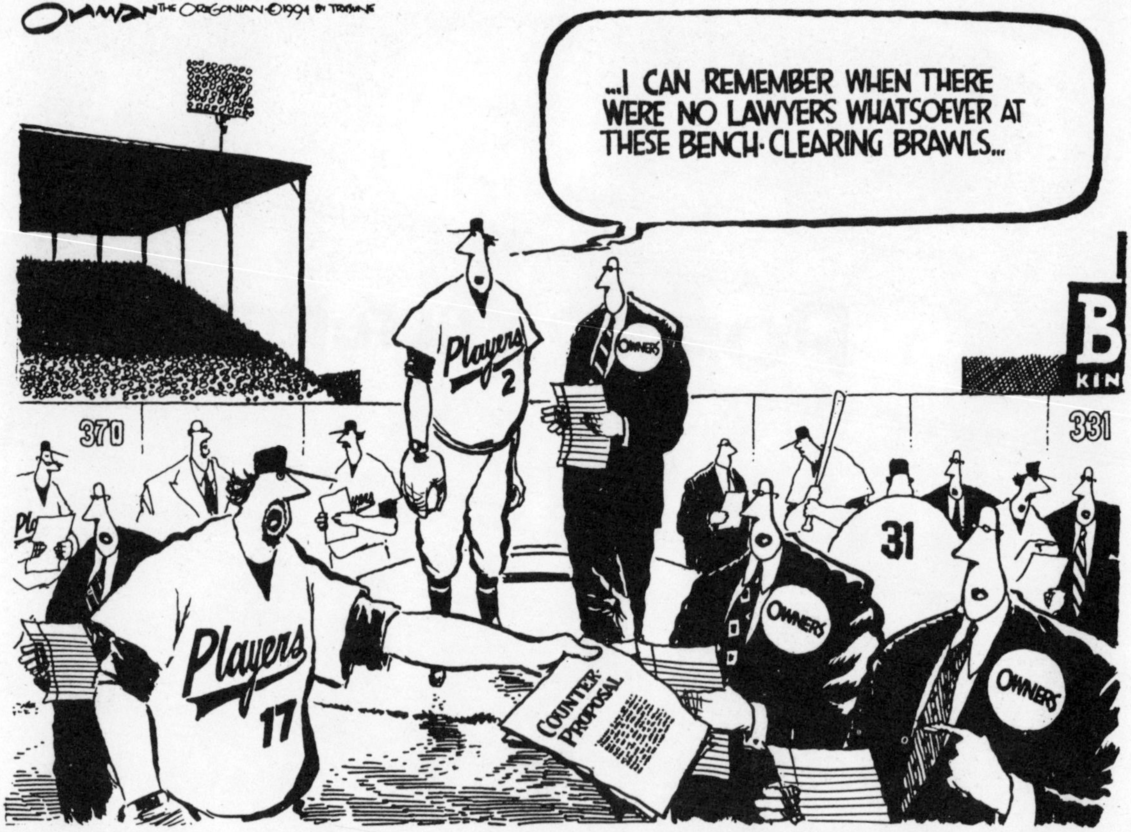
OHMAN THE OREGONIAN ©1994 BY TRIBUNE
...I CAN REMEMBER WHEN THERE WERE NO LAWYERS WHATSOEVER AT THESE BENCH-CLEARING BRAWLS...
Players 2
OWNERS
370
331
B
KIN
31
Players 17
COUNTER-PROPOSAL
OWNERS
OWNERS

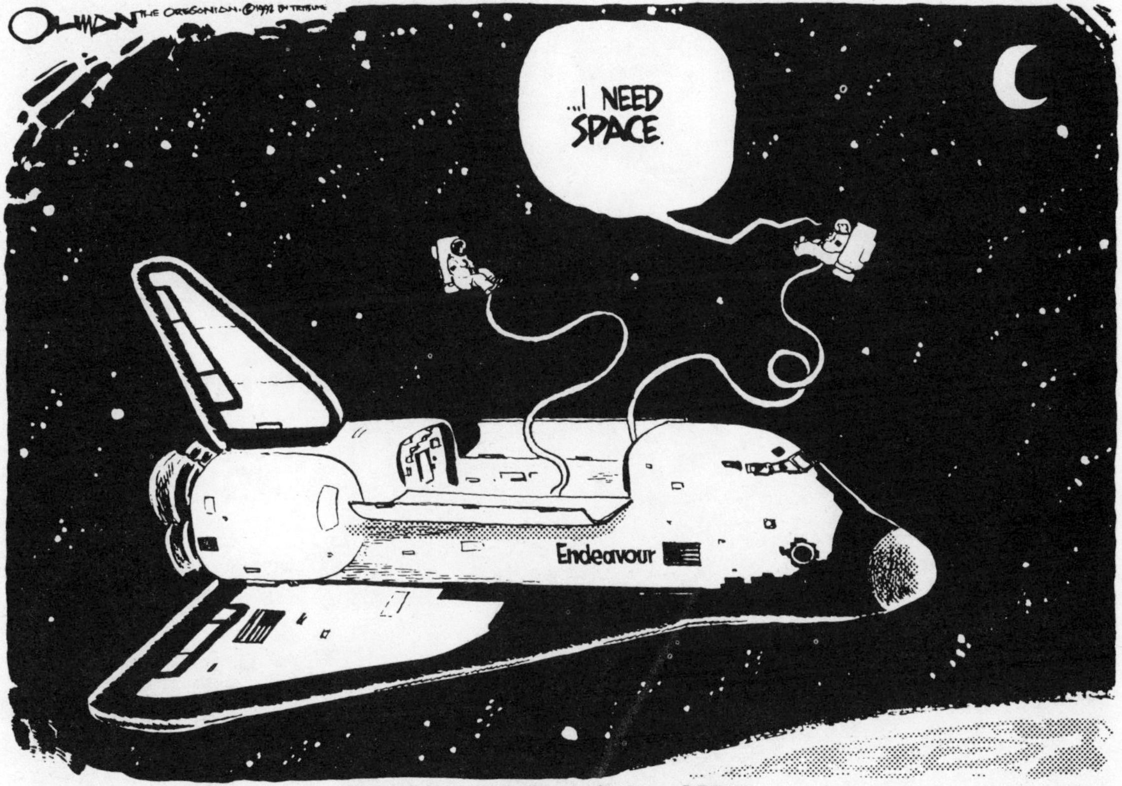
THE OREGONIAN. ©1992
...I NEED SPACE.
Endeavour

THE FIRST MARRIED COUPLE IN ORBIT.

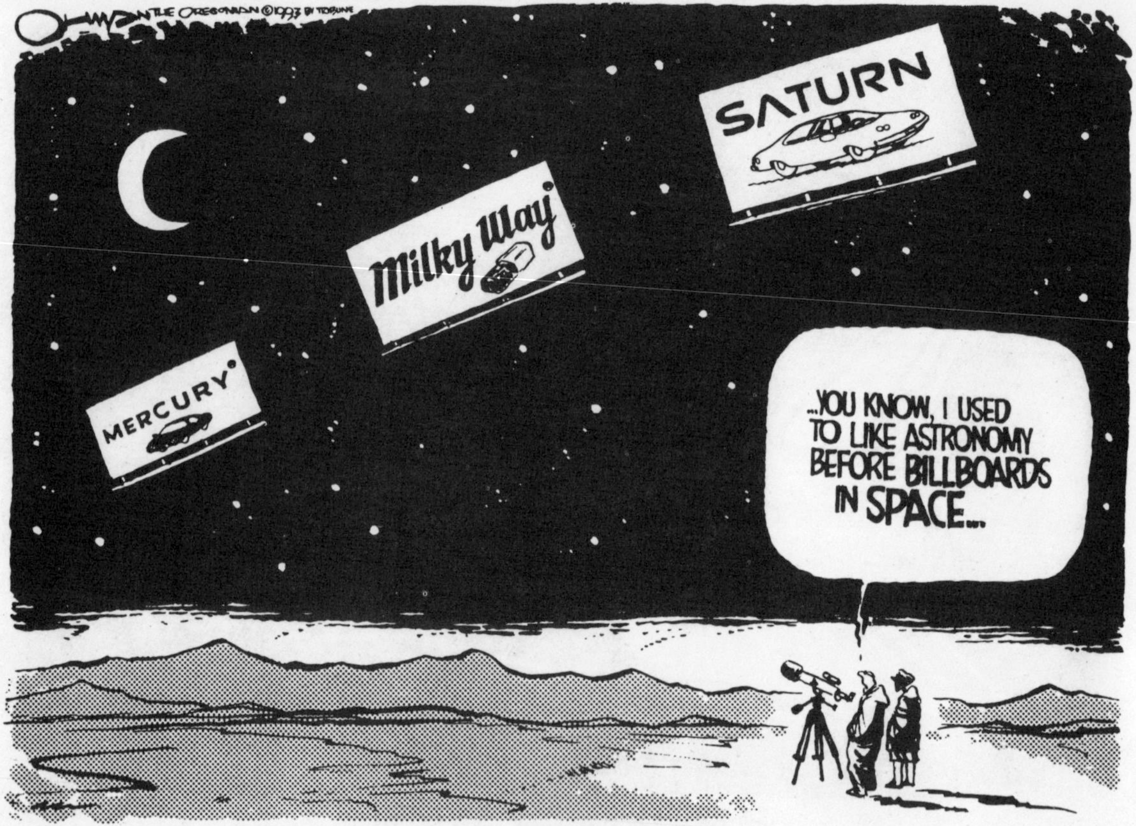
THE OREGONIAN ©1993
SATURN
Milky Way
MERCURY®
...YOU KNOW, I USED TO LIKE ASTRONOMY BEFORE BILLBOARDS IN SPACE...

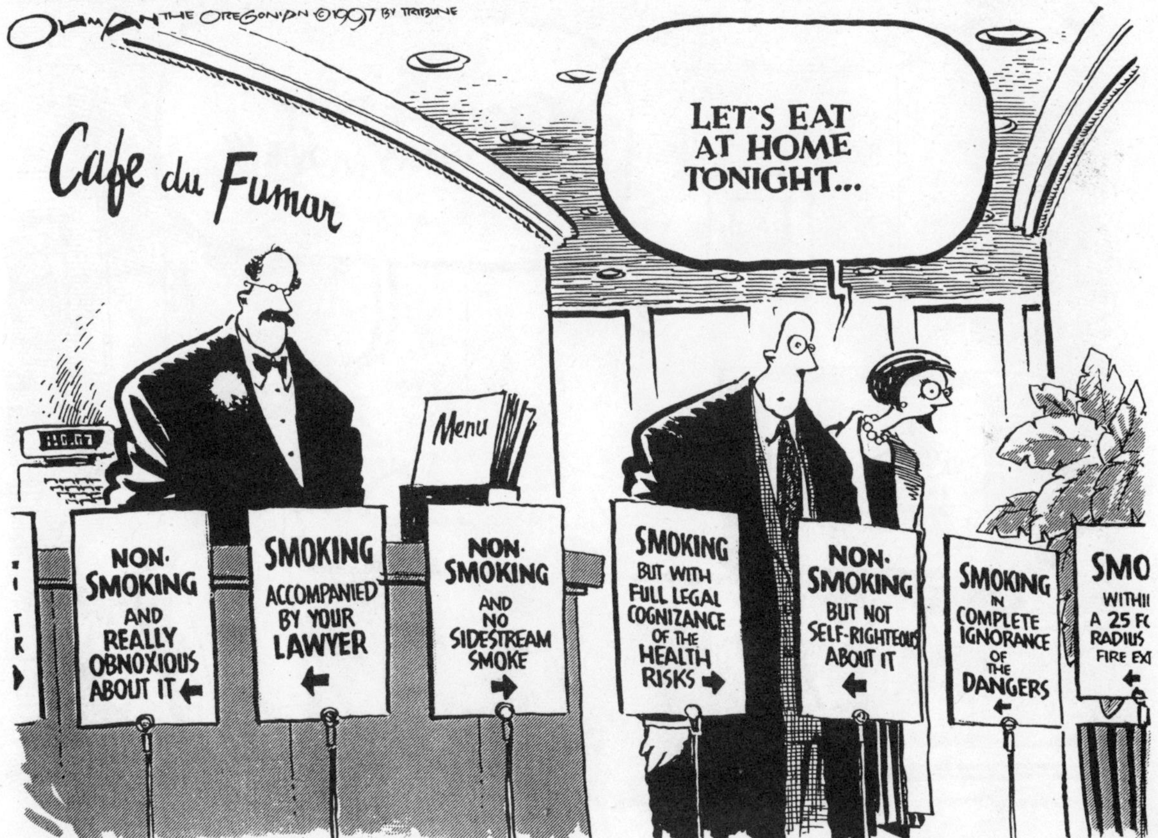
OHMAN THE OREGONIAN ©1997 BY TRIBUNE
Cafe du Fumar
LET'S EAT AT HOME TONIGHT...
Menu
NON-SMOKING AND REALLY OBNOXIOUS ABOUT IT
SMOKING ACCOMPANIED BY YOUR LAWYER
NON-SMOKING AND NO SIDESTREAM SMOKE
SMOKING BUT WITH FULL LEGAL COGNIZANCE OF THE HEALTH RISKS
NON-SMOKING BUT NOT SELF-RIGHTEOUS ABOUT IT
SMOKING IN COMPLETE IGNORANCE OF THE DANGERS

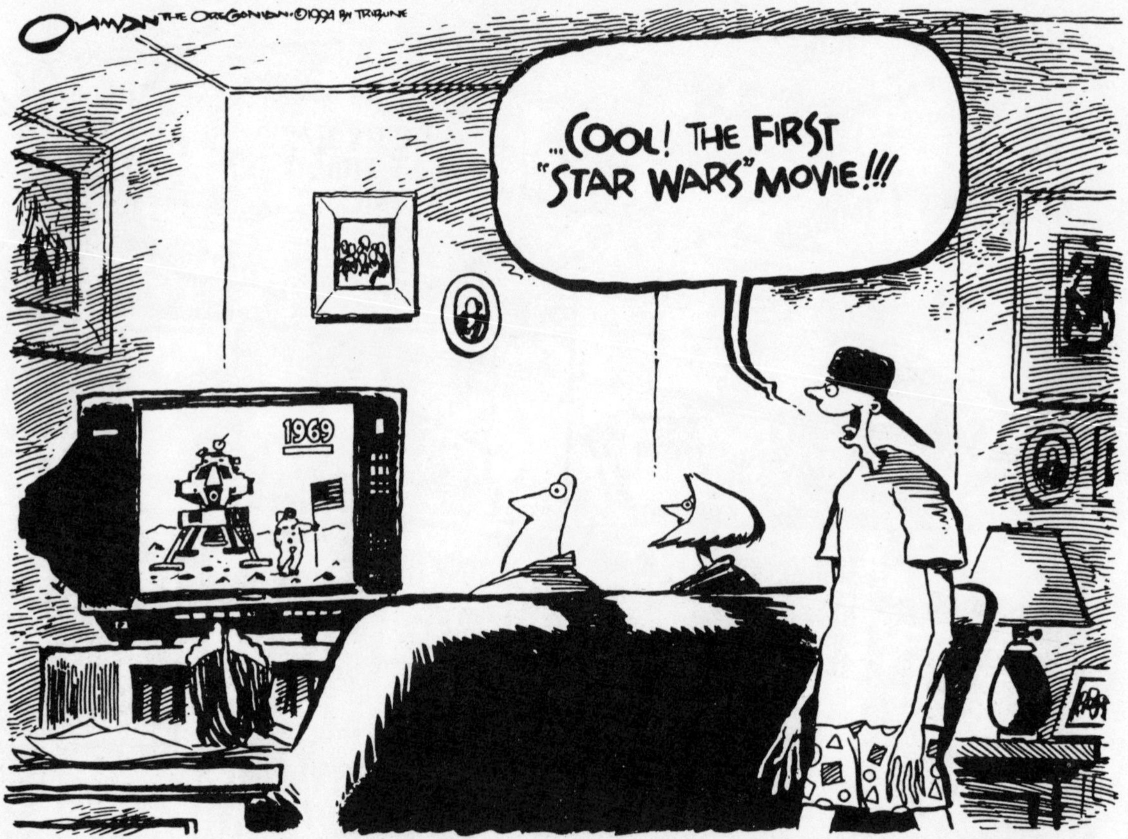
OHMAN THE OREGONIAN ©1994 BY TRIBUNE
1969
...COOL! THE FIRST "STAR WARS" MOVIE!!!

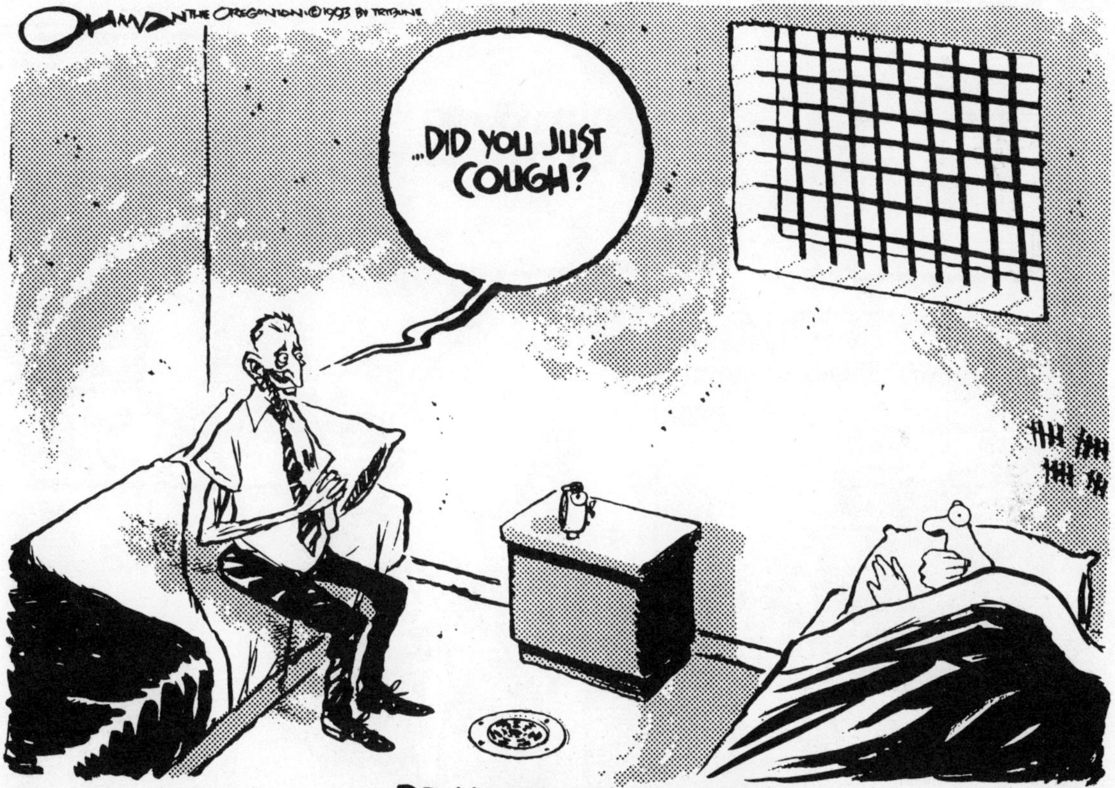
OHMAN THE OREGONIAN ©1993 BY TRIBUNE
...DID YOU JUST COUGH?

DR. KEVORKIAN'S CELLMATE.

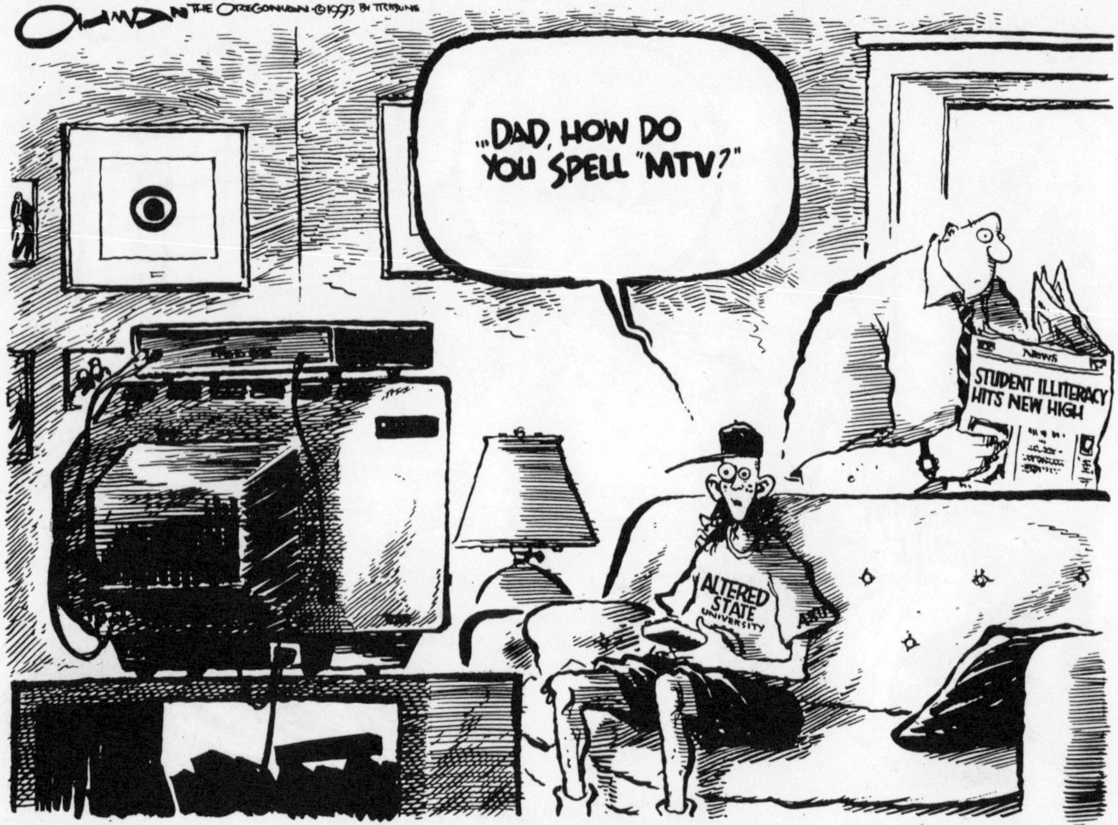

OHMAN THE OREGONIAN ©1993 BY TRIBUNE
...DAD, HOW DO YOU SPELL "MTV?"
NEWS
STUDENT ILLITERACY HITS NEW HIGH
ALTERED STATE UNIVERSITY

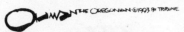
THE OREGONIAN ©1993 BY TRIBUNE

407. The Grape Juice Channel
408. The Patty Duke Channel
409. The Fading Washington Journalist Channel
410. The High-Pitched Whine Channel
411. The Music Video for House-pets Channel
412. The Gay Bowling Channel
413. The Satanic Ping Pong Channel
414. The Nixon Channel
415. The "It's A Wonderful Life" Channel
416. The Mediocre 1947 B-Movie Channel
417. The F-16 Bombing Run Channel
418. The Burned-out Talk Show Host From the '60s Channel
419. The Girls Working Their Lats Channel
420. The Endocrinology Channel
421. The Arrogant Cardiologist Channel
422. The Fiber Channel
423. The Congressional Hypnosis Channel
424. The Crummy 1970s Ma TV Movie Channel
425. The Please Stand By Ch
426. The Scam Channel
427. The Waxy Build-up Chan.
428. The Boiled Carrot Channe
429. The Precocious Brat Cha
430. The Spanish Game S Channel

455. The Asinine Commentary Channel
456. The Inane Rejoinder Channel
457. The Cereal Channel
458. The Neptune Channel
459. The National Anthem Channel
460. The Marxist Dogma Channel
461. The Numbers On The Bottom Of The Screen Channel
462. They're Going Too Fast, The Numbers Channel
463. I Still Can't Read The Numbers Channel
464. Why Don't They Slow The Numbers Down Channel
465. The Smug Financial Analyst Channel
466. The Overly Groomed Real Estate Con Man Channel
467. The Mute Button Channel
468. The Oddball Call-In Channel
469. The Chaucer Channel
470. The Milton Channel
471. The Gratuitous Remark Channel
472. The Smarmy Lie Channel
473. The Mollusk Channel
474. The Sweaty Clinton Jogging Channel

475. The Bush Getting Off Of A Plane Somewhere Channel
476. The Get An Afterlife Channel
477. The Hydrangeia Channel
478. The Ginsu Knife Channel
479. The Salad Shooter Channel
480. The Popeil Pocket Fisherman Channel
481. The Slim Whitman Channel
482. The Zamfir Flute Channel
483. The Obscure Congressman From Oklahoma Channel
484. The School Lunch Menu For Omaha, Nebraska Channel
485. The Precipitation Channel
486. The Blue Glow In The Living Room Channel
487. The Bad Early '60s Sitcom Channel
488. The All-Greg Brady Channel
489. The Al Gore Dental Records Channel
490. The Channel Jay Leno's Gonna Wind Up On Channel
491. The Pathetic Comedians In Front Of A Brick Wall Channel
492. The All-Boy Scout News Channel
493. The News Anchors Getting Ready To Run For Congress Channel
494. The Canadian Parliament Channel
495. The Idaho Senate Channel
496. The Vast Wasteland Channel
497. The .00006 Neilsen Channel
498. The Only A Dog Can Hear Channel
499. The My Thumb Is Worn Out Trying To Get to This Channel

500 CABLE CHANNELS

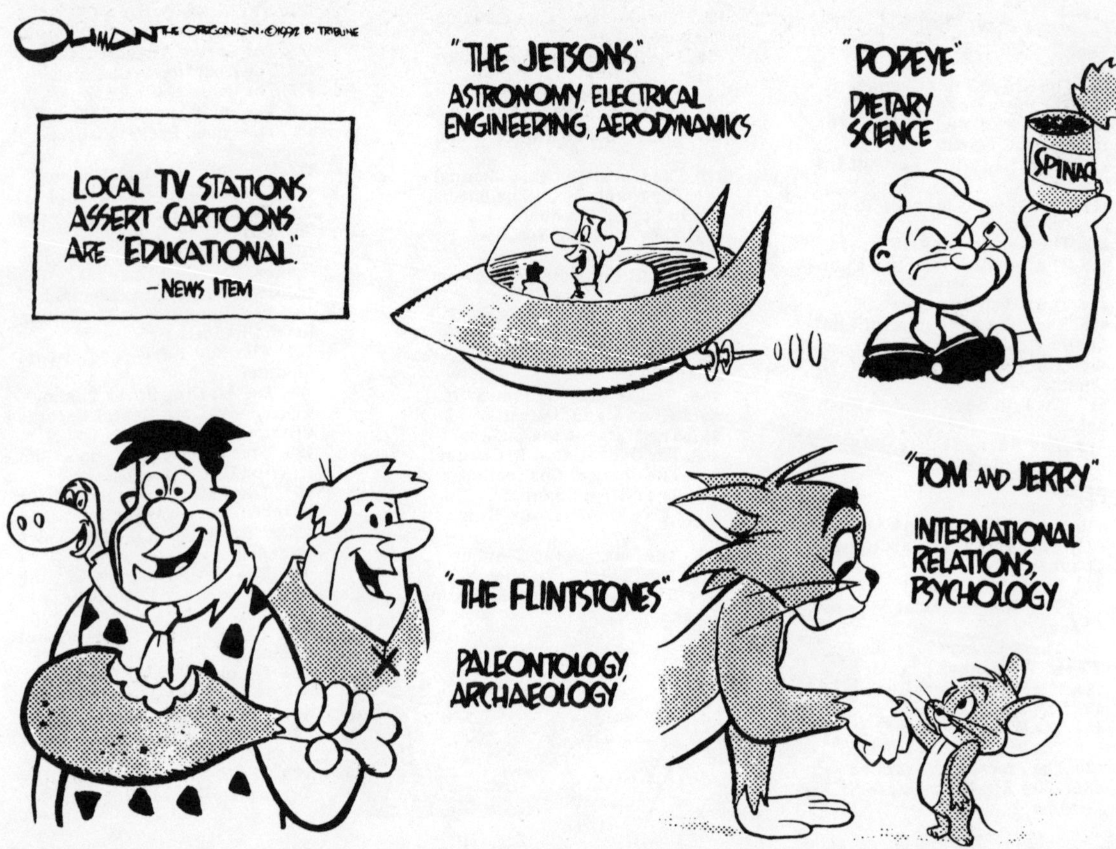
OLIPHANT THE OREGONIAN ©1992 BY TRIBUNE
LOCAL TV STATIONS ASSERT CARTOONS ARE "EDUCATIONAL."
-NEWS ITEM
"THE JETSONS"
ASTRONOMY, ELECTRICAL ENGINEERING, AERODYNAMICS
"POPEYE"
DIETARY SCIENCE
SPINAC
"THE FLINTSTONES"
PALEONTOLOGY, ARCHAEOLOGY
"TOM AND JERRY"
INTERNATIONAL RELATIONS, PSYCHOLOGY

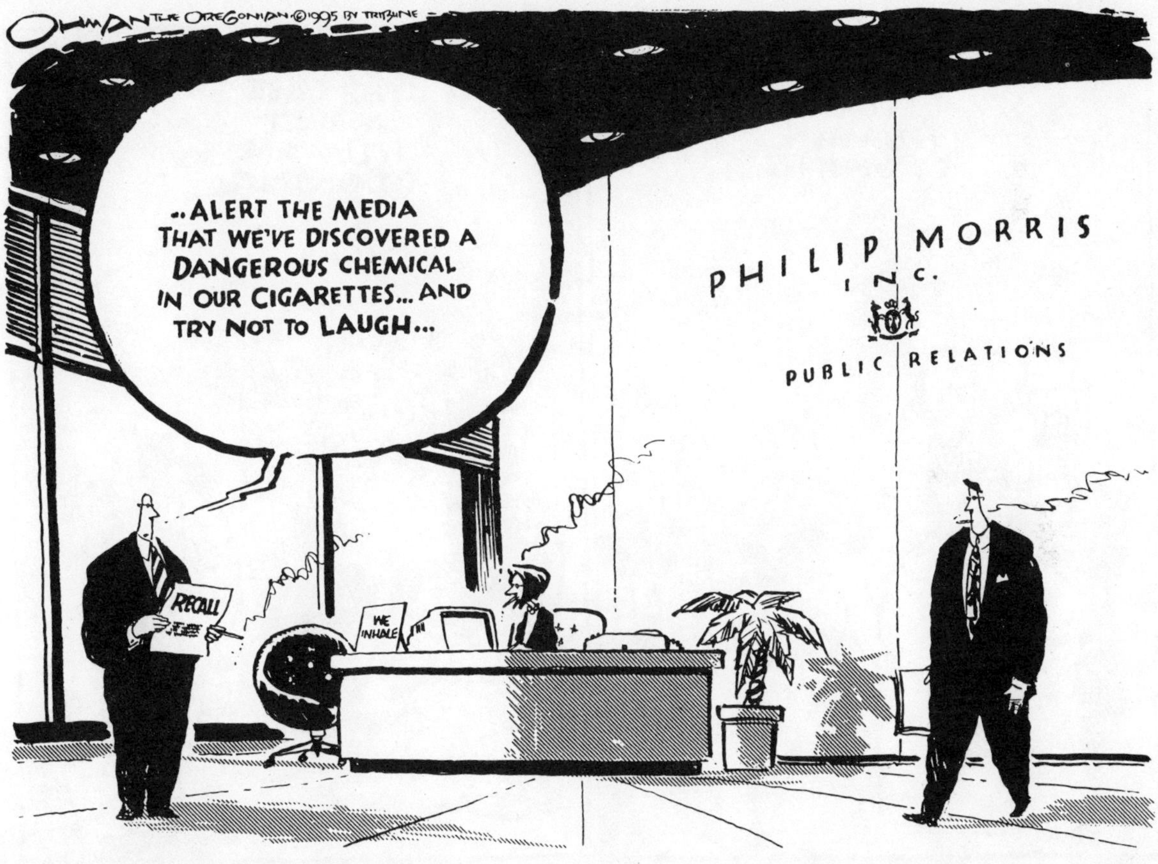
OHMAN THE OREGONIAN ©1995 BY TRIBUNE
..ALERT THE MEDIA THAT WE'VE DISCOVERED A DANGEROUS CHEMICAL IN OUR CIGARETTES... AND TRY NOT TO LAUGH...
PHILIP MORRIS INC.
PUBLIC RELATIONS
RECALL
WE INHALE

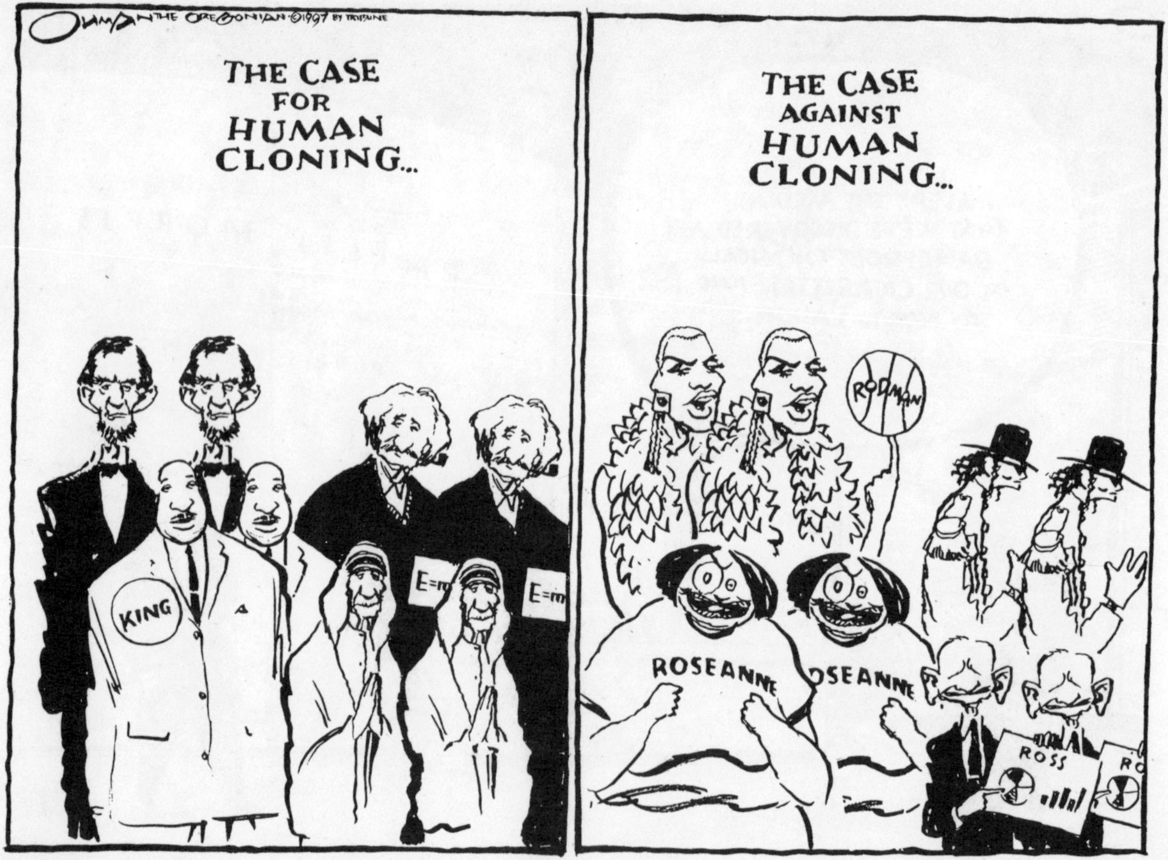
OHMAN THE OREGONIAN ©1997 BY TRIBUNE
THE CASE FOR HUMAN CLONING...
KING
E=m
E=m
THE CASE AGAINST HUMAN CLONING...
RODMAN
ROSEANNE
OSEANNE
ROSS
RO

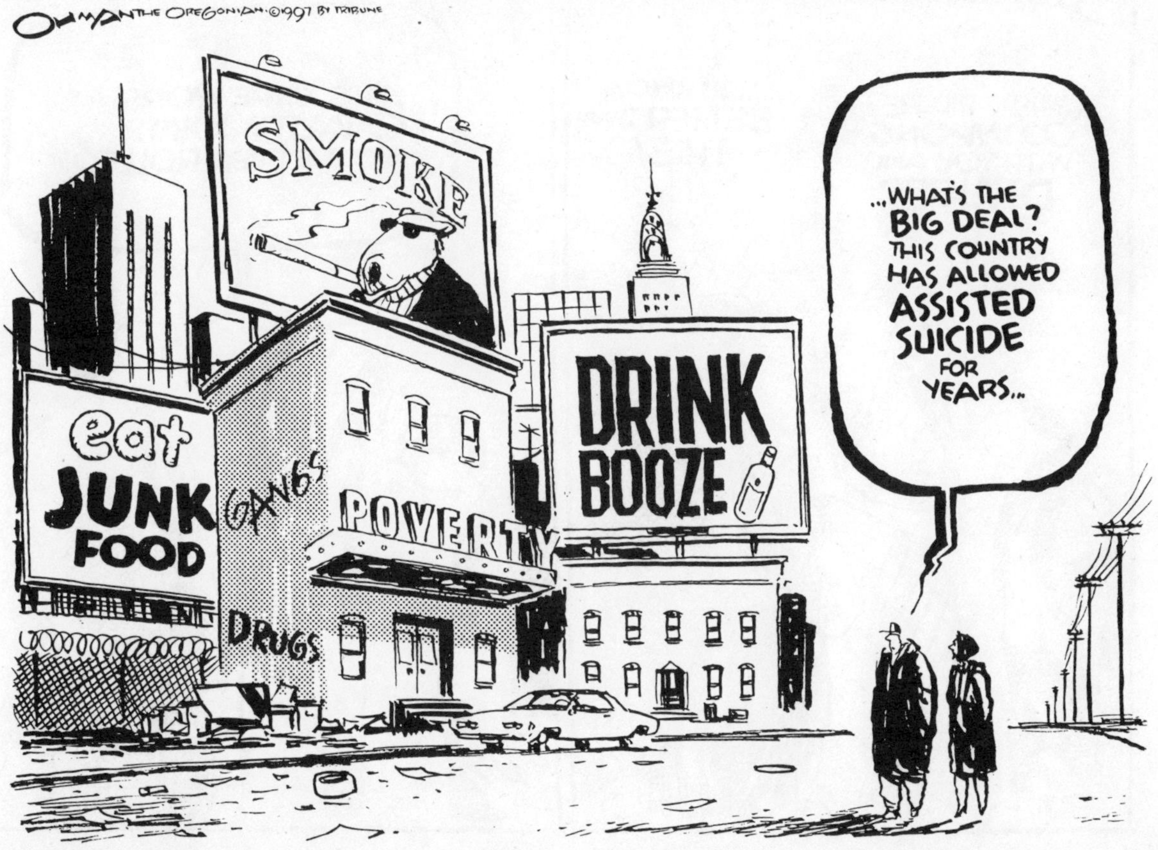
OHMAN THE OREGONIAN ©1997 BY TRIBUNE
SMOKE
eat JUNK FOOD
GANGS
POVERTY
DRUGS
DRINK BOOZE
...WHAT'S THE BIG DEAL? THIS COUNTRY HAS ALLOWED ASSISTED SUICIDE FOR YEARS...

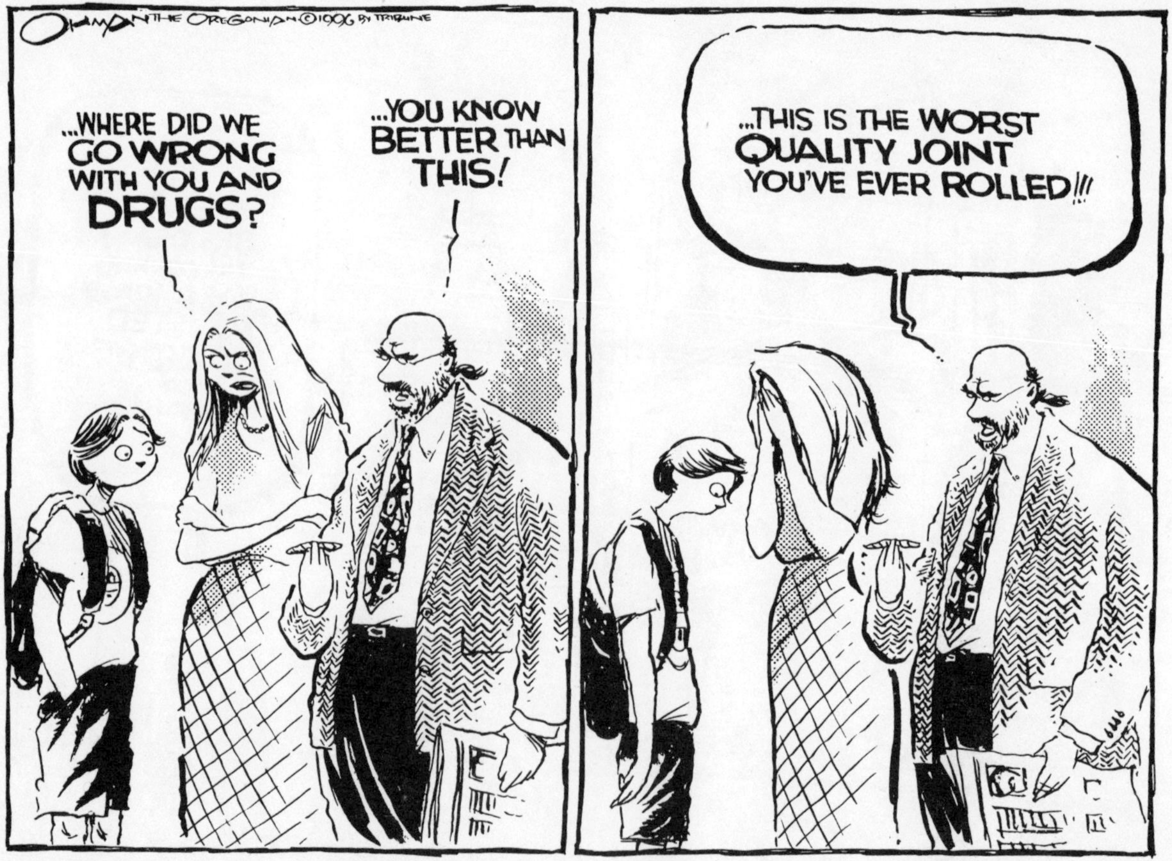
OHMAN THE OREGONIAN ©1996 BY TRIBUNE
...WHERE DID WE GO WRONG WITH YOU AND DRUGS?
...YOU KNOW BETTER THAN THIS!
...THIS IS THE WORST QUALITY JOINT YOU'VE EVER ROLLED!!!

IT'S NOT EASY BEING GREEN

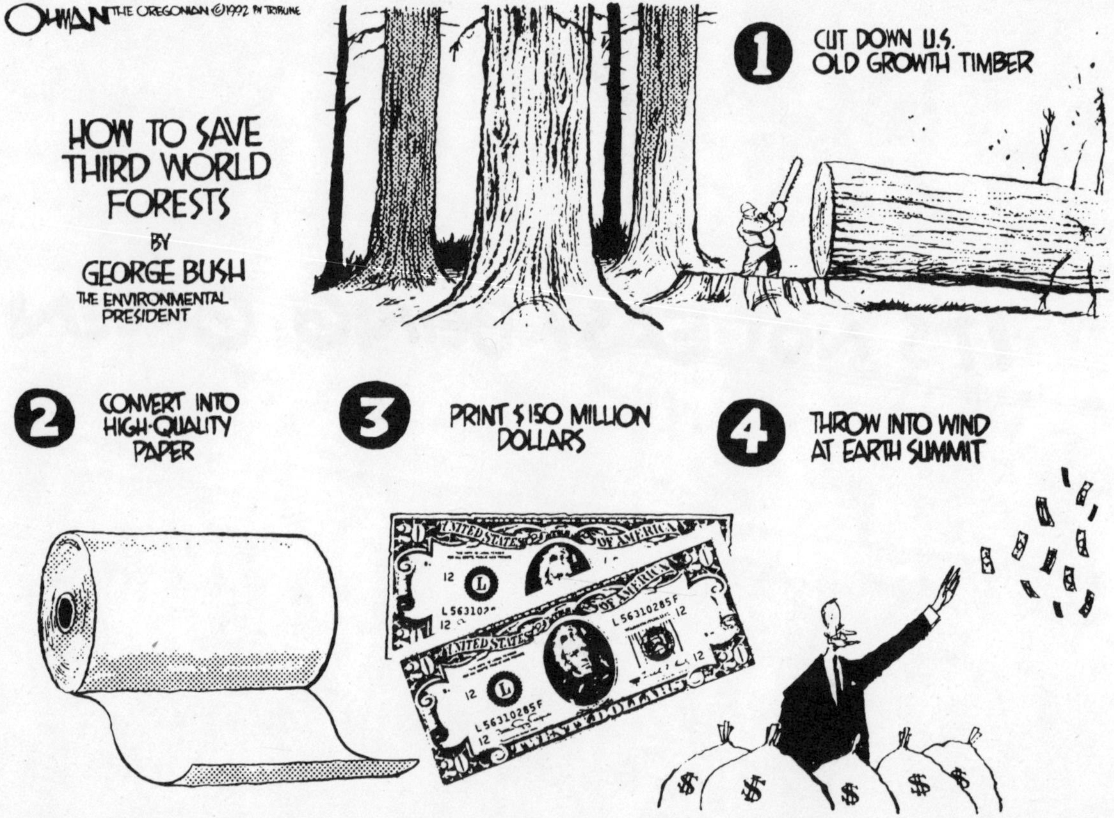

OHMAN THE OREGONIAN ©1992 NY TRIBUNE
HOW TO SAVE THIRD WORLD FORESTS
BY
GEORGE BUSH
THE ENVIRONMENTAL PRESIDENT
1 CUT DOWN U.S. OLD GROWTH TIMBER
2 CONVERT INTO HIGH-QUALITY PAPER
3 PRINT $150 MILLION DOLLARS
4 THROW INTO WIND AT EARTH SUMMIT

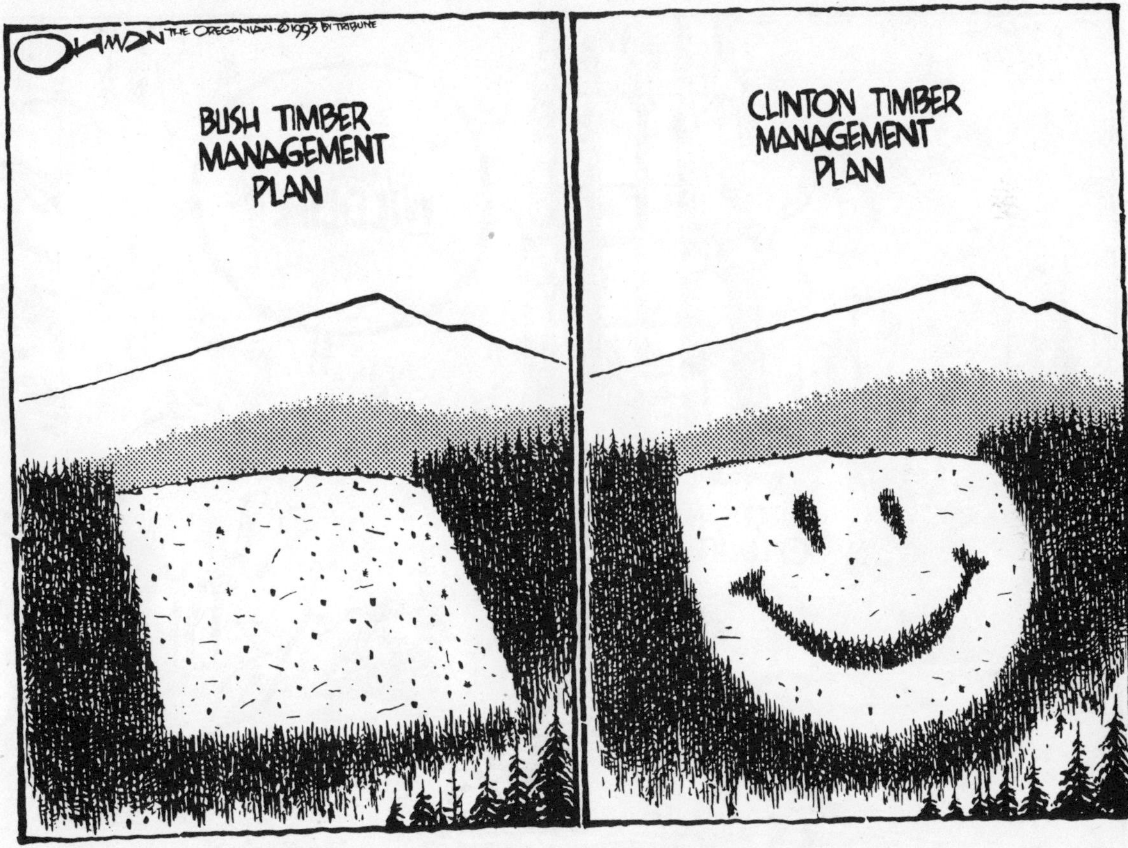

OLIPHANT THE OREGONIAN ©1993 BY TRIBUNE
BUSH TIMBER MANAGEMENT PLAN
CLINTON TIMBER MANAGEMENT PLAN

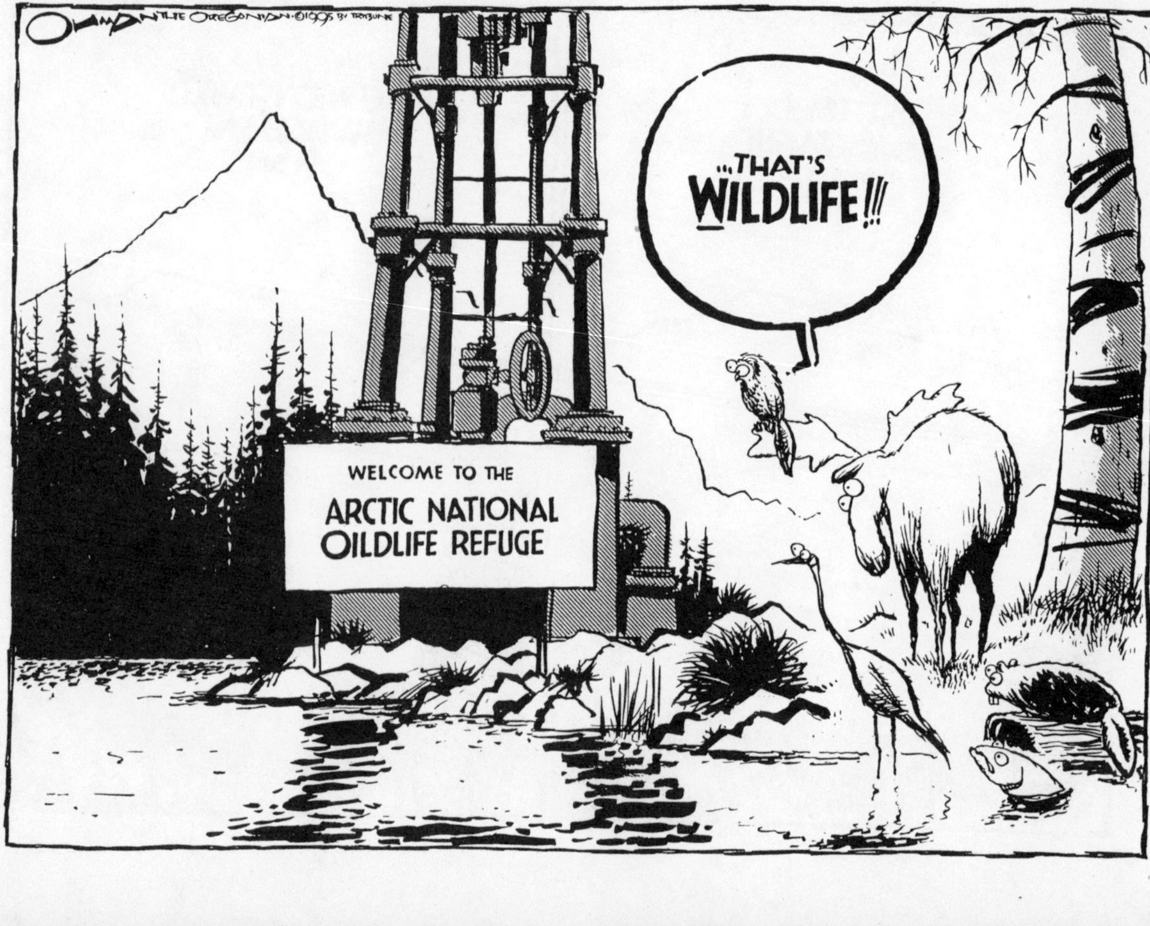
WELCOME TO THE
ARCTIC NATIONAL
OILDLIFE REFUGE
...THAT'S WILDLIFE!!!

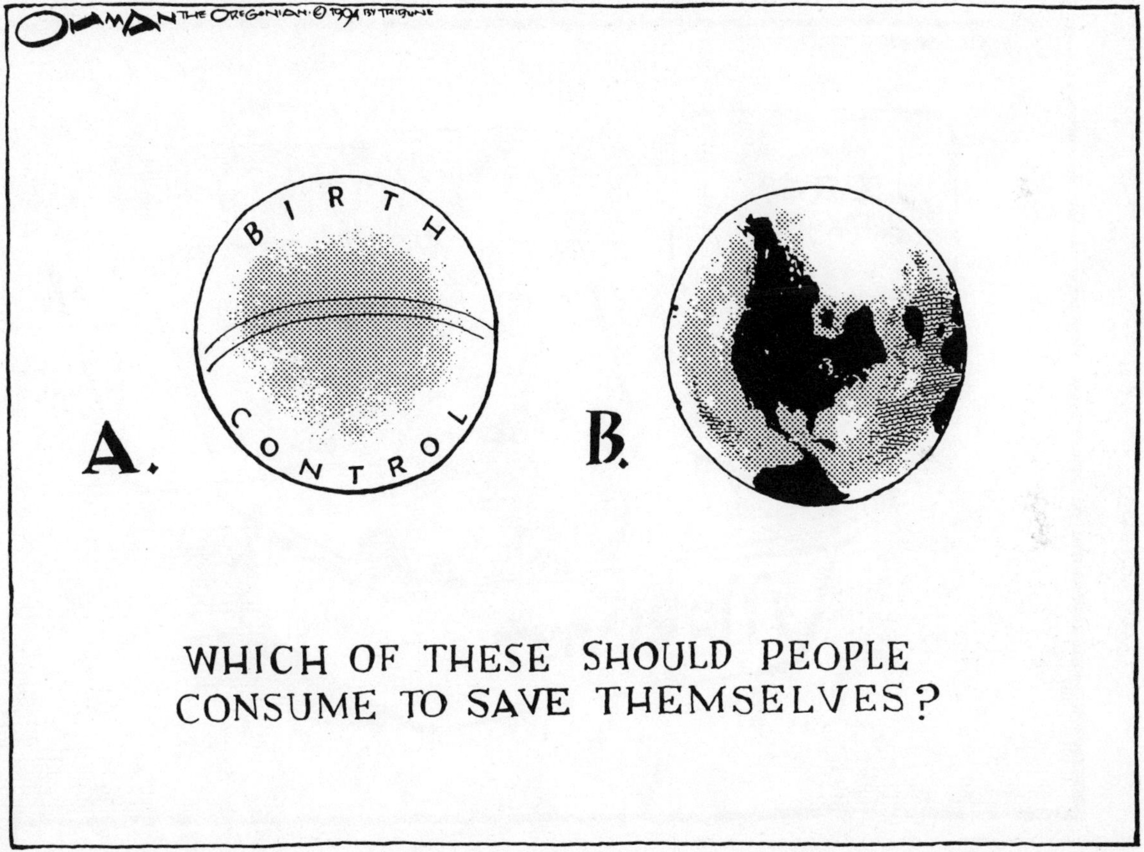
OHMAN THE OREGONIAN · © 1994 BY TRIBUNE
A.
BIRTH CONTROL
B.
WHICH OF THESE SHOULD PEOPLE CONSUME TO SAVE THEMSELVES?

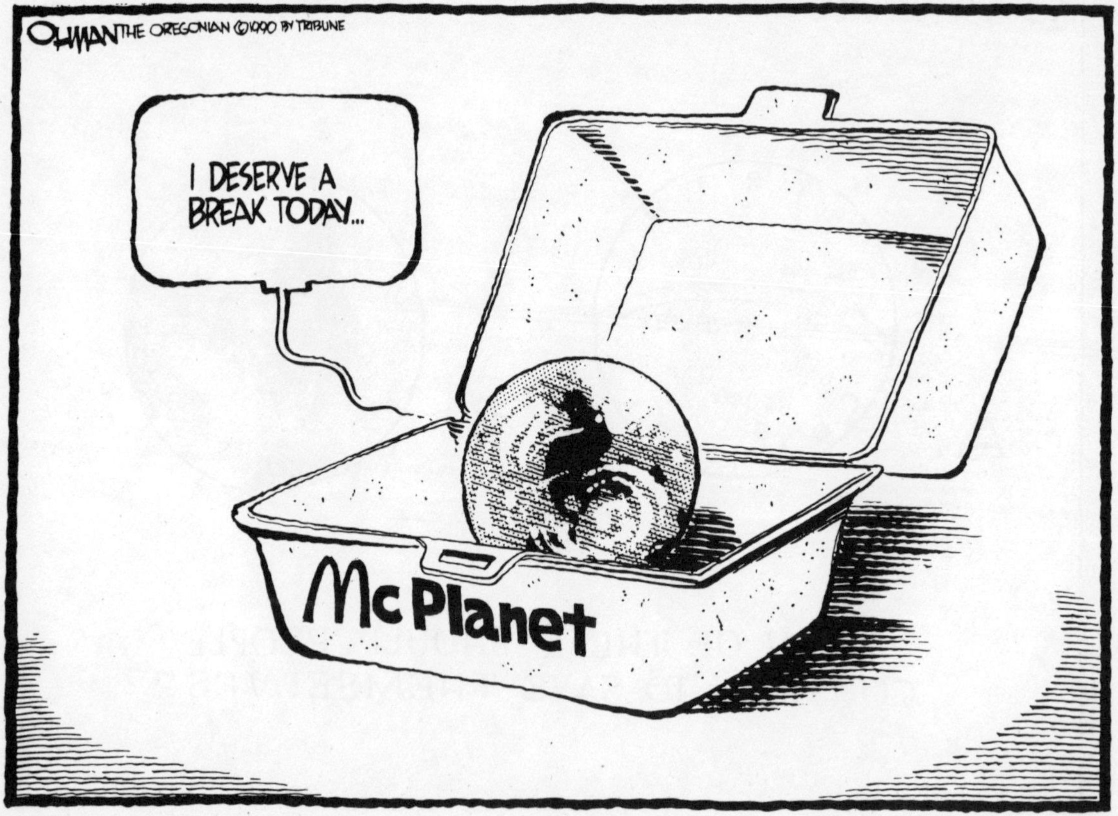
OHMAN THE OREGONIAN ©1990 BY TRIBUNE
I DESERVE A BREAK TODAY...
McPlanet

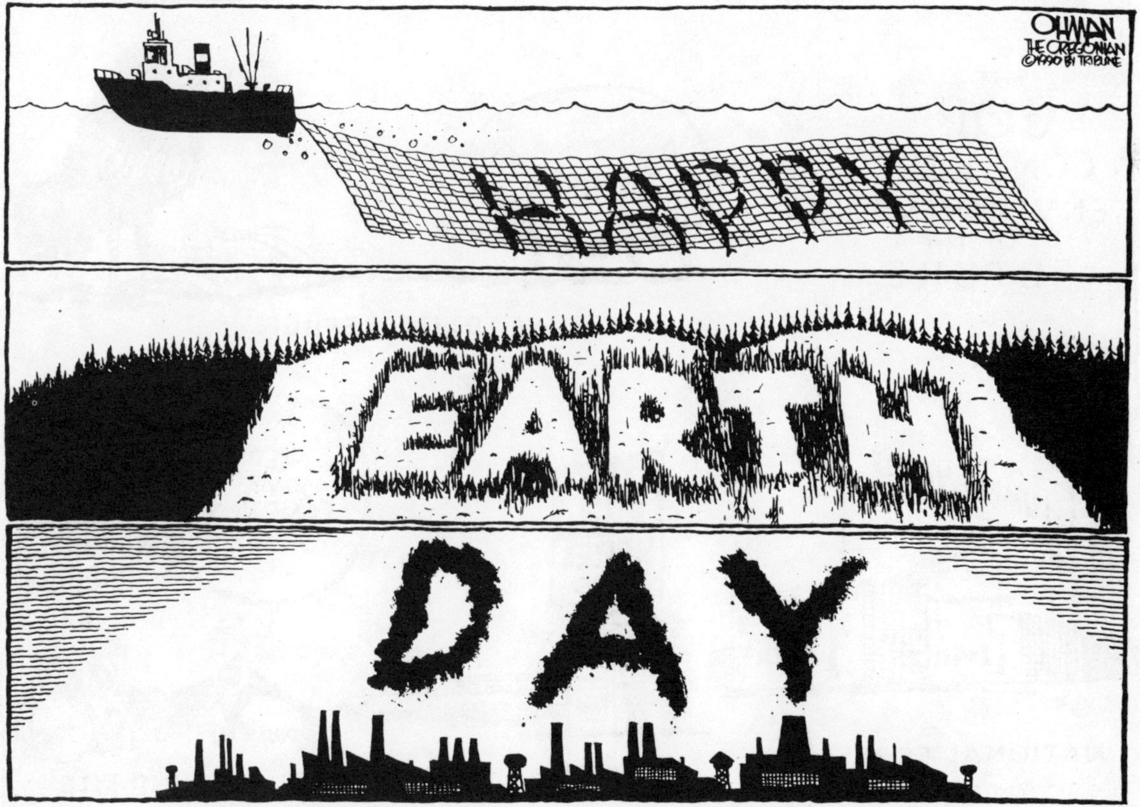
OHMAN
THE OREGONIAN
©1990 BY TRIBUNE
HAPPY
EARTH
DAY

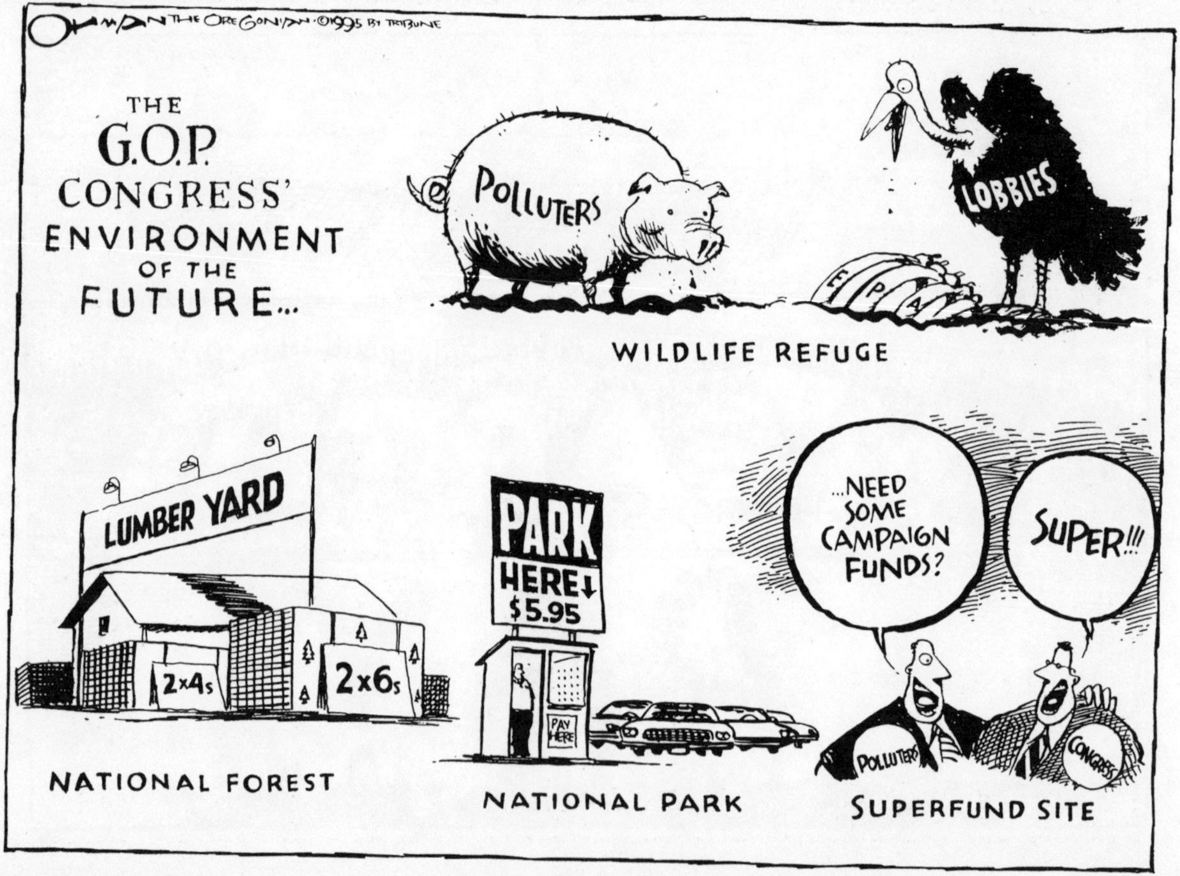
OHMAN THE OREGONIAN ©1995 BY TRIBUNE
THE G.O.P. CONGRESS' ENVIRONMENT OF THE FUTURE...
POLLUTERS
LOBBIES
EPA
WILDLIFE REFUGE
LUMBER YARD
2x4s
2x6s
NATIONAL FOREST
PARK HERE↓ $5.95
PAY HERE
NATIONAL PARK
...NEED SOME CAMPAIGN FUNDS?
SUPER!!!
POLLUTERS
CONGRESS
SUPERFUND SITE

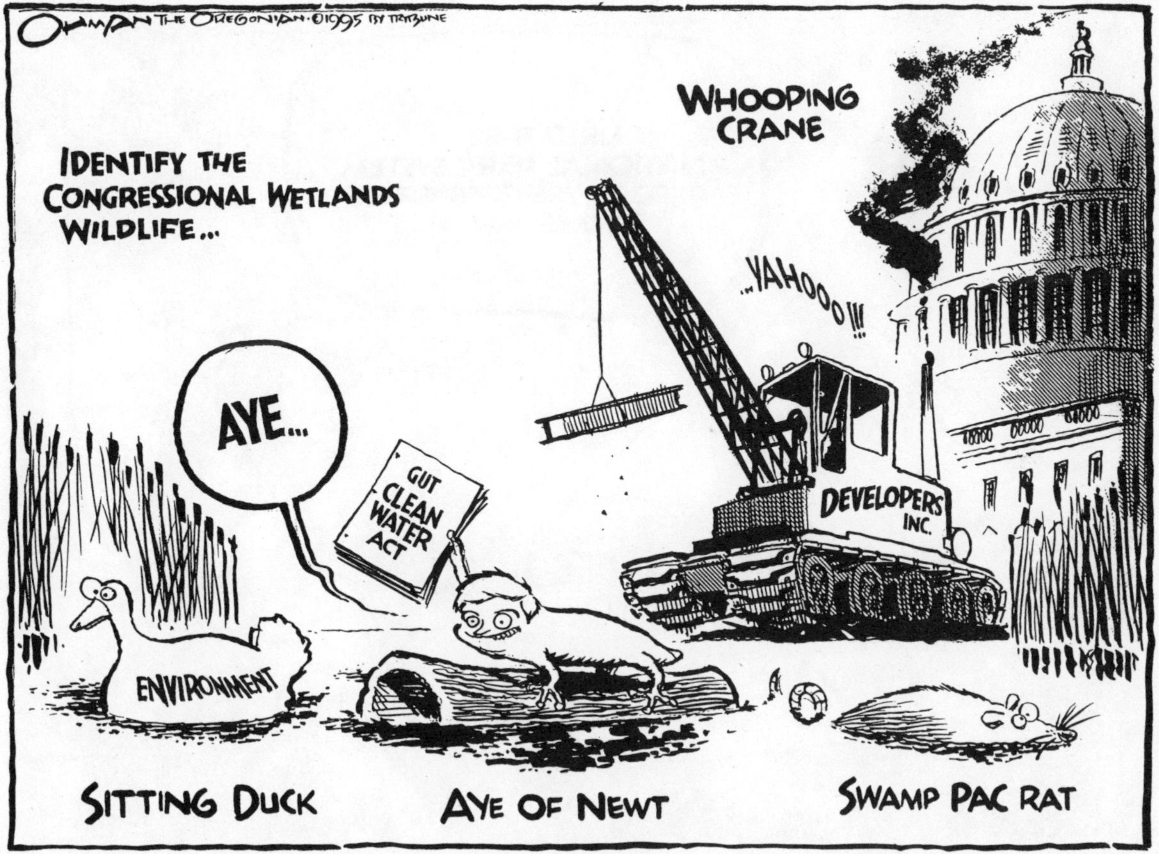
OHMAN THE OREGONIAN ©1995 BY TRIBUNE
IDENTIFY THE CONGRESSIONAL WETLANDS WILDLIFE...
WHOOPING CRANE
...YAHOOOO!!!
DEVELOPERS INC.
AYE...
GUT CLEAN WATER ACT
ENVIRONMENT
SITTING DUCK
AYE OF NEWT
SWAMP PAC RAT

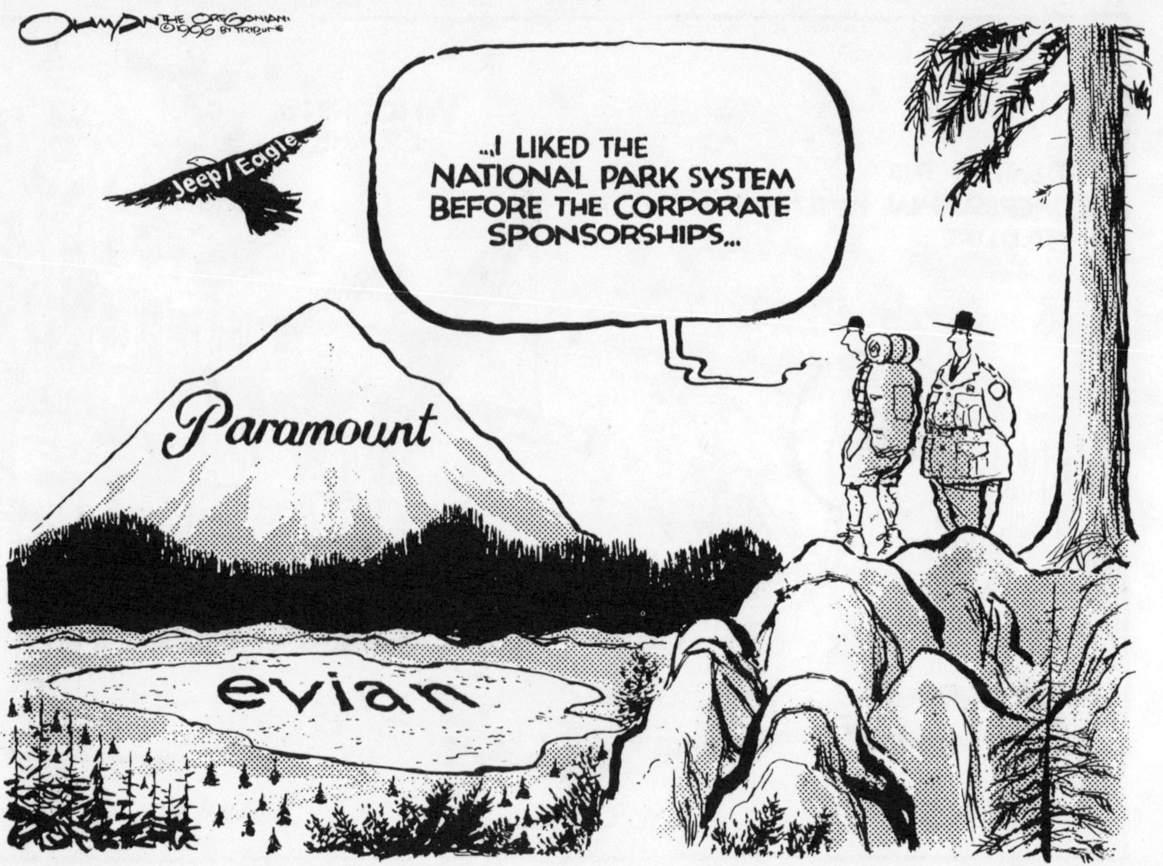
OHMAN THE OREGONIAN ©1996 BY TRIBUNE
Jeep/Eagle
...I LIKED THE NATIONAL PARK SYSTEM BEFORE THE CORPORATE SPONSORSHIPS...
Paramount
evian

# BILL ME LATER

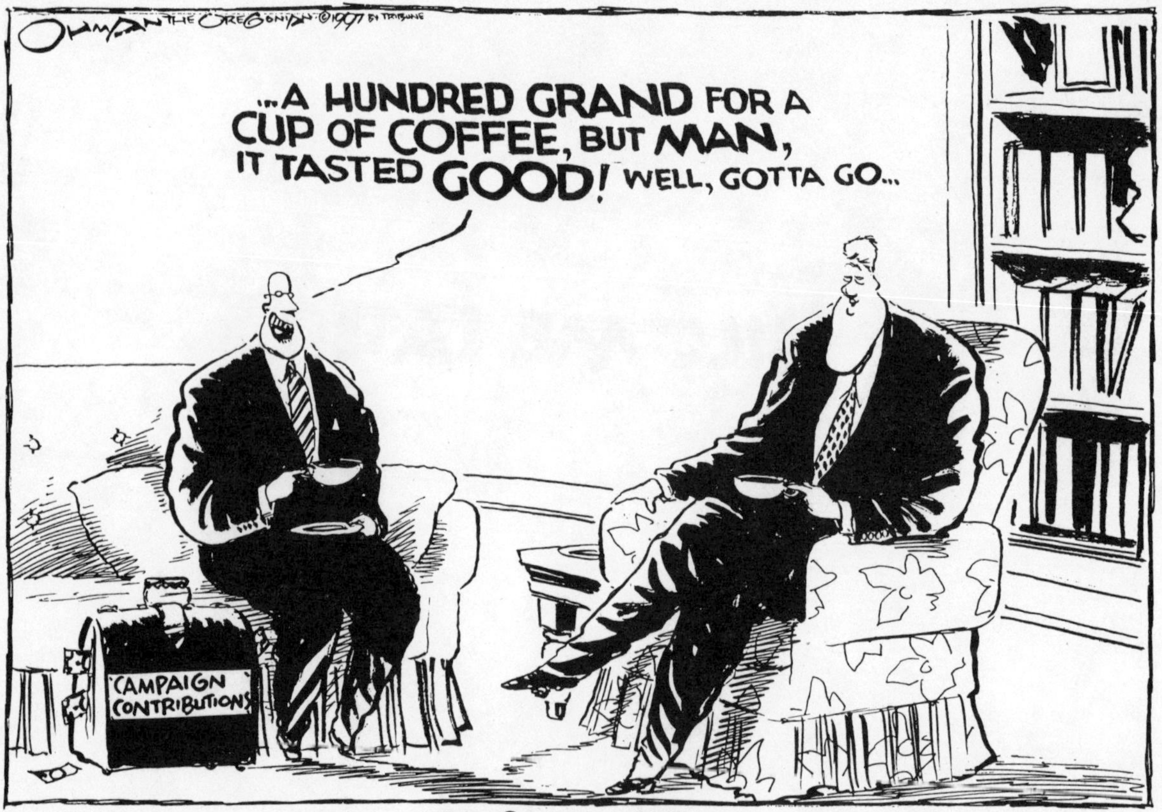
OHMAN THE OREGONIAN ©1997 BY TRIBUNE
...A HUNDRED GRAND FOR A CUP OF COFFEE, BUT MAN, IT TASTED GOOD! WELL, GOTTA GO...
CAMPAIGN CONTRIBUTIONS

THE CLINTON VERSION...

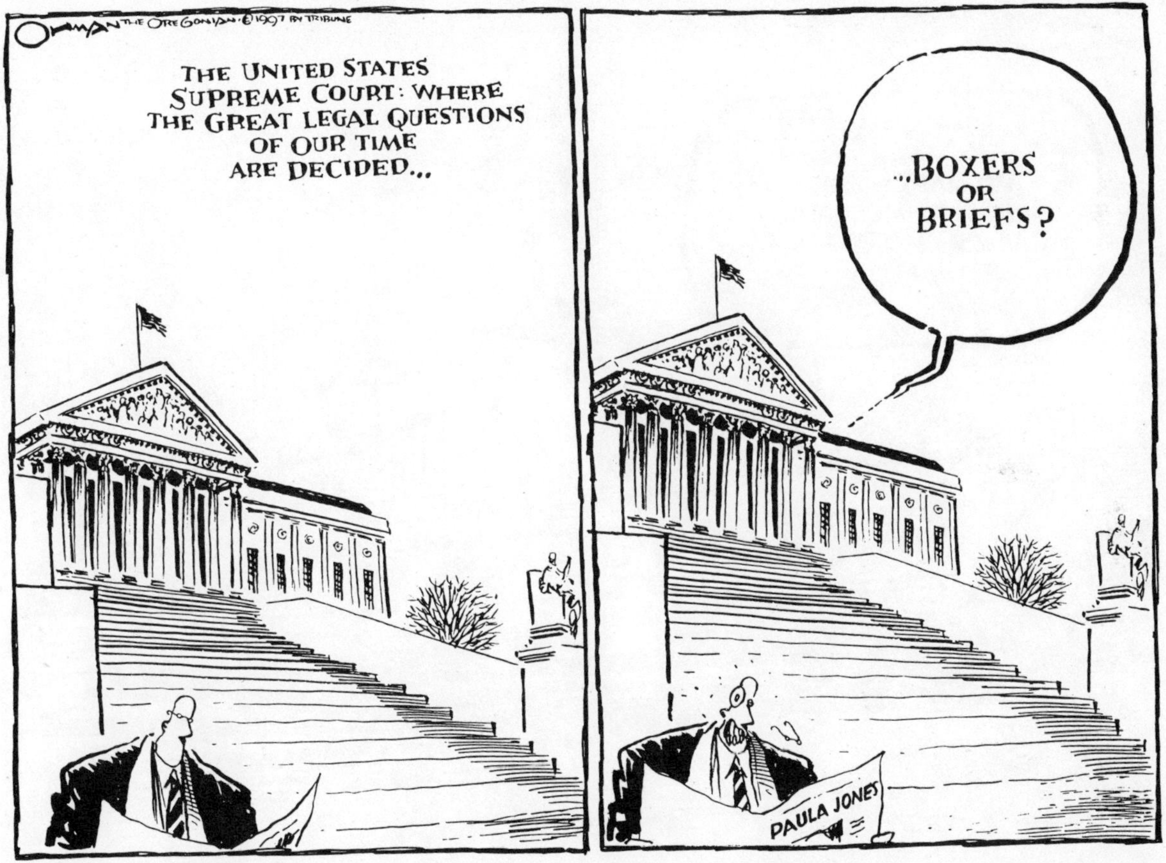
OHMAN THE OREGONIAN ©1997 BY TRIBUNE
THE UNITED STATES SUPREME COURT: WHERE THE GREAT LEGAL QUESTIONS OF OUR TIME ARE DECIDED...
...BOXERS OR BRIEFS?
PAULA JONES

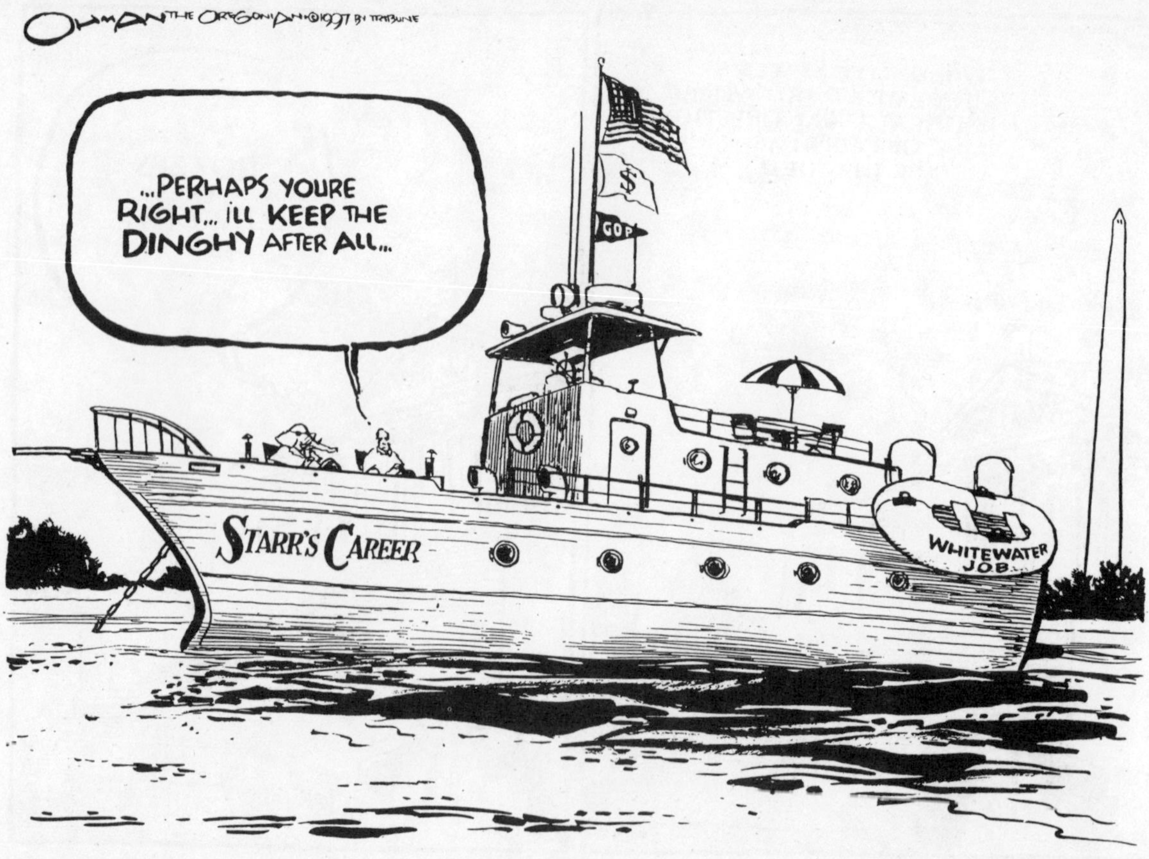

OHMAN THE OREGONIAN ©1997 BY TRIBUNE
...PERHAPS YOURE RIGHT... ILL KEEP THE DINGHY AFTER ALL...
$
GOP
STARR'S CAREER
WHITEWATER JOB

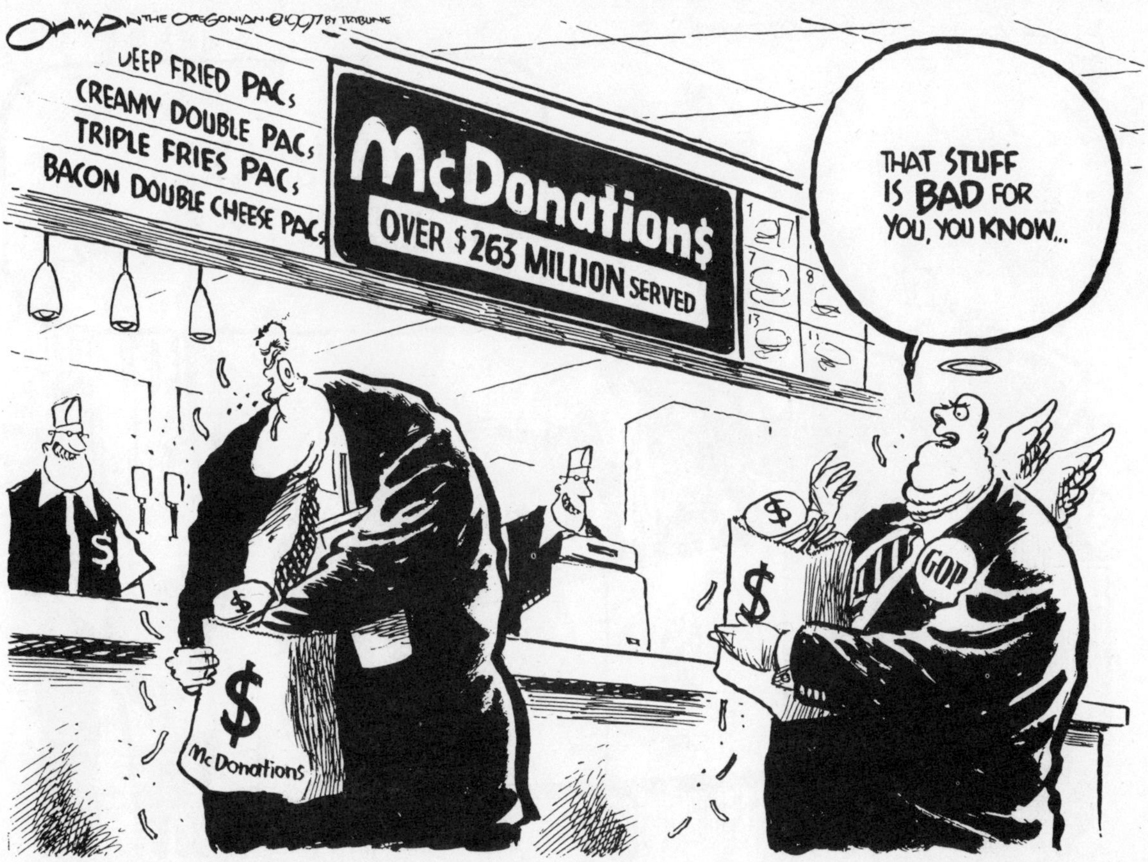
OHMAN THE OREGONIAN ©1997 BY TRIBUNE
DEEP FRIED PACs
CREAMY DOUBLE PACs
TRIPLE FRIES PACs
BACON DOUBLE CHEESE PACs
McDonation$
OVER $263 MILLION SERVED
THAT STUFF IS BAD FOR YOU, YOU KNOW...
GOP
$
McDonations

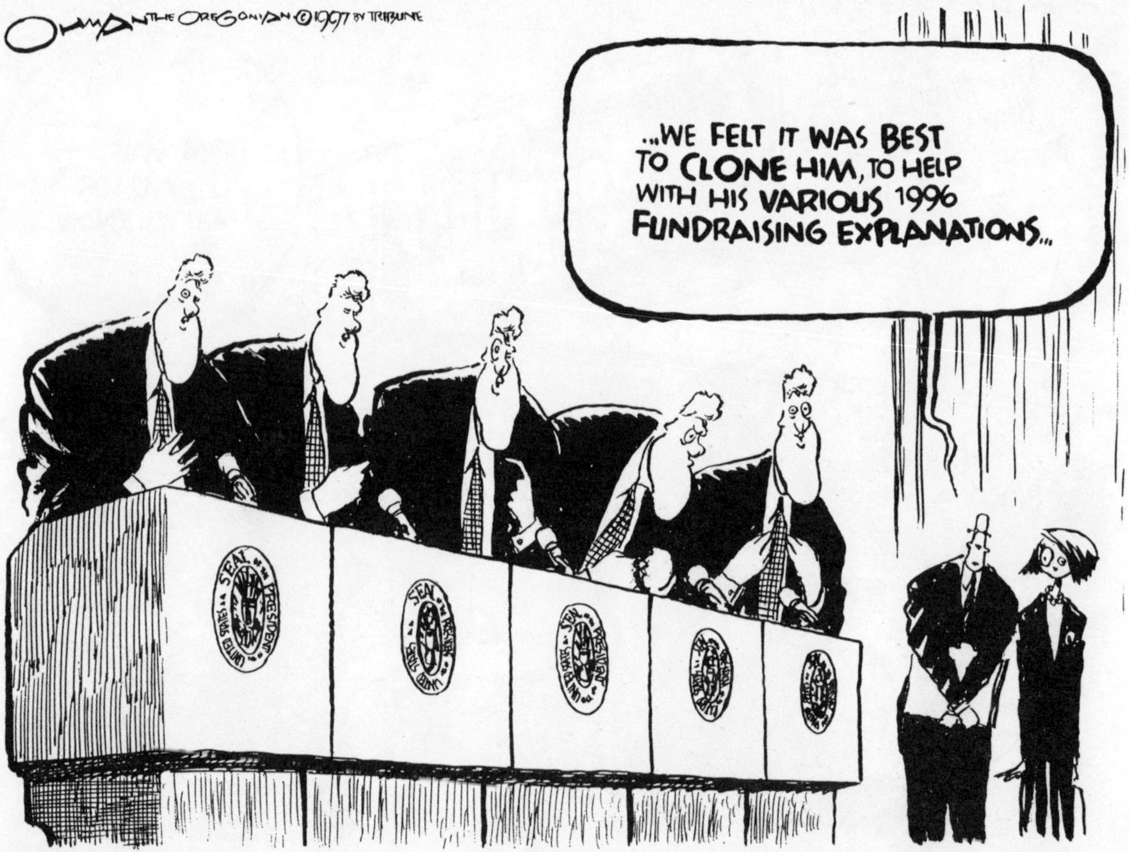
OHMAN THE OREGONIAN ©1997 BY TRIBUNE
...WE FELT IT WAS BEST TO CLONE HIM, TO HELP WITH HIS VARIOUS 1996 FUNDRAISING EXPLANATIONS...

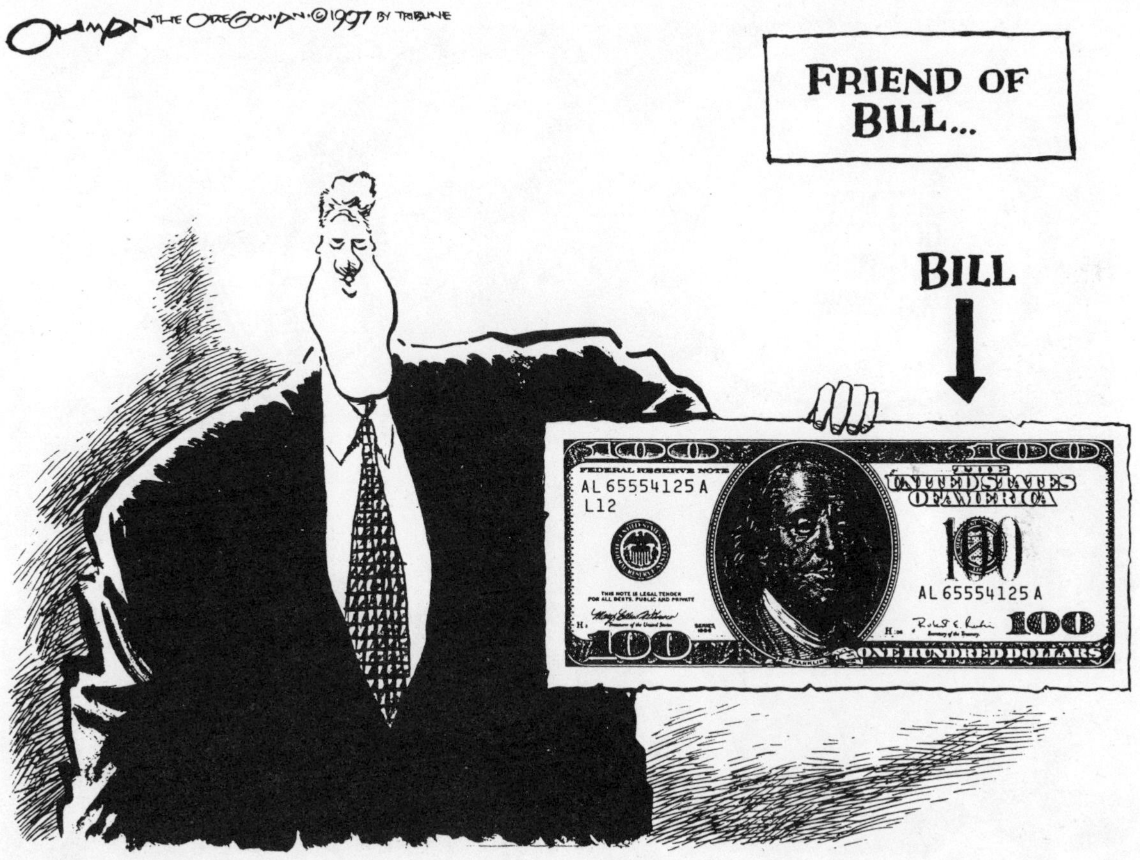

OHMAN THE OREGONIAN ©1997 BY TRIBUNE
FRIEND OF BILL...
BILL
FEDERAL RESERVE NOTE
AL 65554125 A
L12
THE UNITED STATES OF AMERICA
100
AL 65554125 A
ONE HUNDRED DOLLARS

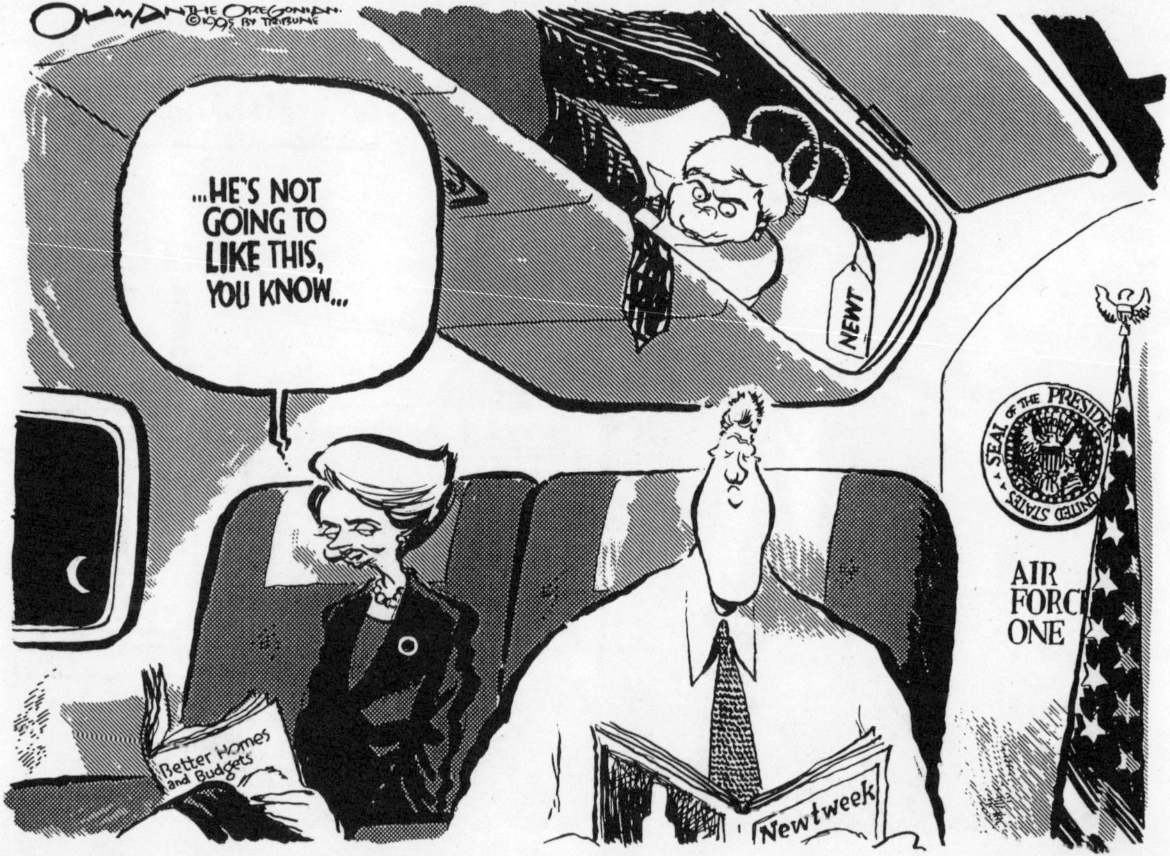

OHMAN THE OREGONIAN ©1995 BY TRIBUNE
...HE'S NOT GOING TO LIKE THIS, YOU KNOW...
NEWT
SEAL OF THE PRESIDENT OF THE UNITED STATES
AIR FORCE ONE
Better Homes and Budgets
Newtweek

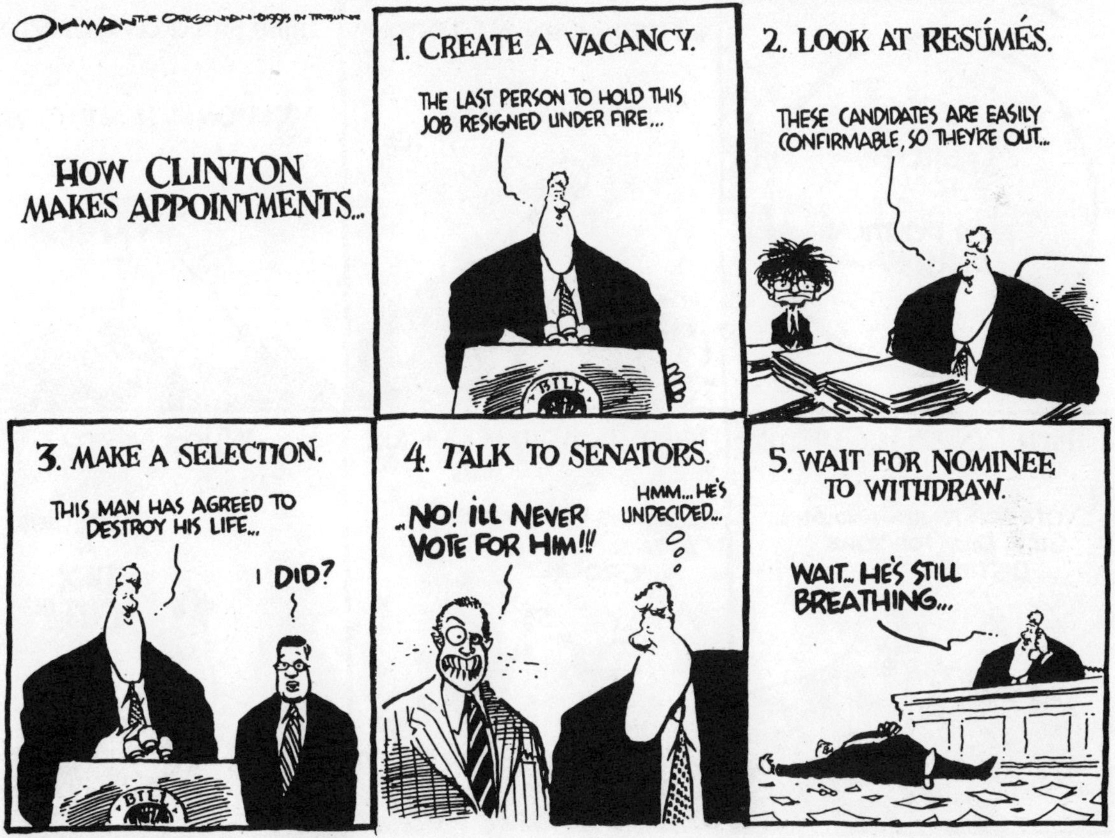
OHMAN THE OREGONIAN ©1995 TRIBUNE
HOW CLINTON MAKES APPOINTMENTS...
1. CREATE A VACANCY.
THE LAST PERSON TO HOLD THIS JOB RESIGNED UNDER FIRE...
BILL
2. LOOK AT RESÚMÉS.
THESE CANDIDATES ARE EASILY CONFIRMABLE, SO THEY'RE OUT...
3. MAKE A SELECTION.
THIS MAN HAS AGREED TO DESTROY HIS LIFE...
I DID?
BILL
4. TALK TO SENATORS.
...NO! I'LL NEVER VOTE FOR HIM!!!
HMM... HE'S UNDECIDED...
5. WAIT FOR NOMINEE TO WITHDRAW.
WAIT... HE'S STILL BREATHING...

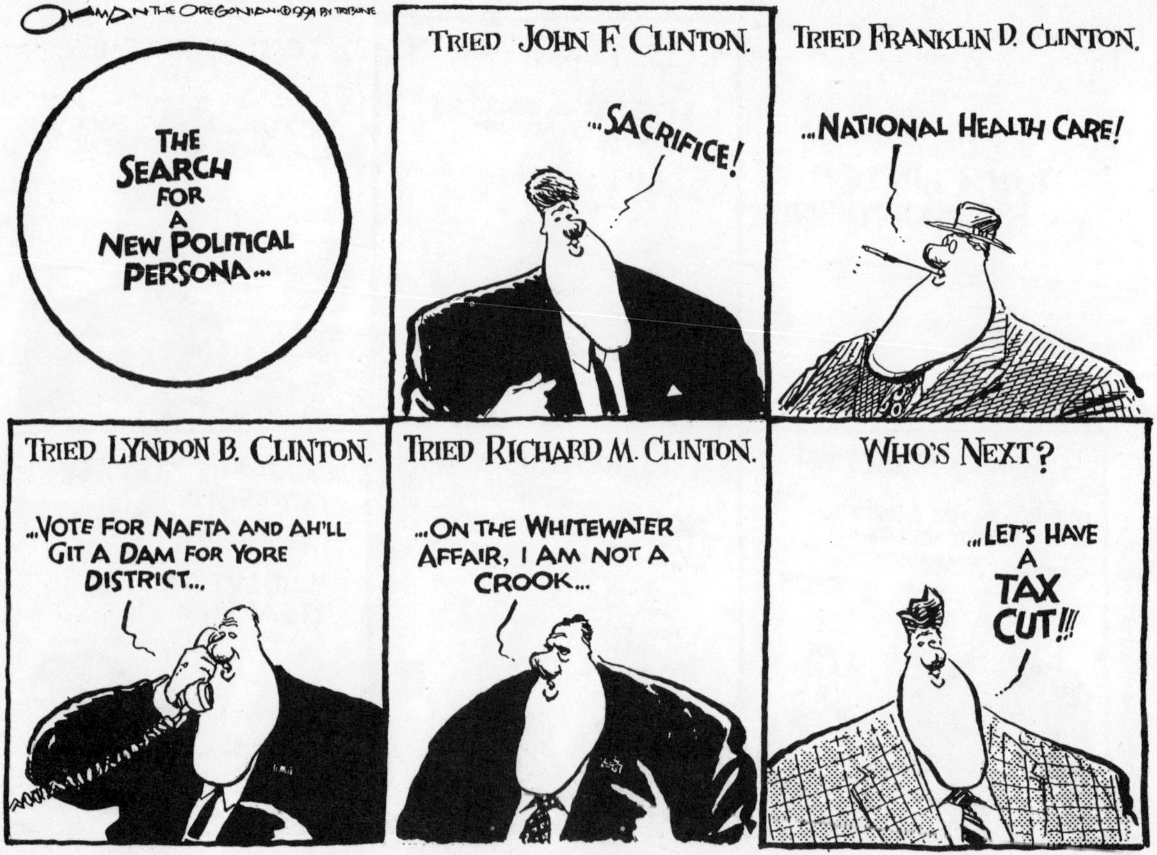
OHMAN THE OREGONIAN ©1994 BY TRIBUNE
THE SEARCH FOR A NEW POLITICAL PERSONA...
TRIED JOHN F. CLINTON.
...SACRIFICE!
TRIED FRANKLIN D. CLINTON.
...NATIONAL HEALTH CARE!
TRIED LYNDON B. CLINTON.
...VOTE FOR NAFTA AND AH'LL GIT A DAM FOR YORE DISTRICT...
TRIED RICHARD M. CLINTON.
...ON THE WHITEWATER AFFAIR, I AM NOT A CROOK...
WHO'S NEXT?
...LET'S HAVE A TAX CUT!!!

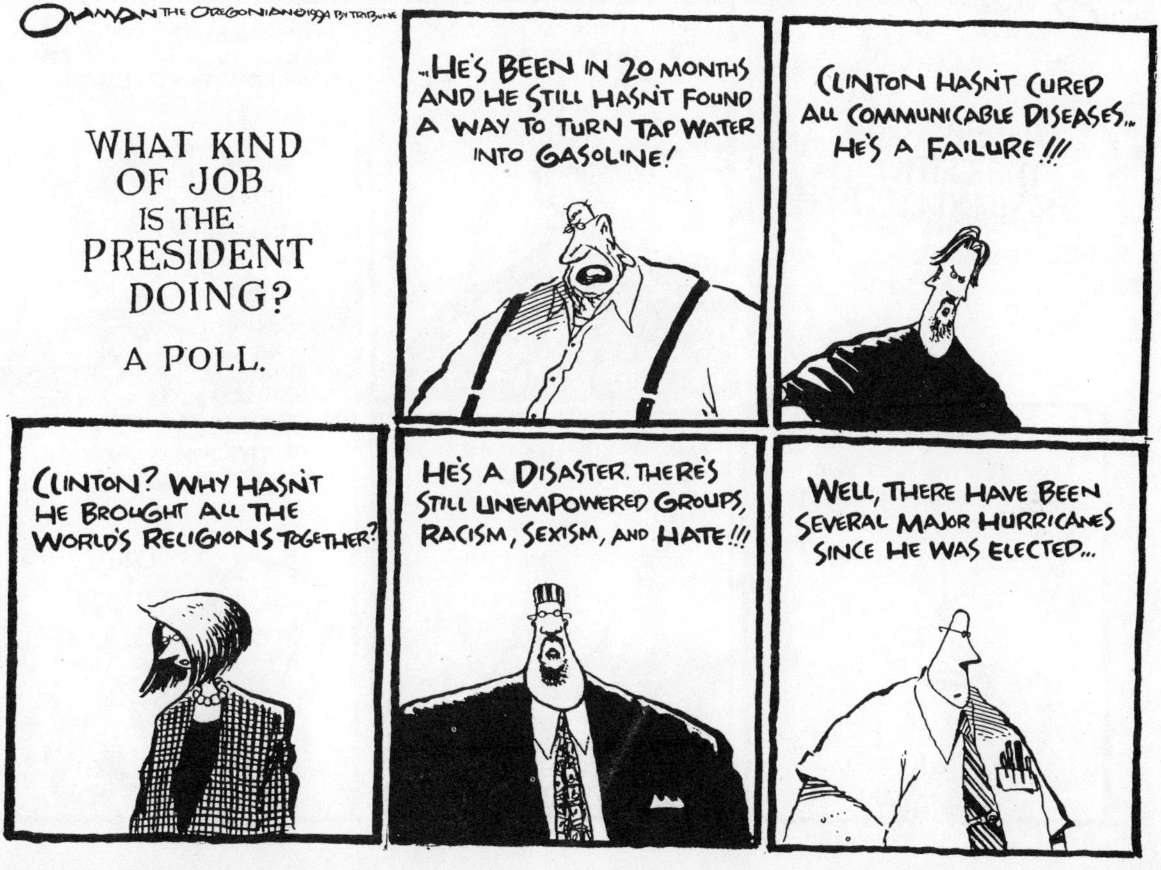
OHMAN THE OREGONIAN ©1994 BY TRIBUNE
WHAT KIND OF JOB IS THE PRESIDENT DOING?
A POLL.
...HE'S BEEN IN 20 MONTHS AND HE STILL HASN'T FOUND A WAY TO TURN TAP WATER INTO GASOLINE!
CLINTON HASN'T CURED ALL COMMUNICABLE DISEASES... HE'S A FAILURE!!!
CLINTON? WHY HASN'T HE BROUGHT ALL THE WORLD'S RELIGIONS TOGETHER?
HE'S A DISASTER. THERE'S STILL UNEMPOWERED GROUPS, RACISM, SEXISM, AND HATE!!!
WELL, THERE HAVE BEEN SEVERAL MAJOR HURRICANES SINCE HE WAS ELECTED...

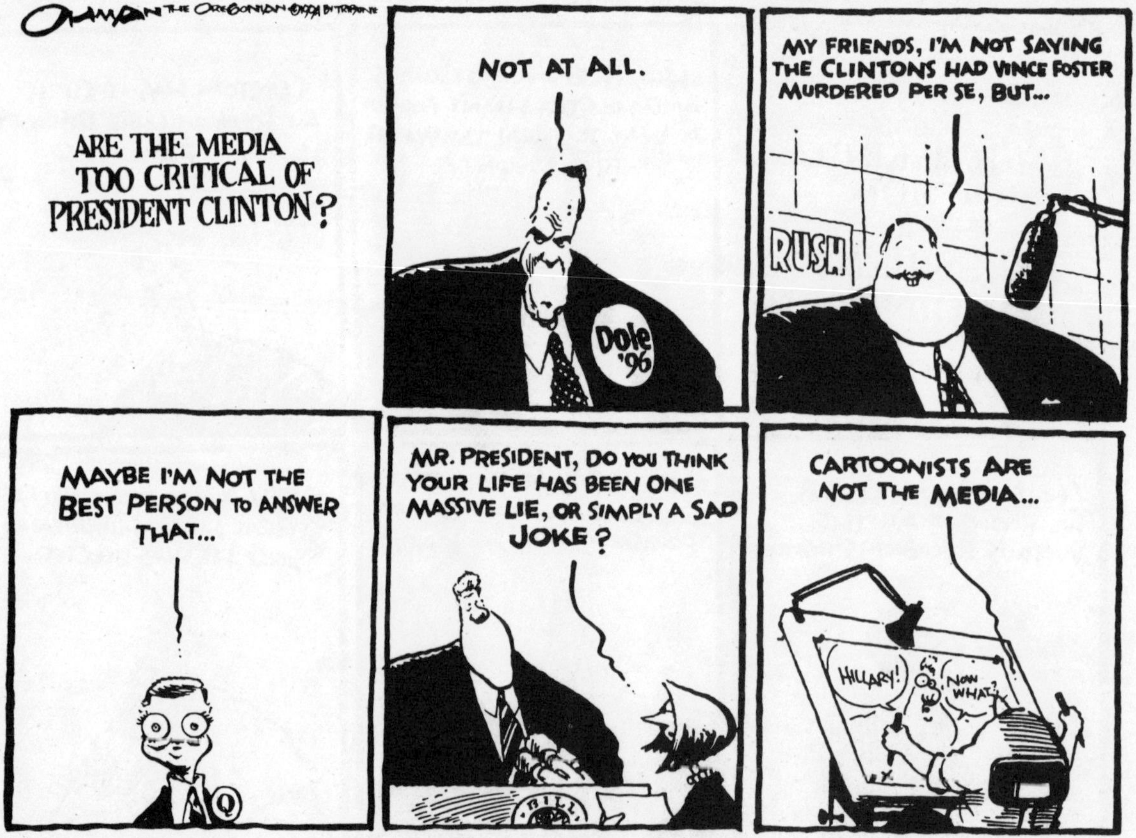
OHMAN THE OREGONIAN ©1994 BY TRIBUNE
ARE THE MEDIA TOO CRITICAL OF PRESIDENT CLINTON?
NOT AT ALL.
Dole '96
MY FRIENDS, I'M NOT SAYING THE CLINTONS HAD VINCE FOSTER MURDERED PER SE, BUT...
RUSH
MAYBE I'M NOT THE BEST PERSON TO ANSWER THAT...
Q
MR. PRESIDENT, DO YOU THINK YOUR LIFE HAS BEEN ONE MASSIVE LIE, OR SIMPLY A SAD JOKE?
BILL
CARTOONISTS ARE NOT THE MEDIA...
HILLARY!
NOW WHAT?

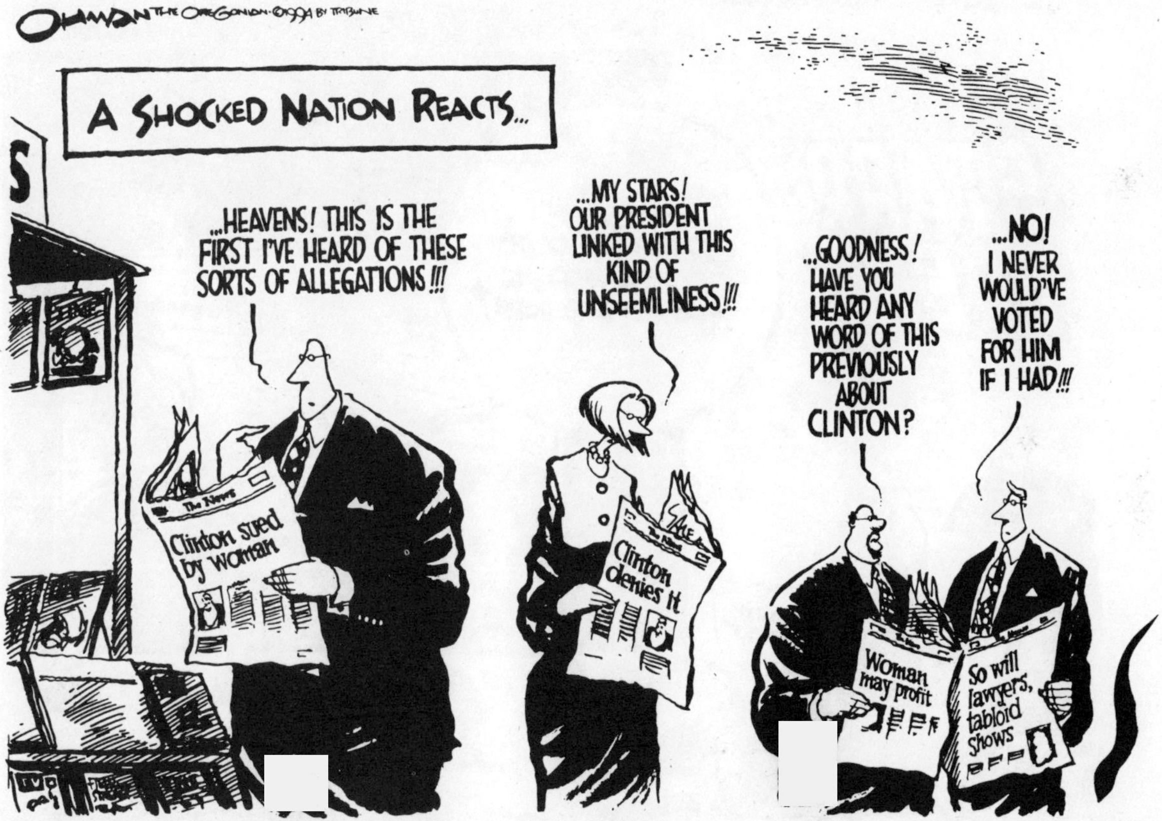
OHMAN THE OREGONIAN ©1994 BY TRIBUNE
A SHOCKED NATION REACTS...
...HEAVENS! THIS IS THE FIRST I'VE HEARD OF THESE SORTS OF ALLEGATIONS!!!
The News
Clinton sued by woman
...MY STARS! OUR PRESIDENT LINKED WITH THIS KIND OF UNSEEMLINESS!!!
Clinton denies it
...GOODNESS! HAVE YOU HEARD ANY WORD OF THIS PREVIOUSLY ABOUT CLINTON?
Woman may profit
...NO! I NEVER WOULD'VE VOTED FOR HIM IF I HAD!!!
So will lawyers, tabloid shows

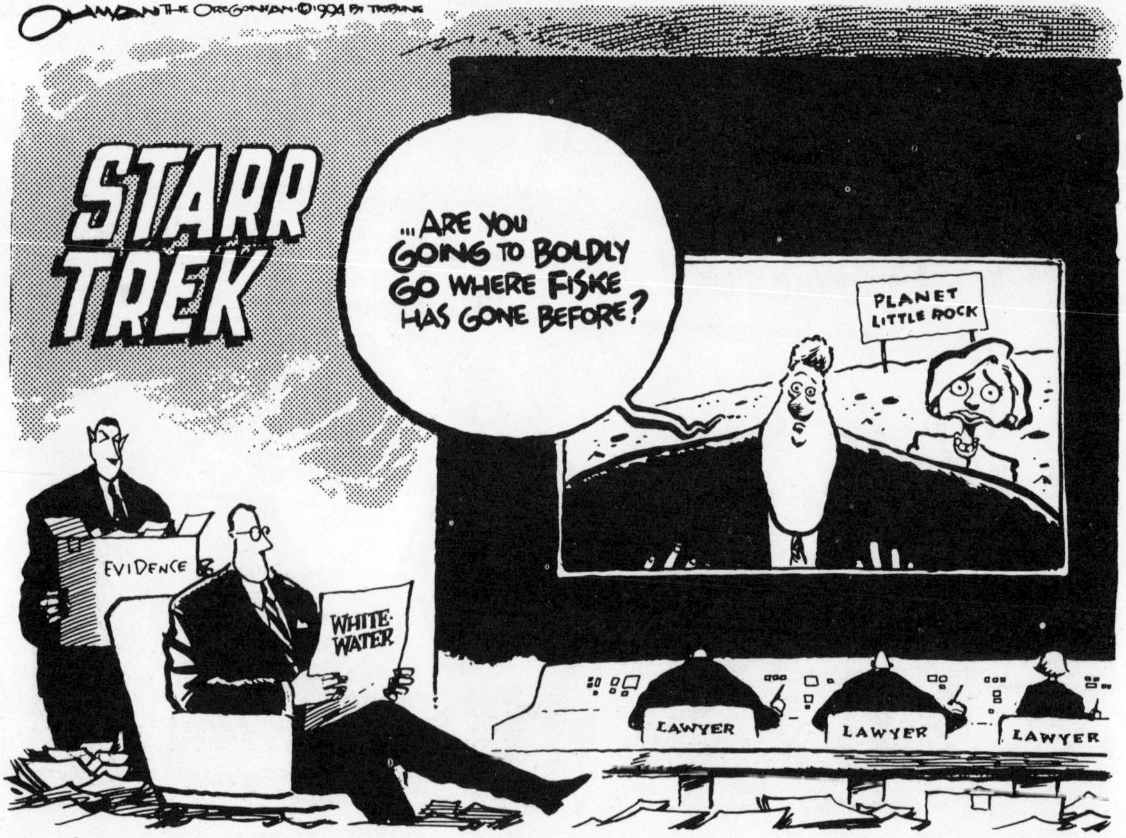

OHMAN THE OREGONIAN ©1994 BY TRIBUNE
STARR TREK
...ARE YOU GOING TO BOLDLY GO WHERE FISKE HAS GONE BEFORE?
PLANET LITTLE ROCK
EVIDENCE
WHITE-WATER
LAWYER
LAWYER
LAWYER

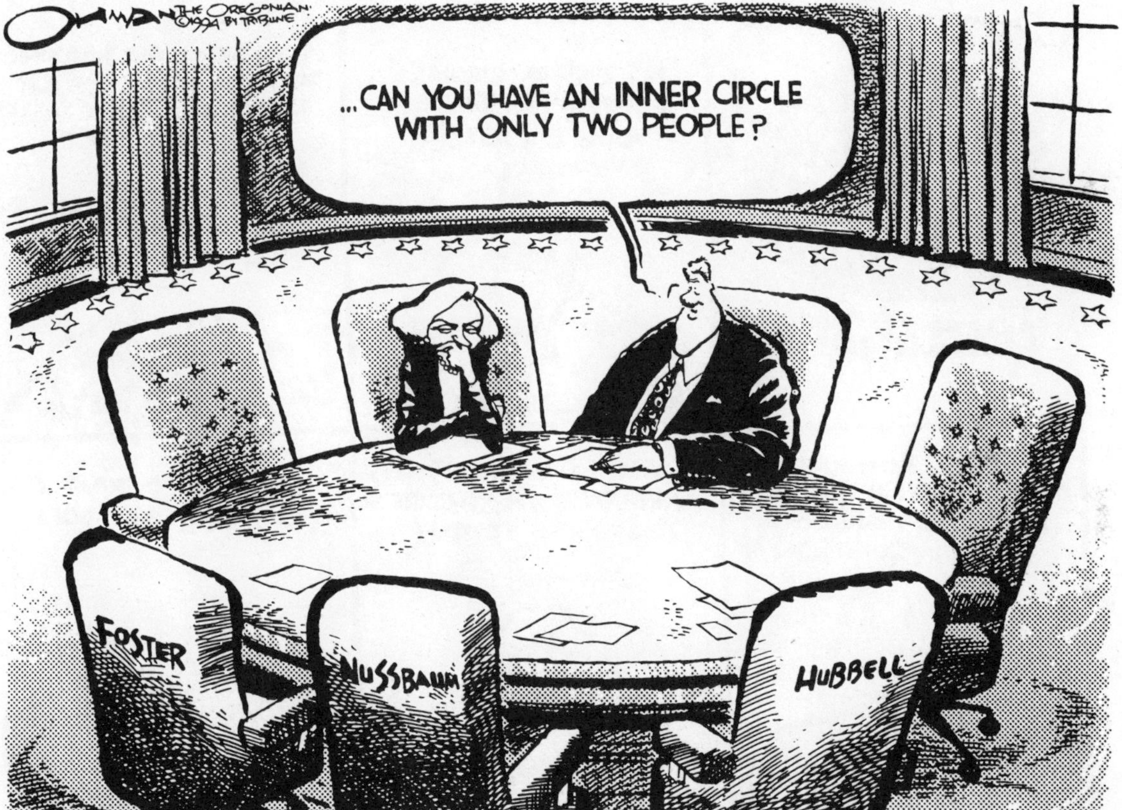
OHMAN THE OREGONIAN ©1994 BY TRIBUNE
...CAN YOU HAVE AN INNER CIRCLE WITH ONLY TWO PEOPLE?
FOSTER
NUSSBAUM
HUBBELL

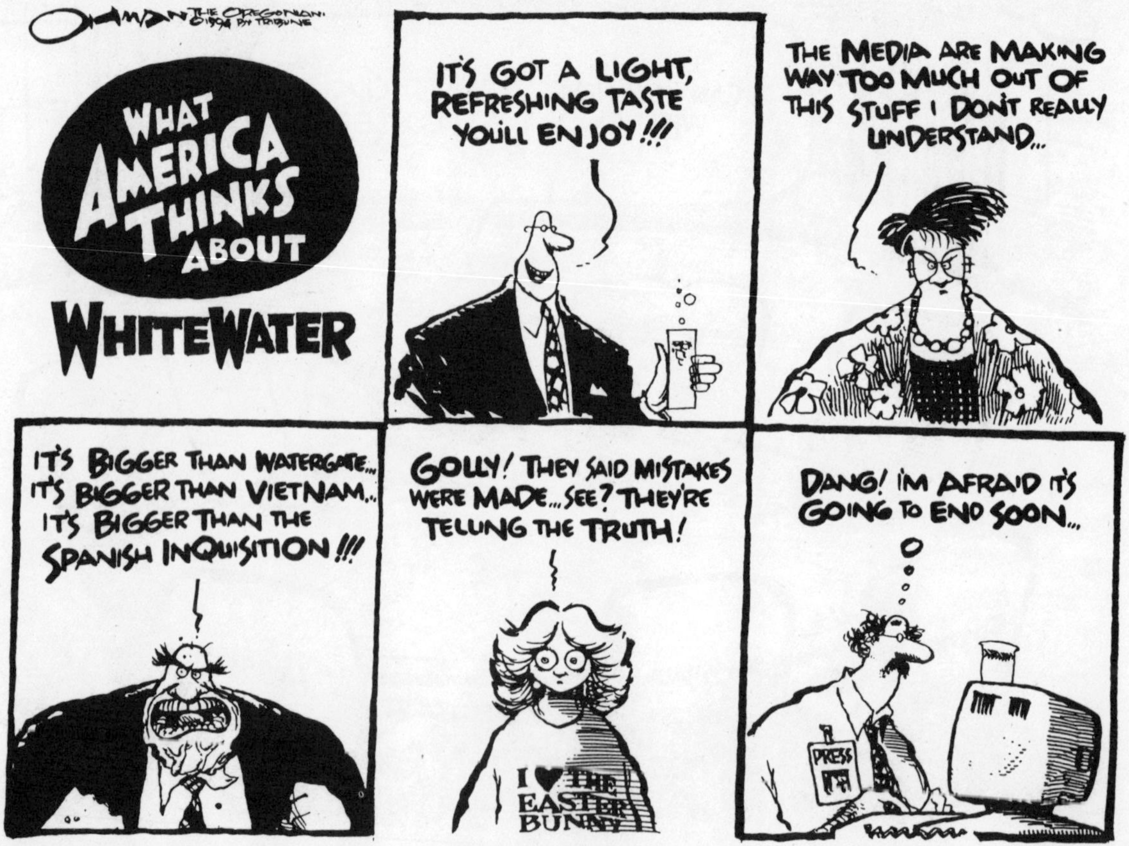
OHMAN THE OREGONIAN ©1994 BY TRIBUNE
WHAT AMERICA THINKS ABOUT WHITEWATER
IT'S GOT A LIGHT, REFRESHING TASTE YOU'LL ENJOY!!!
THE MEDIA ARE MAKING WAY TOO MUCH OUT OF THIS STUFF I DON'T REALLY UNDERSTAND...
IT'S BIGGER THAN WATERGATE... IT'S BIGGER THAN VIETNAM... IT'S BIGGER THAN THE SPANISH INQUISITION!!!
GOLLY! THEY SAID MISTAKES WERE MADE... SEE? THEY'RE TELLING THE TRUTH!
I ♥ THE EASTER BUNNY
DANG! I'M AFRAID IT'S GOING TO END SOON...
PRESS

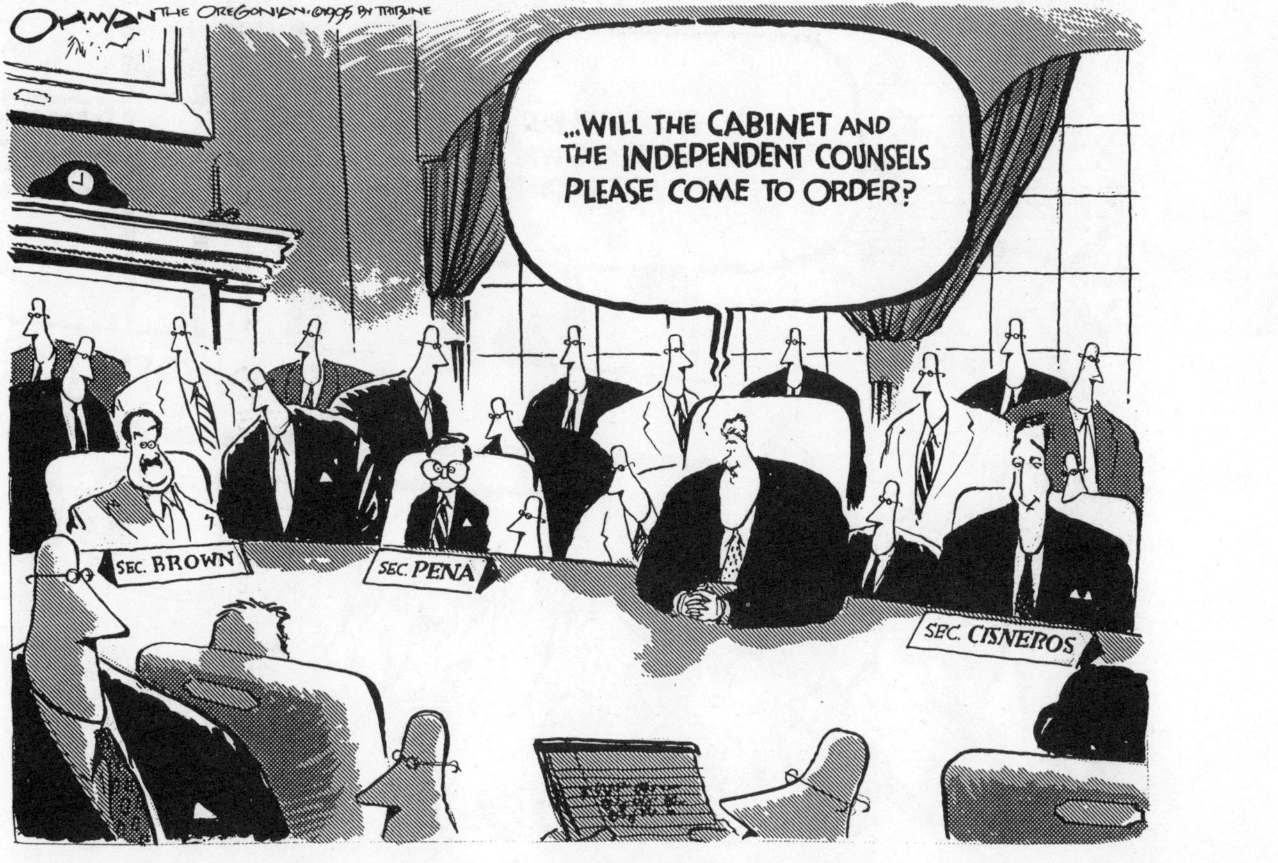
OHMAN THE OREGONIAN ©1995 BY TRIBUNE
...WILL THE CABINET AND THE INDEPENDENT COUNSELS PLEASE COME TO ORDER?
SEC. BROWN
SEC. PENA
SEC. CISNEROS

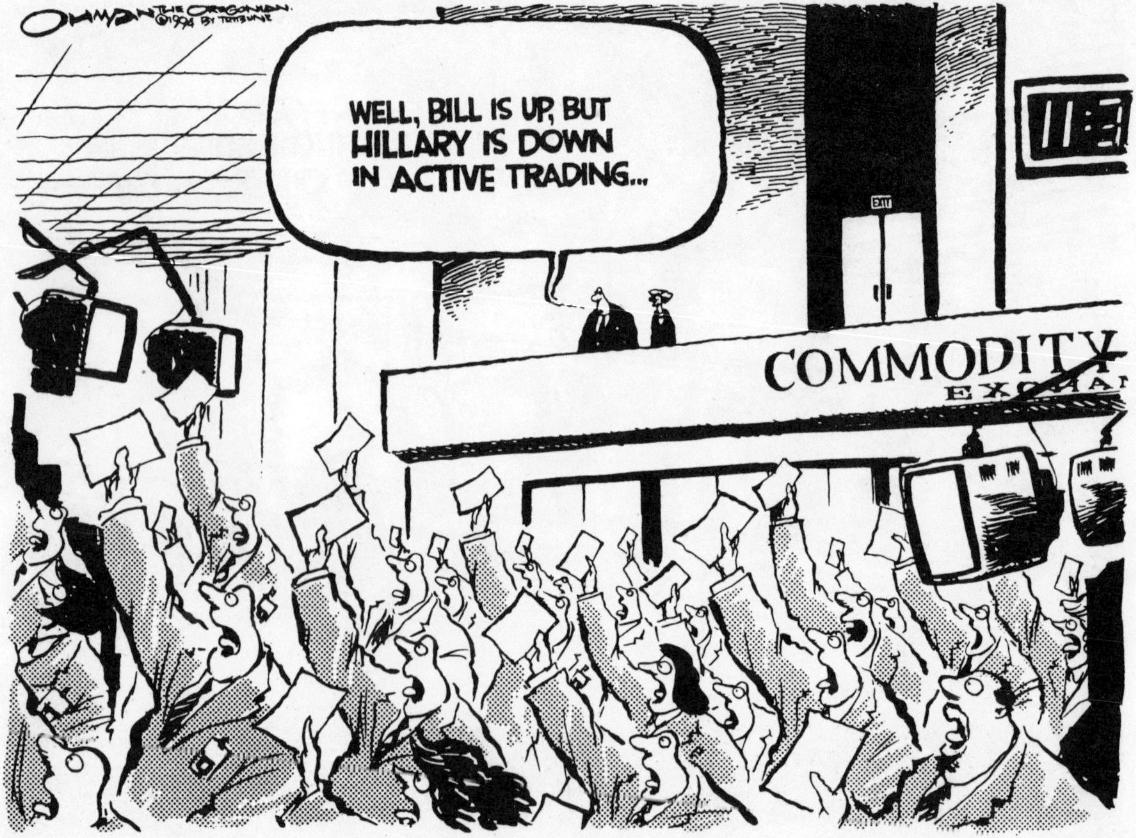
OHMAN THE OREGONIAN ©1994 BY TRIBUNE
WELL, BILL IS UP, BUT HILLARY IS DOWN IN ACTIVE TRADING...
EXIT
COMMODITY

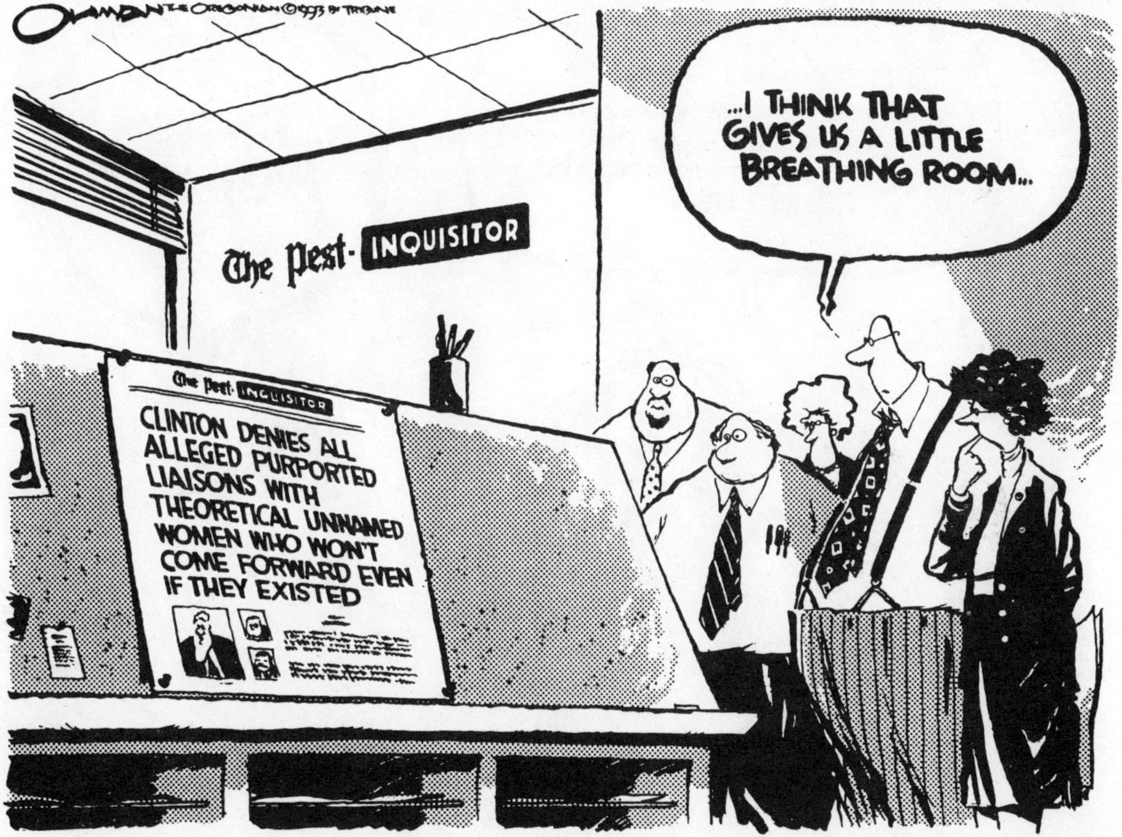
OLIPHANT THE OREGONIAN ©1993 BY TRIBUNE
...I THINK THAT GIVES US A LITTLE BREATHING ROOM...
The Pest-INQUISITOR
The Pest-INQUISITOR
CLINTON DENIES ALL ALLEGED PURPORTED LIAISONS WITH THEORETICAL UNNAMED WOMEN WHO WON'T COME FORWARD EVEN IF THEY EXISTED

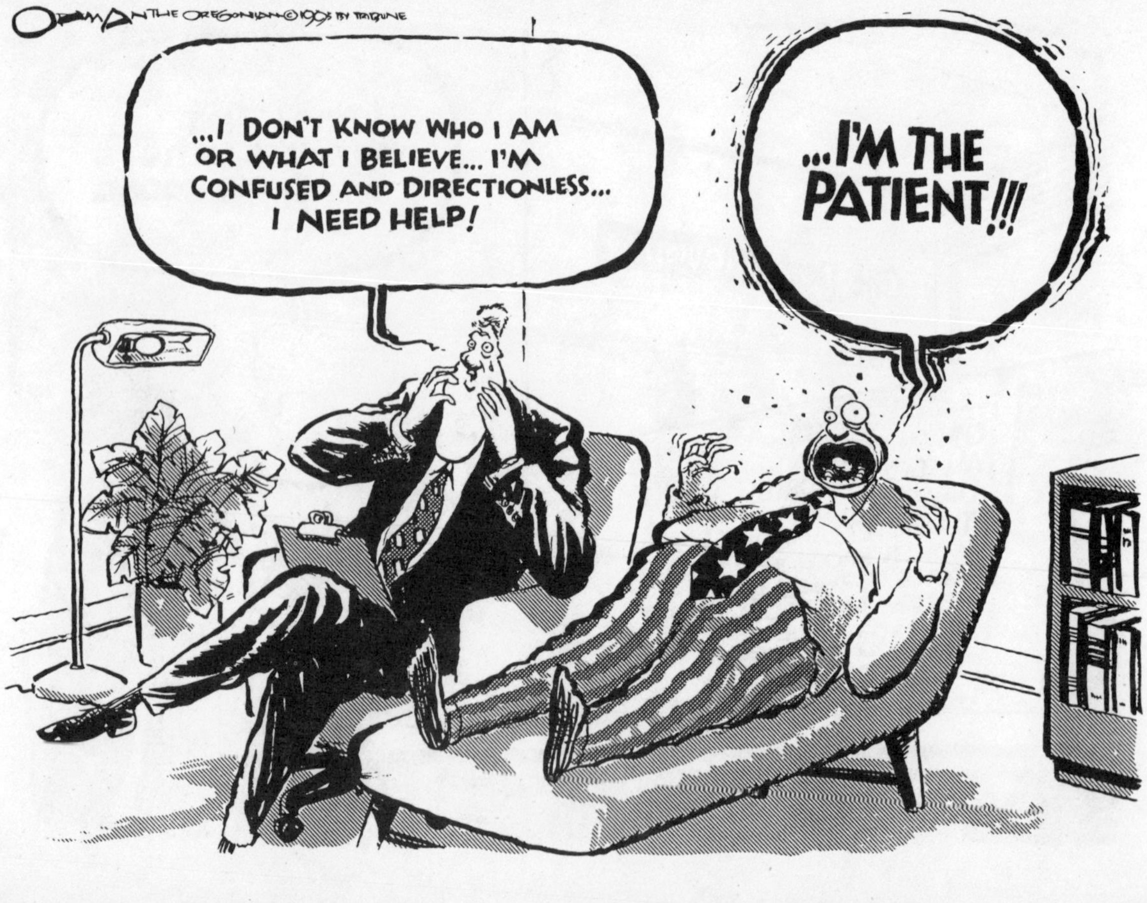
OHMAN THE OREGONIAN ©1995 BY TRIBUNE
...I DON'T KNOW WHO I AM OR WHAT I BELIEVE... I'M CONFUSED AND DIRECTIONLESS... I NEED HELP!
...I'M THE PATIENT!!!

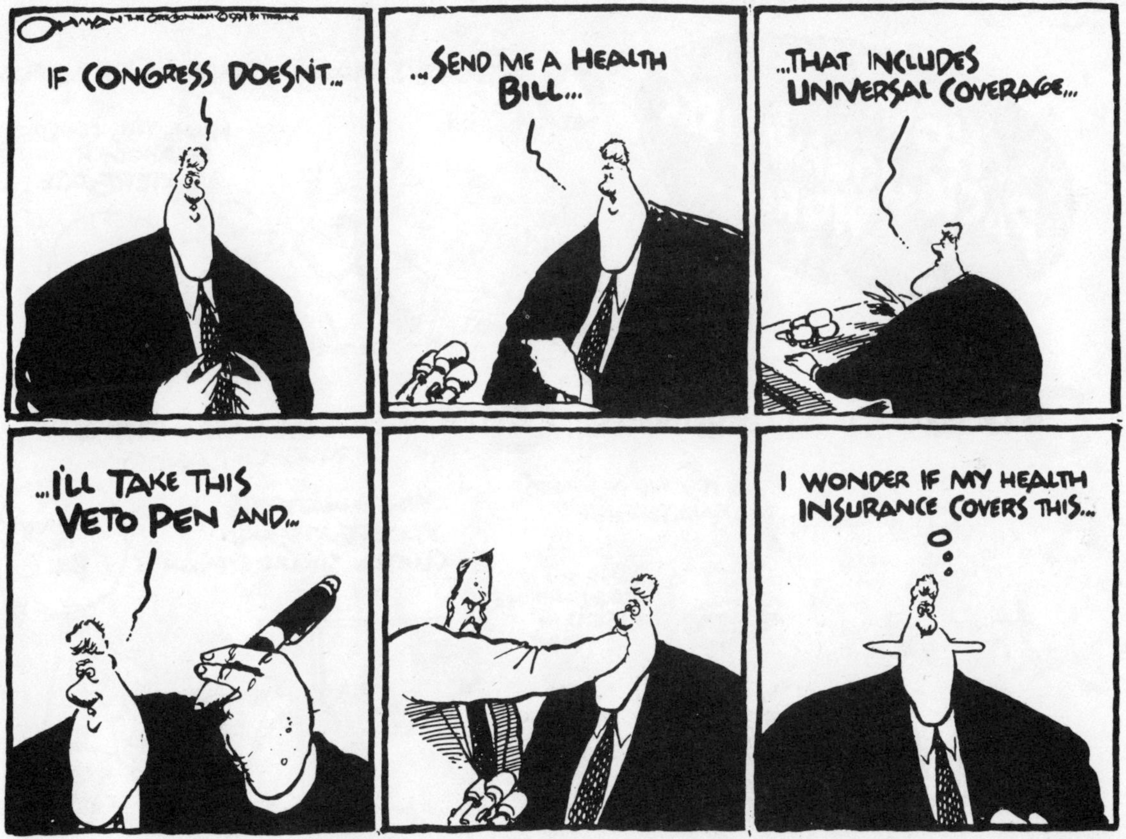

OHMAN THE OREGONIAN ©1994
IF CONGRESS DOESN'T...
...SEND ME A HEALTH BILL...
...THAT INCLUDES UNIVERSAL COVERAGE...
...I'LL TAKE THIS VETO PEN AND...
I WONDER IF MY HEALTH INSURANCE COVERS THIS...

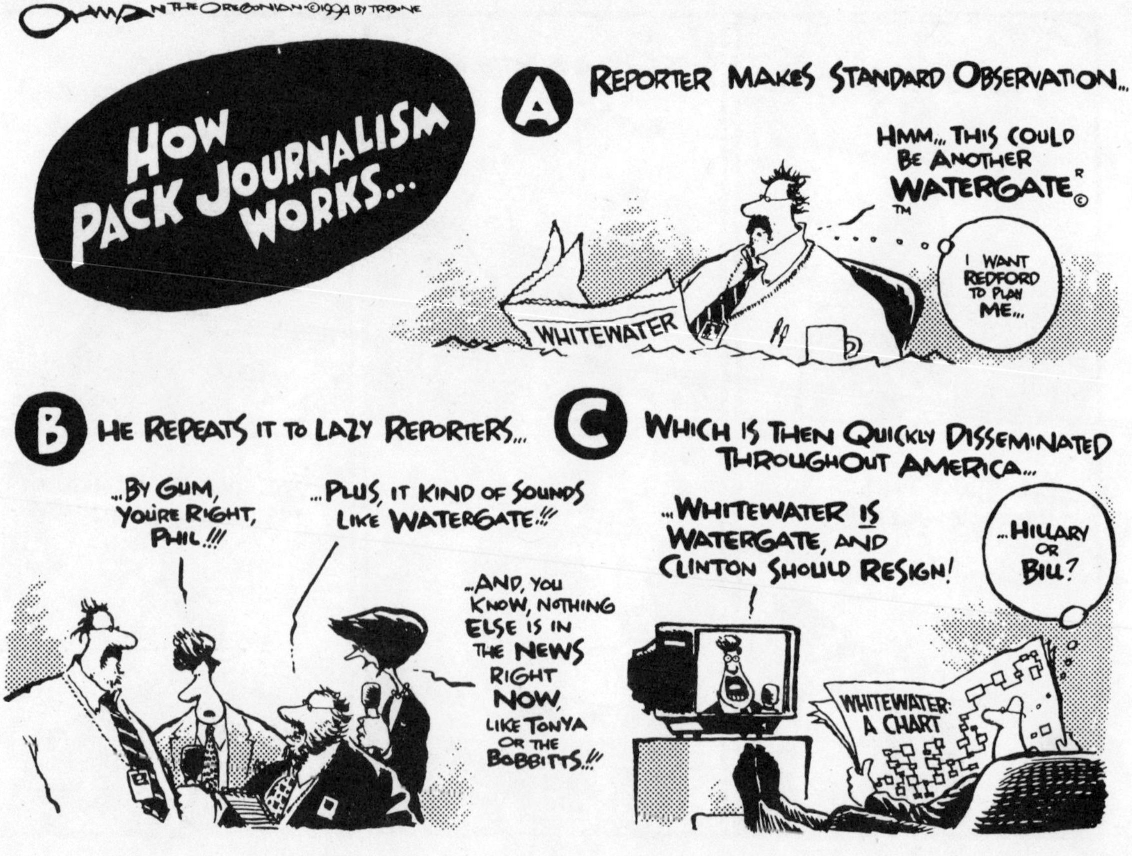
OHMAN IN THE OREGONIAN ©1994 BY TRIBUNE
HOW PACK JOURNALISM WORKS...
A REPORTER MAKES STANDARD OBSERVATION...
HMM... THIS COULD BE ANOTHER WATERGATE
I WANT REDFORD TO PLAY ME...
WHITEWATER
B HE REPEATS IT TO LAZY REPORTERS...
...BY GUM, YOU'RE RIGHT, PHIL!!!
...PLUS, IT KIND OF SOUNDS LIKE WATERGATE!!!
...AND, YOU KNOW, NOTHING ELSE IS IN THE NEWS RIGHT NOW, LIKE TONYA OR THE BOBBITTS!!!
C WHICH IS THEN QUICKLY DISSEMINATED THROUGHOUT AMERICA...
...WHITEWATER IS WATERGATE, AND CLINTON SHOULD RESIGN!
...HILLARY OR BILL?
WHITEWATER: A CHART

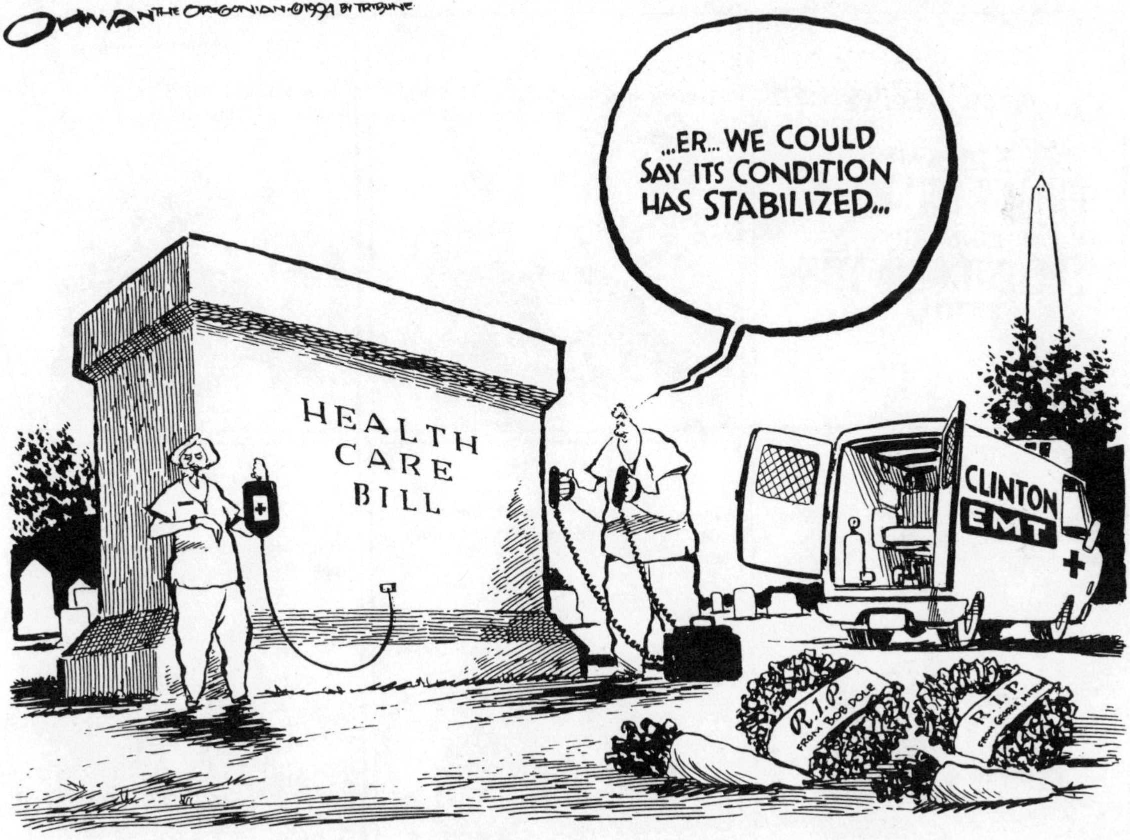
OHMAN THE OREGONIAN ©1994 BY TRIBUNE
...ER... WE COULD SAY ITS CONDITION HAS STABILIZED...
HEALTH CARE BILL
CLINTON EMT
R.I.P. FROM BOB DOLE
R.I.P. FROM GEORGE MITCH

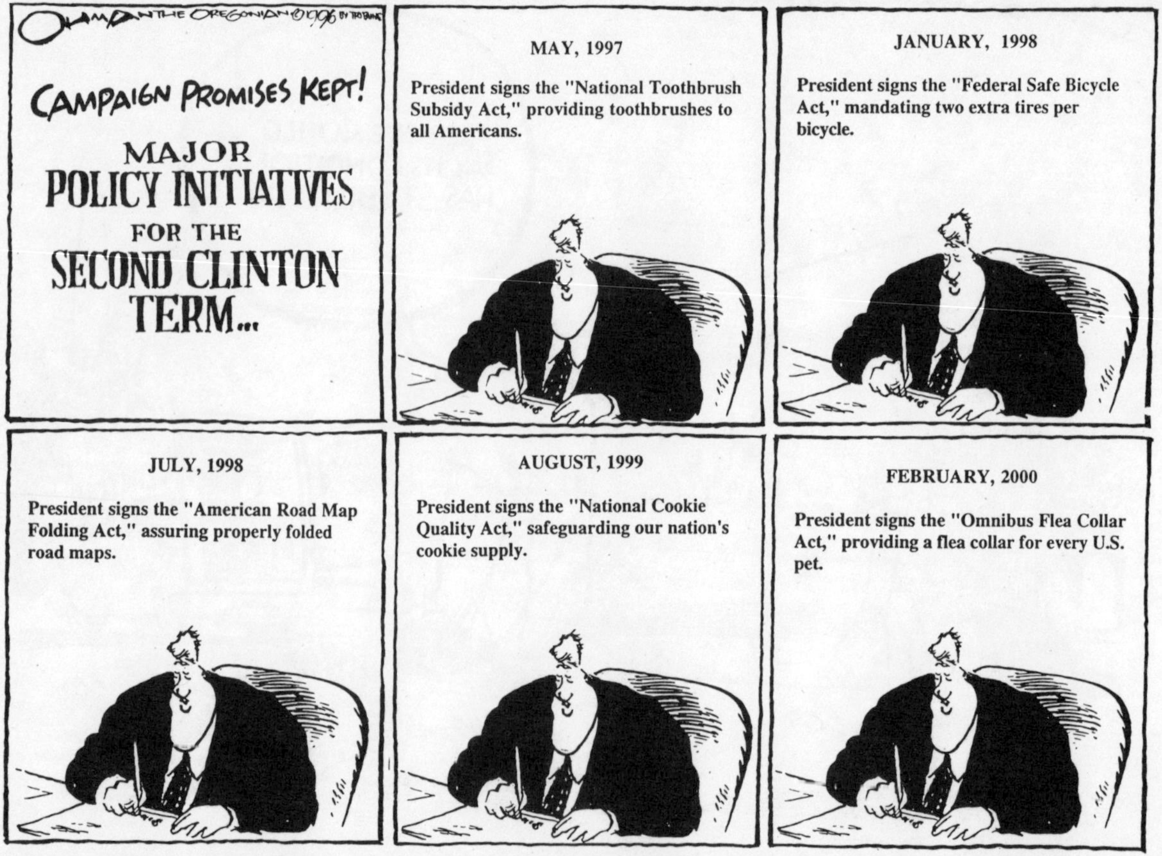
OLIPHANT THE OREGONIAN ©1996
CAMPAIGN PROMISES KEPT!
MAJOR POLICY INITIATIVES FOR THE SECOND CLINTON TERM...
MAY, 1997
President signs the "National Toothbrush Subsidy Act," providing toothbrushes to all Americans.
JANUARY, 1998
President signs the "Federal Safe Bicycle Act," mandating two extra tires per bicycle.
JULY, 1998
President signs the "American Road Map Folding Act," assuring properly folded road maps.
AUGUST, 1999
President signs the "National Cookie Quality Act," safeguarding our nation's cookie supply.
FEBRUARY, 2000
President signs the "Omnibus Flea Collar Act," providing a flea collar for every U.S. pet.

# SEX, RACE, GUNS, AND NUTS

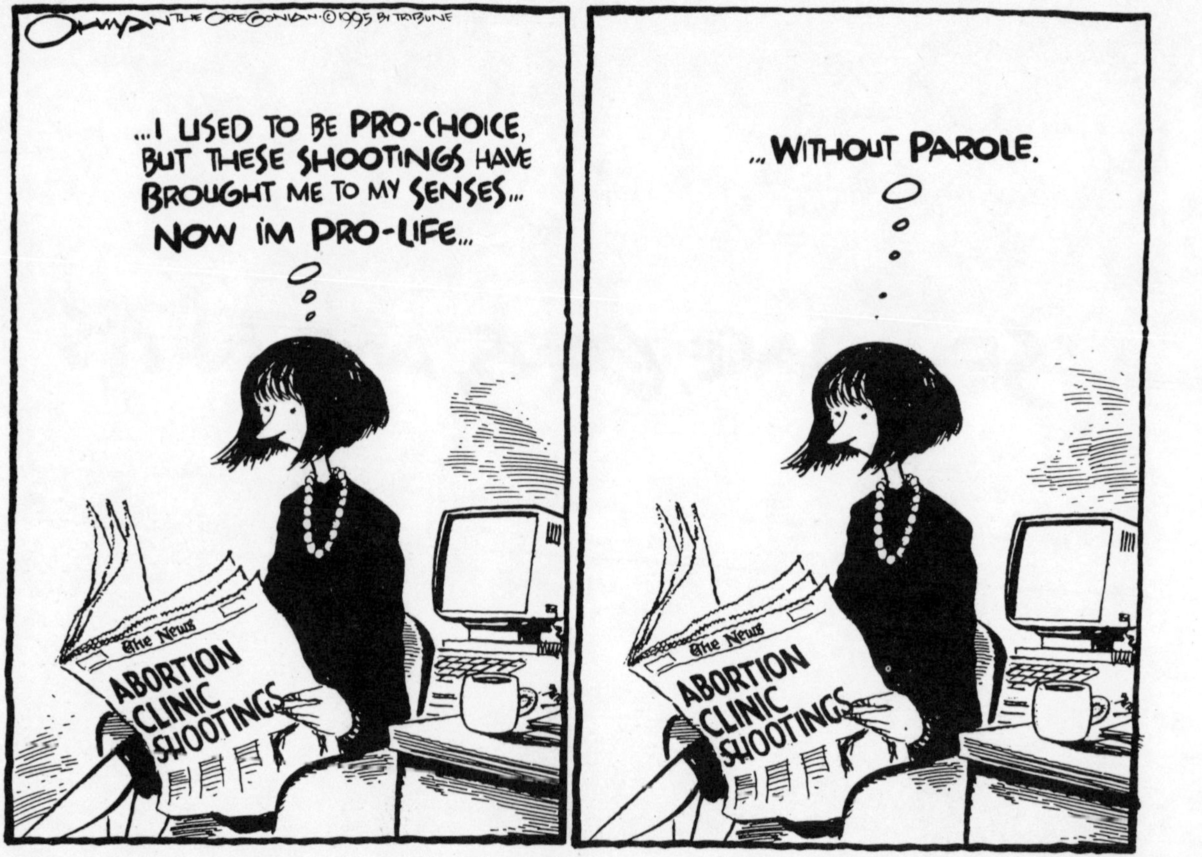
OHMAN THE OREGONIAN ©1995 BY TRIBUNE
...I USED TO BE PRO-CHOICE, BUT THESE SHOOTINGS HAVE BROUGHT ME TO MY SENSES... NOW IM PRO-LIFE...
The News
ABORTION CLINIC SHOOTINGS
...WITHOUT PAROLE.
The News
ABORTION CLINIC SHOOTINGS

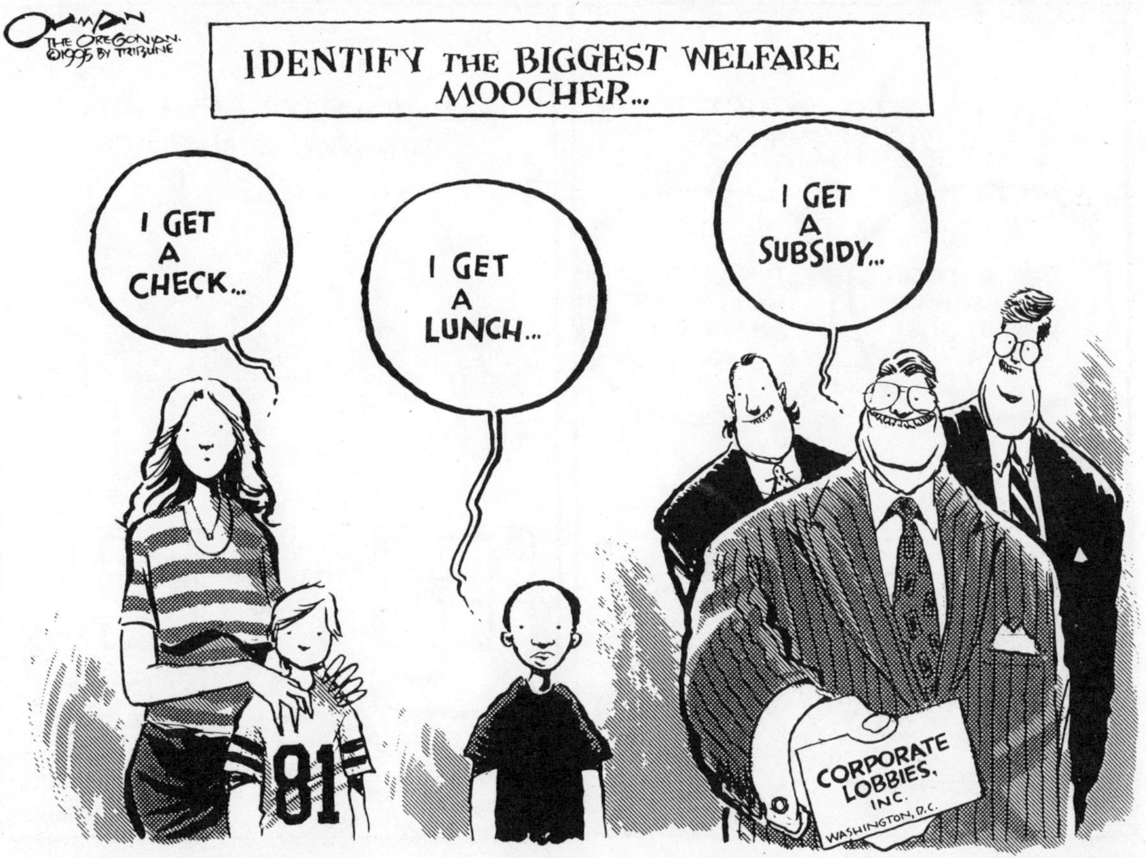
OHMAN
THE OREGONIAN
©1995 BY TRIBUNE
IDENTIFY THE BIGGEST WELFARE MOOCHER...
I GET A CHECK...
I GET A LUNCH...
I GET A SUBSIDY...
81
CORPORATE LOBBIES, INC.
WASHINGTON, D.C.

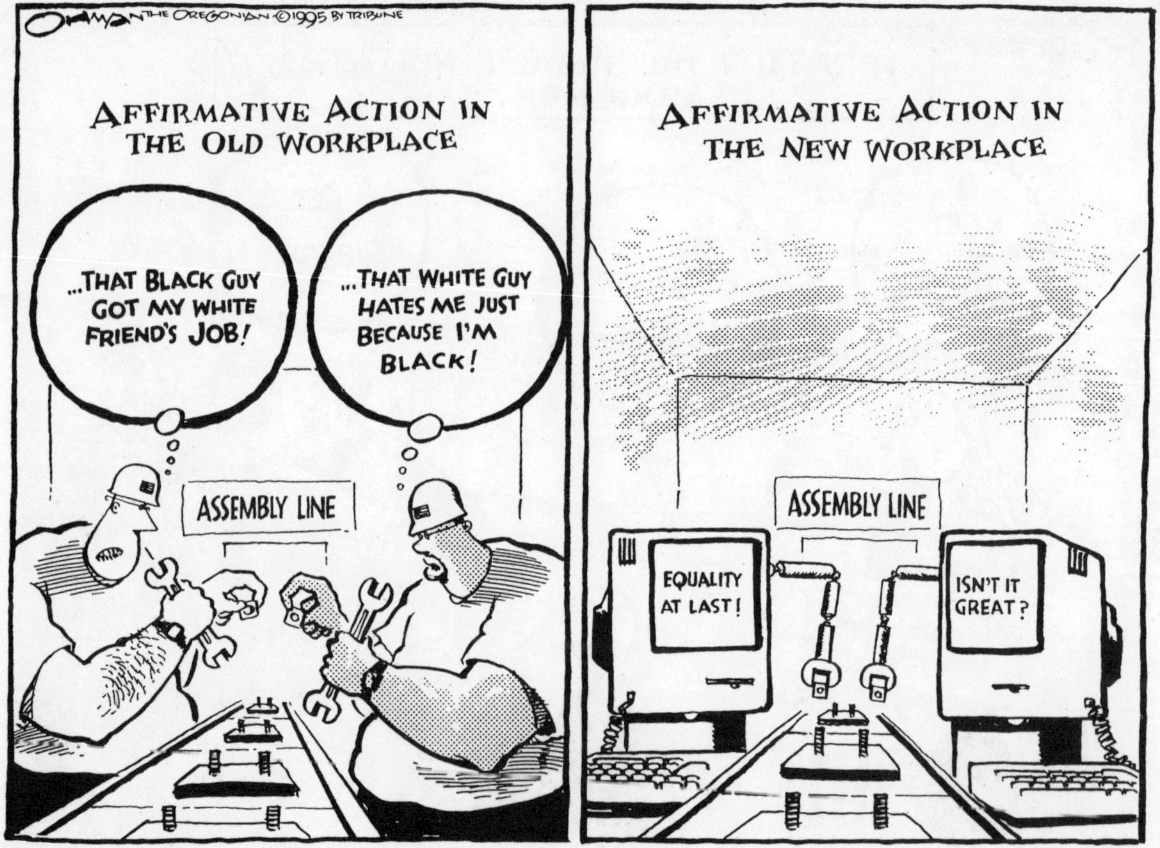
OHMAN THE OREGONIAN ©1995 BY TRIBUNE
AFFIRMATIVE ACTION IN THE OLD WORKPLACE
...THAT BLACK GUY GOT MY WHITE FRIEND'S JOB!
...THAT WHITE GUY HATES ME JUST BECAUSE I'M BLACK!
ASSEMBLY LINE
AFFIRMATIVE ACTION IN THE NEW WORKPLACE
ASSEMBLY LINE
EQUALITY AT LAST!
ISN'T IT GREAT?

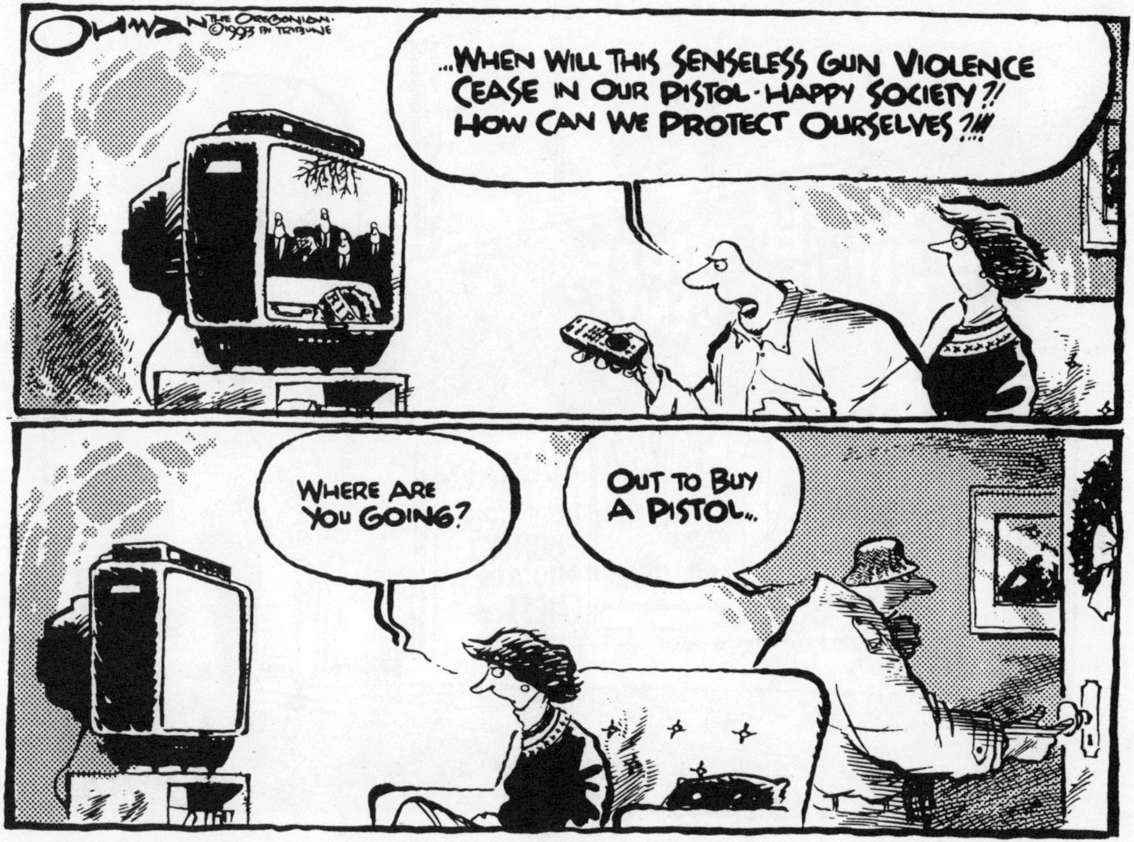
OHMAN THE OREGONIAN ©1993 BY TRIBUNE
...WHEN WILL THIS SENSELESS GUN VIOLENCE CEASE IN OUR PISTOL-HAPPY SOCIETY?! HOW CAN WE PROTECT OURSELVES?!!!
RIP
WHERE ARE YOU GOING?
OUT TO BUY A PISTOL...

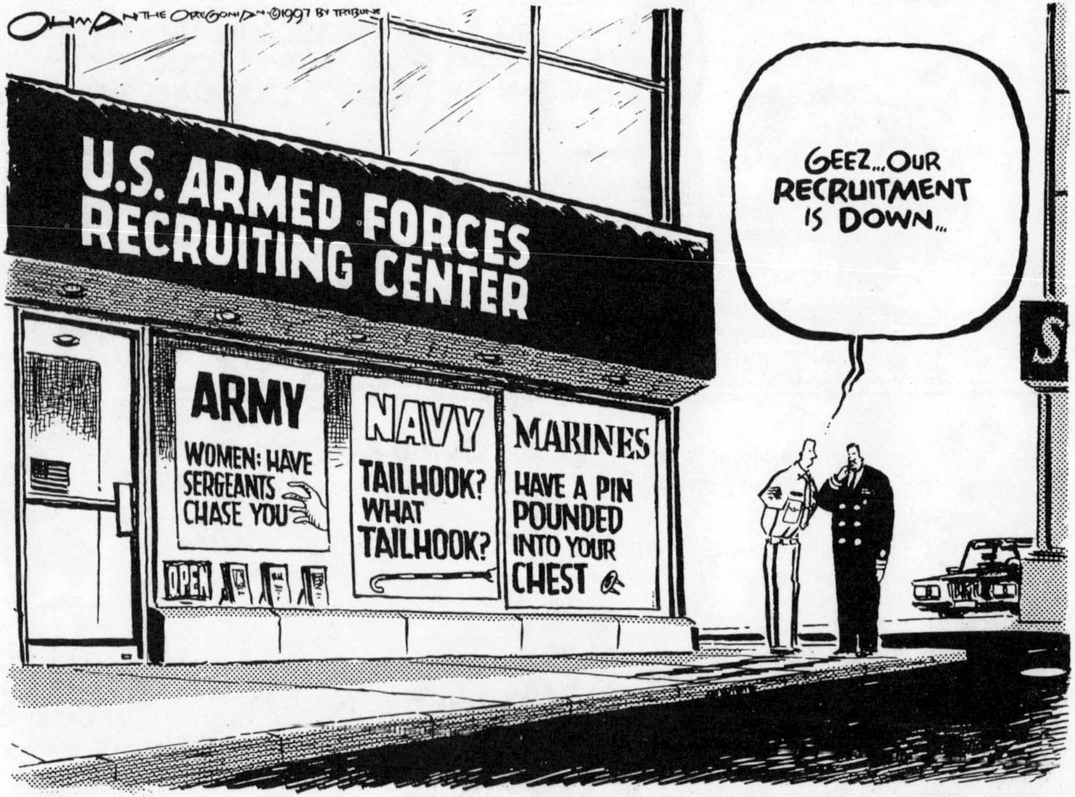
OLIPHANT THE OREGONIAN ©1997 BY TRIBUNE
U.S. ARMED FORCES RECRUITING CENTER
ARMY
WOMEN: HAVE SERGEANTS CHASE YOU
OPEN
NAVY
TAILHOOK? WHAT TAILHOOK?
MARINES
HAVE A PIN POUNDED INTO YOUR CHEST
GEEZ... OUR RECRUITMENT IS DOWN...

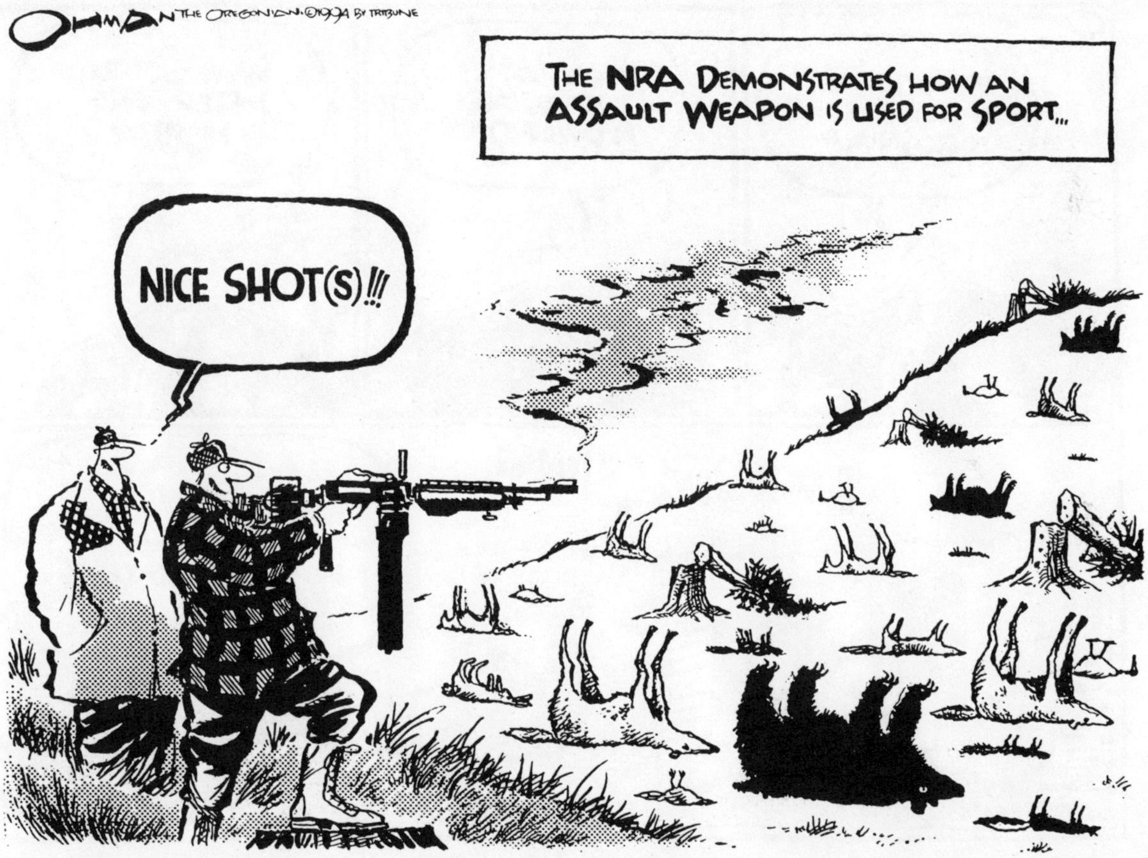
OHMAN THE OREGONIAN ©1994 BY TRIBUNE
THE NRA DEMONSTRATES HOW AN ASSAULT WEAPON IS USED FOR SPORT...
NICE SHOT(S)!!!

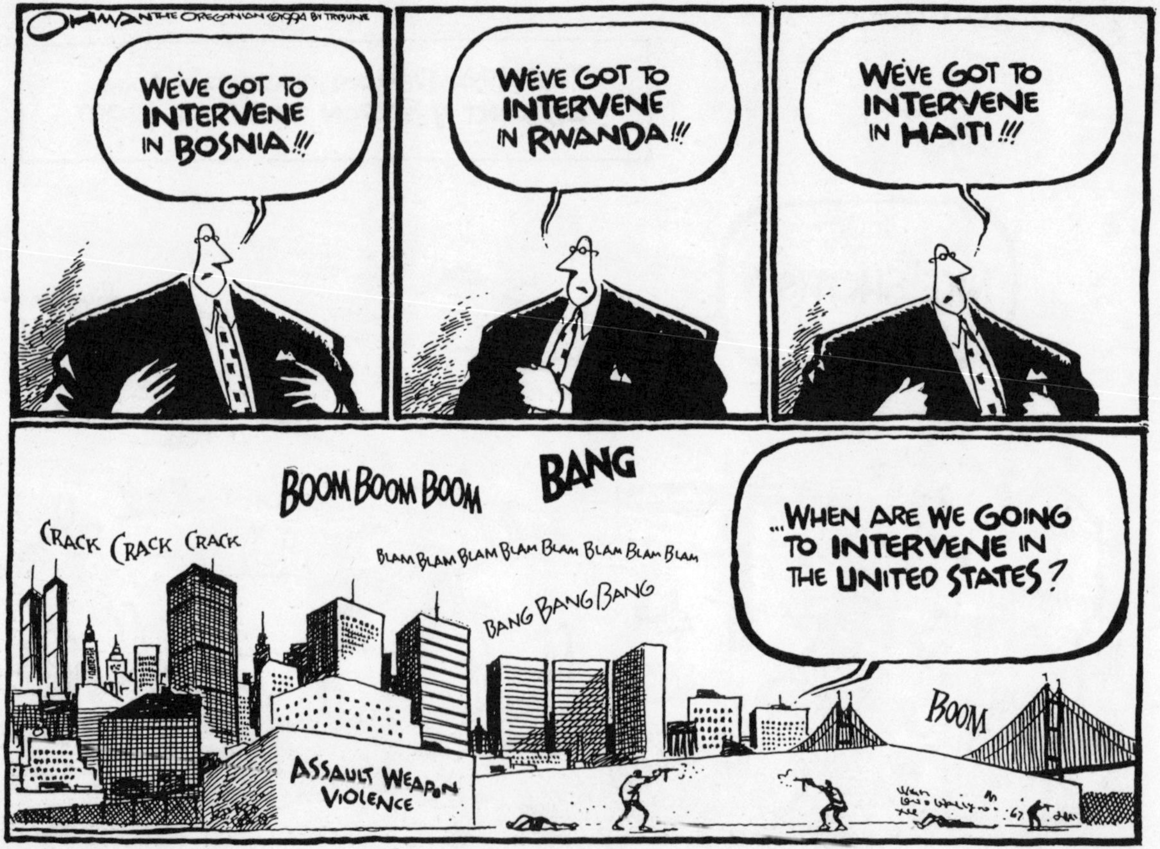
OHMAN THE OREGONIAN ©1994 BY TRIBUNE
WE'VE GOT TO INTERVENE IN BOSNIA!!!
WE'VE GOT TO INTERVENE IN RWANDA!!!
WE'VE GOT TO INTERVENE IN HAITI!!!
BOOM BOOM BOOM
BANG
CRACK CRACK CRACK
BLAM BLAM BLAM BLAM BLAM BLAM BLAM BLAM
BANG BANG BANG
...WHEN ARE WE GOING TO INTERVENE IN THE UNITED STATES?
BOOM
ASSAULT WEAPON VIOLENCE

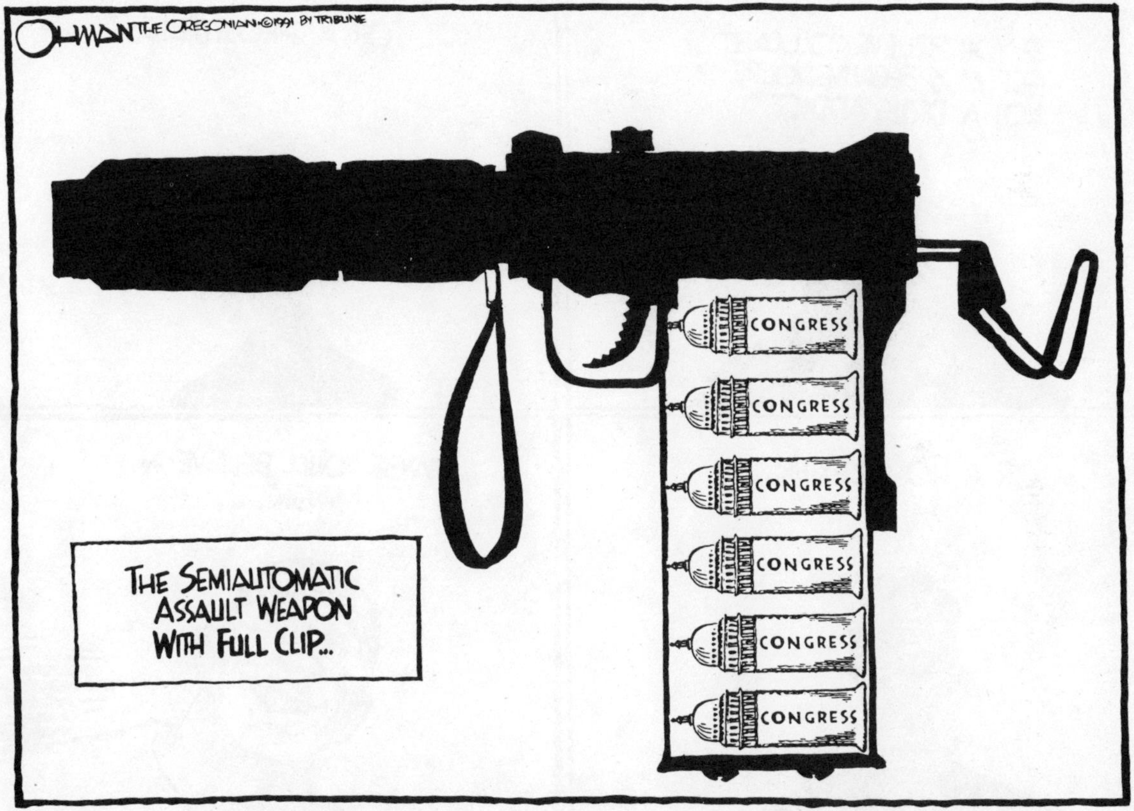
OHMAN THE OREGONIAN ©1991 BY TRIBUNE
CONGRESS
CONGRESS
CONGRESS
CONGRESS
CONGRESS
CONGRESS
THE SEMIAUTOMATIC ASSAULT WEAPON WITH FULL CLIP...

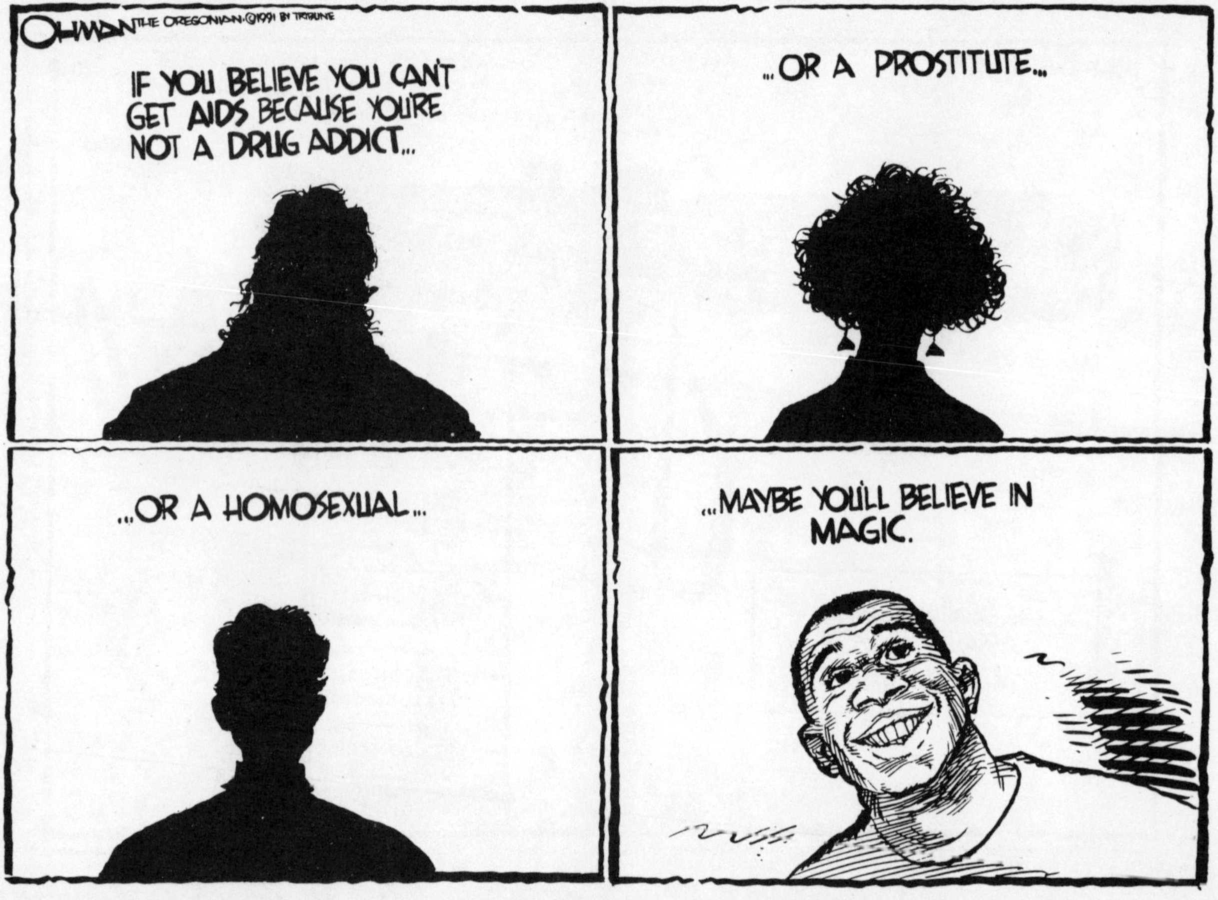
OHMAN THE OREGONIAN ©1991 BY TRIBUNE
IF YOU BELIEVE YOU CAN'T GET AIDS BECAUSE YOU'RE NOT A DRUG ADDICT...
...OR A PROSTITUTE...
...OR A HOMOSEXUAL...
...MAYBE YOU'LL BELIEVE IN MAGIC.

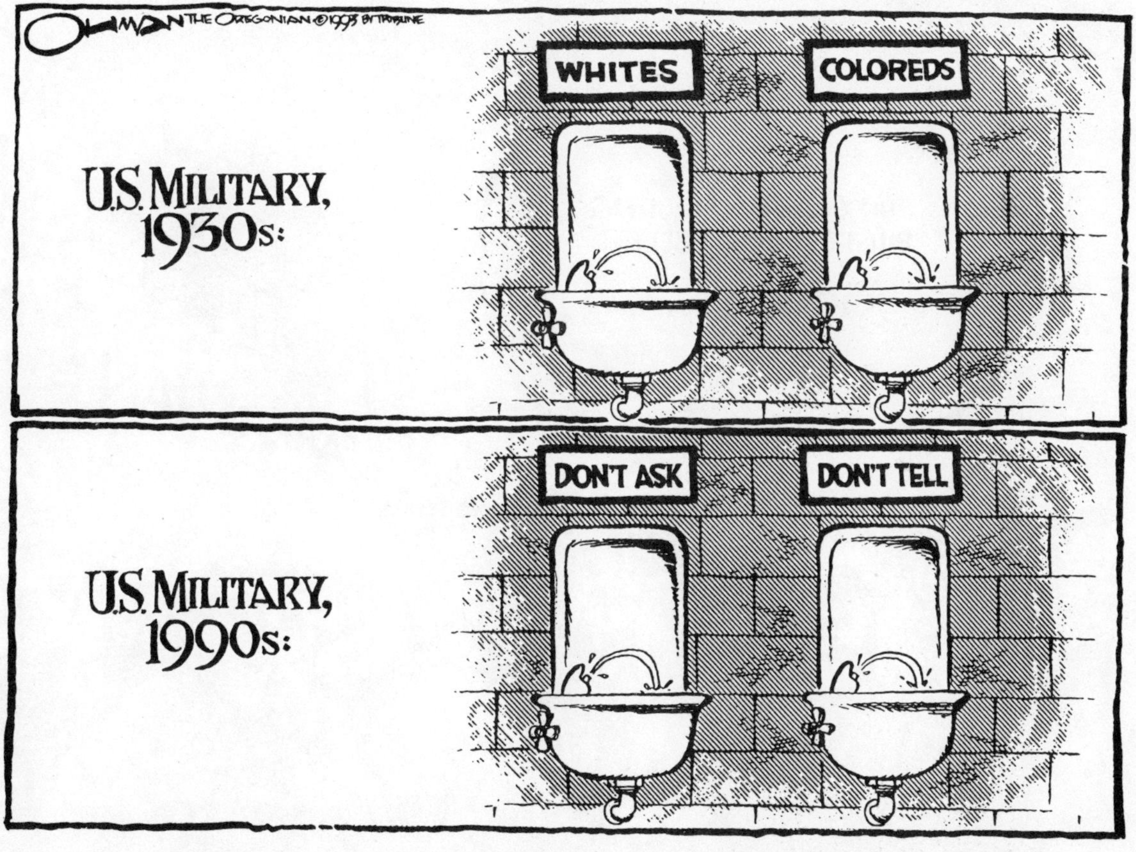
OHMAN THE OREGONIAN ©1993 BY TRIBUNE
U.S. MILITARY, 1930s:
WHITES
COLOREDS
U.S. MILITARY, 1990s:
DON'T ASK
DON'T TELL

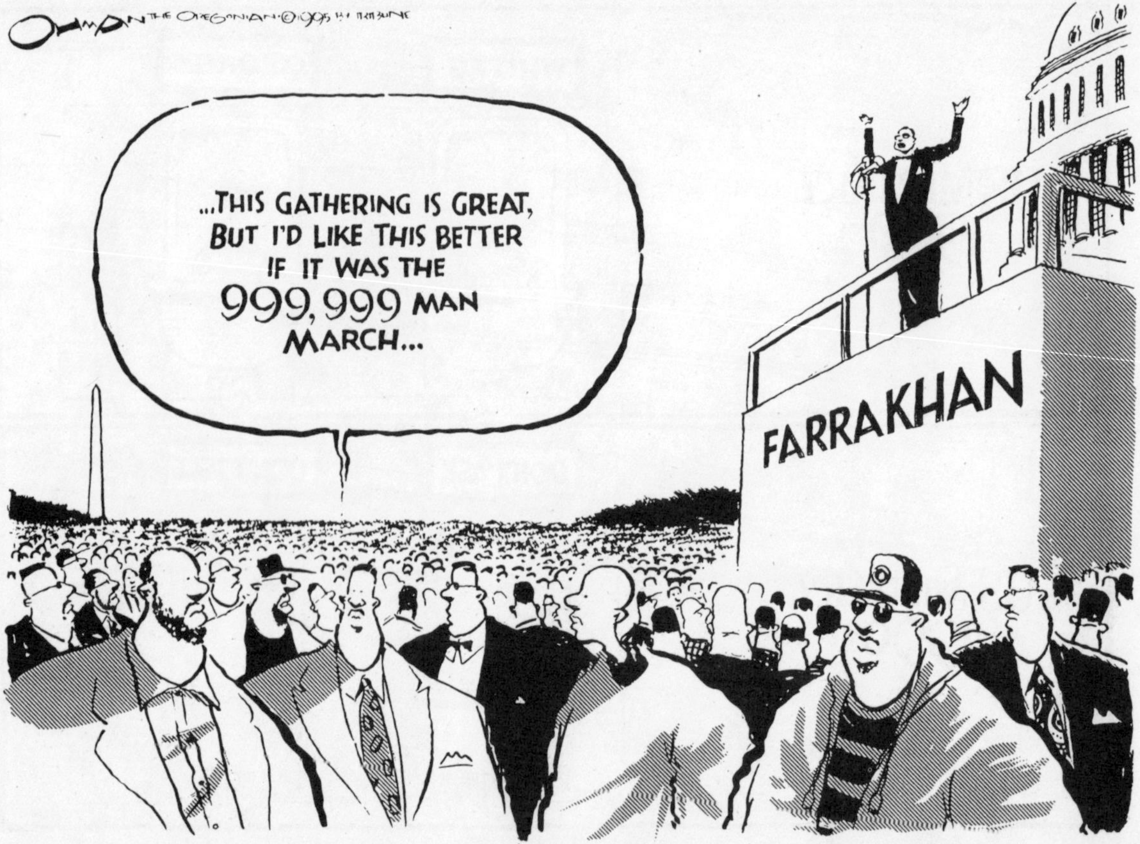
OHMAN THE OREGONIAN ©1995 TRIBUNE
...THIS GATHERING IS GREAT, BUT I'D LIKE THIS BETTER IF IT WAS THE 999,999 MAN MARCH...
FARRAKHAN

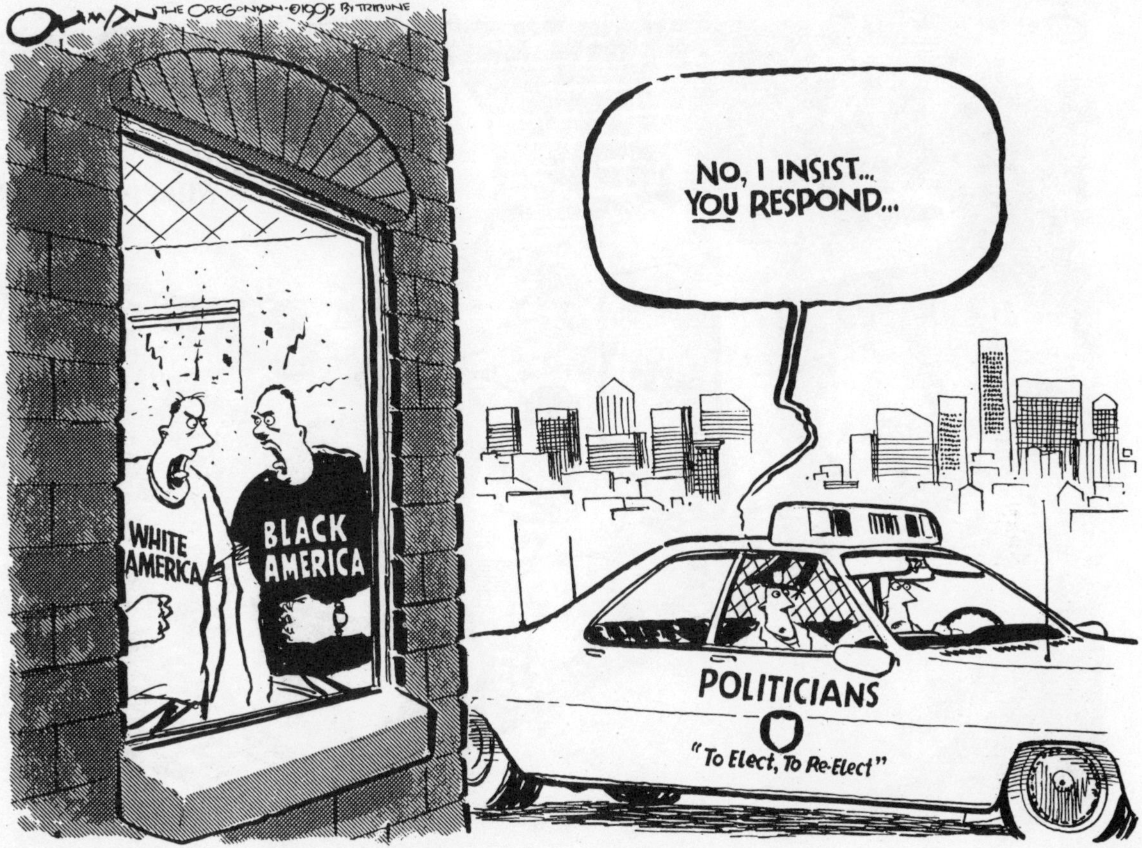
OHMAN THE OREGONIAN ©1995 BY TRIBUNE
NO, I INSIST... YOU RESPOND...
WHITE AMERICA
BLACK AMERICA
POLITICIANS
"To Elect, To Re-Elect"

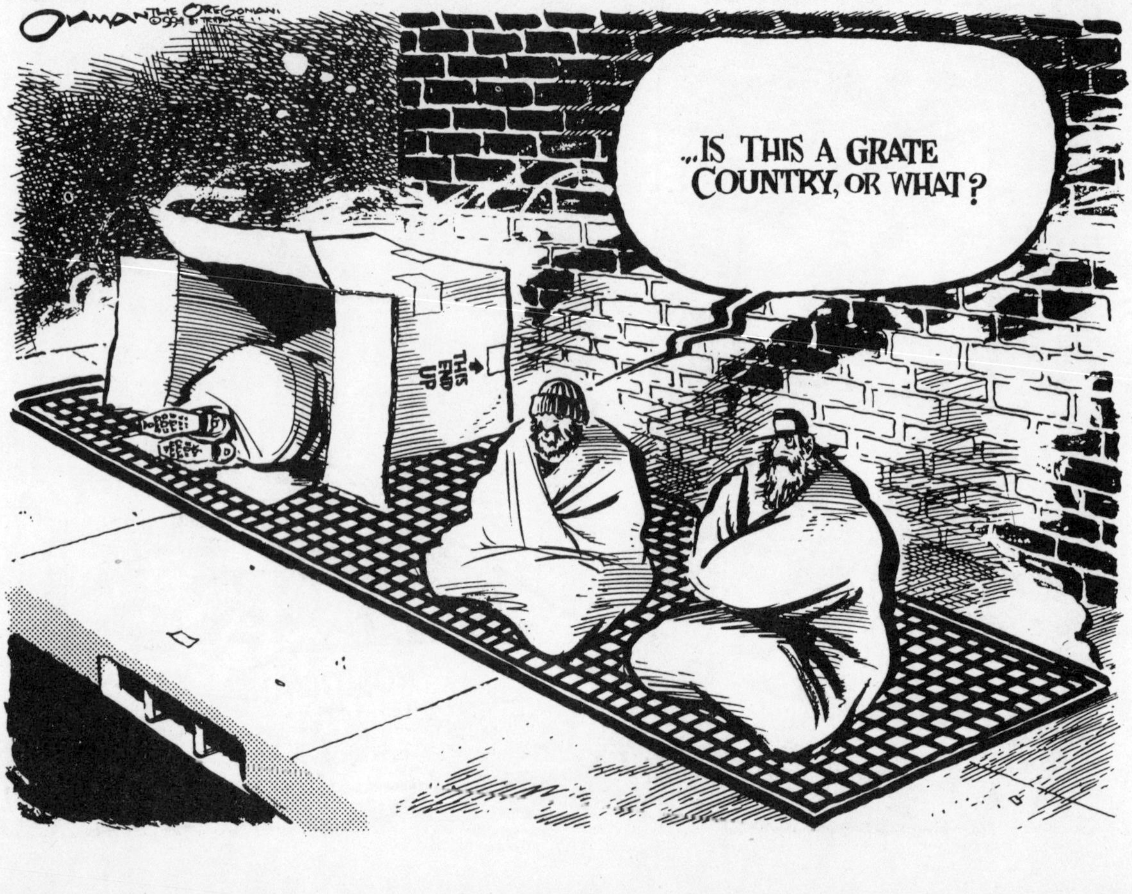
THE OREGONIAN
...IS THIS A GRATE COUNTRY, OR WHAT?
THIS END UP

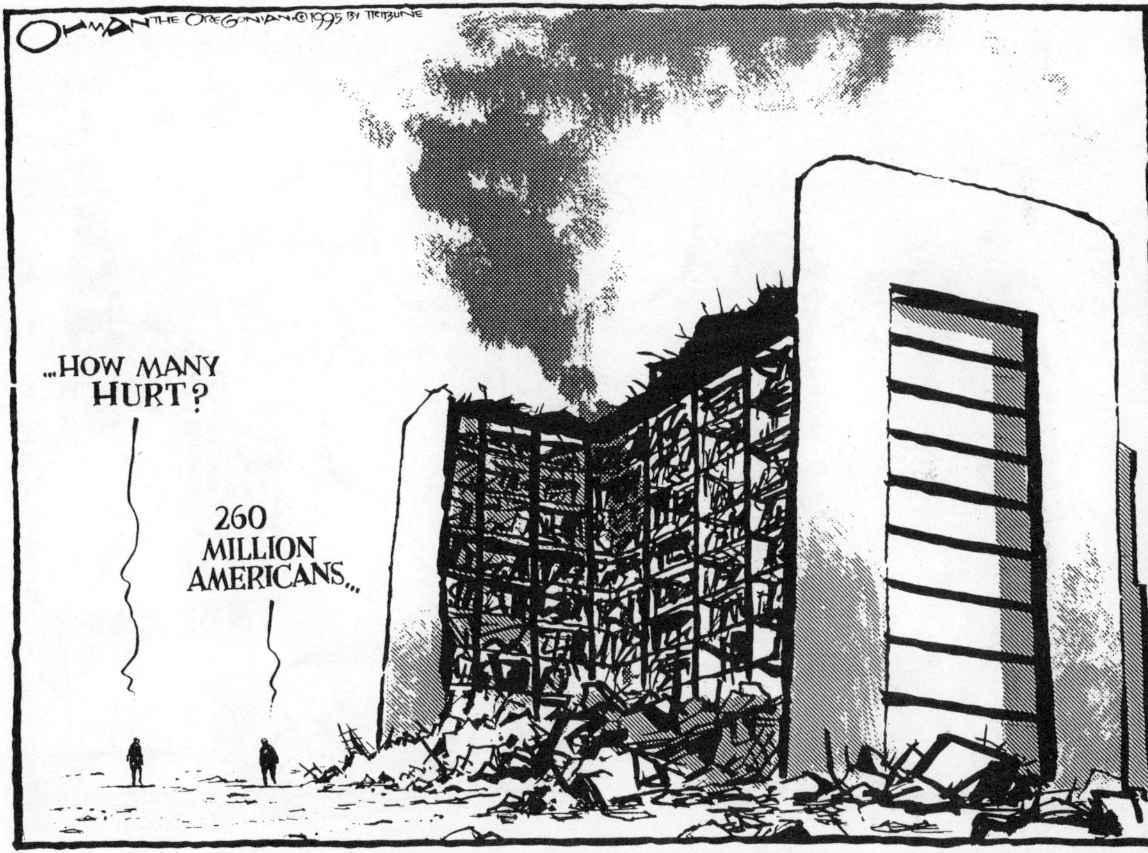
OHMAN THE OREGONIAN ©1995 BY TRIBUNE
...HOW MANY HURT?
260 MILLION AMERICANS...

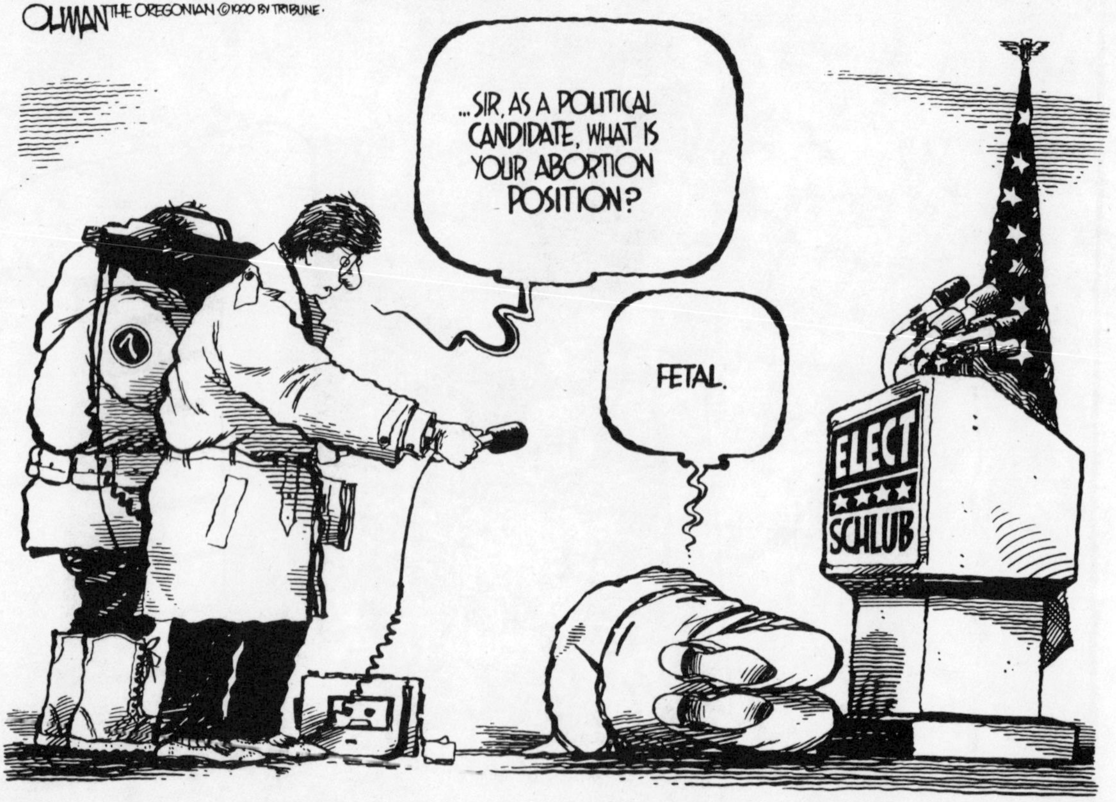
OHMAN THE OREGONIAN ©1990 BY TRIBUNE
...SIR, AS A POLITICAL CANDIDATE, WHAT IS YOUR ABORTION POSITION?
FETAL.
7
ELECT
SCHLUB

# THE POLITICS OF MEANINGLESSNESS

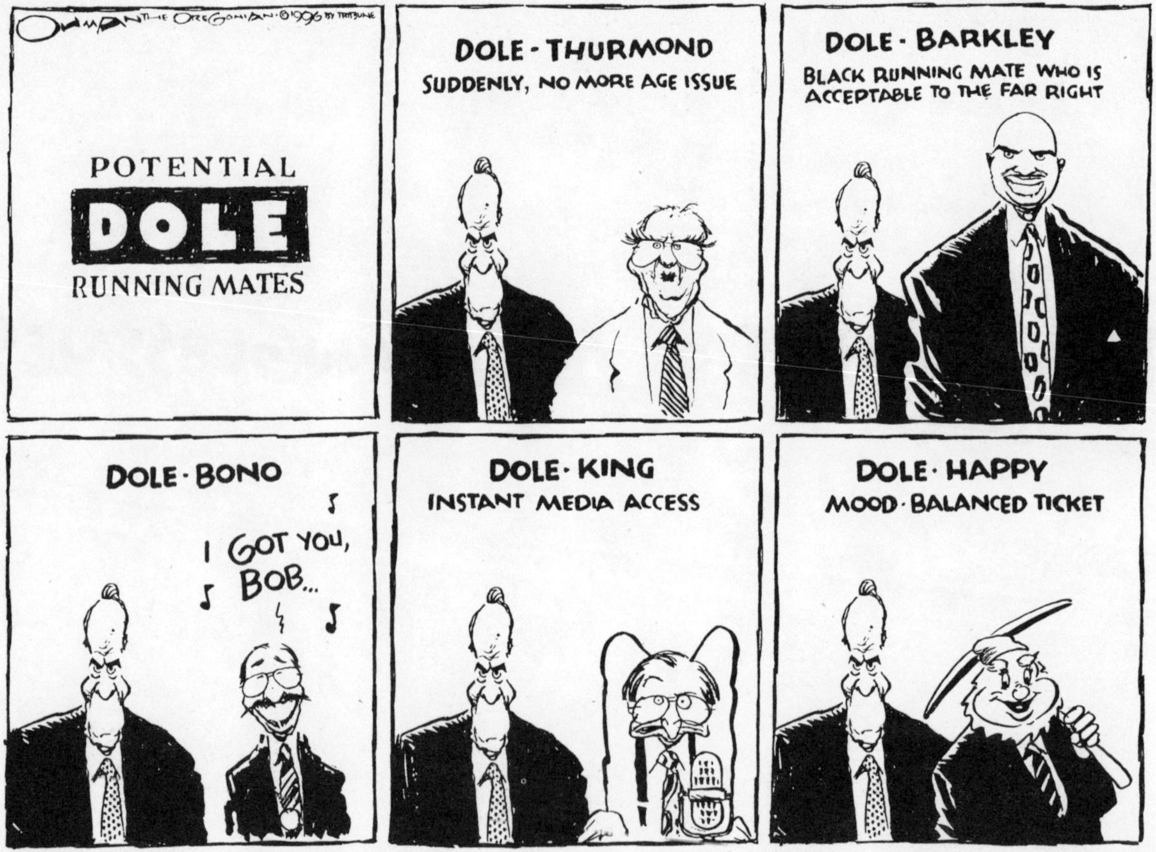
OHMAN THE OREGONIAN ©1996 BY TRIBUNE
POTENTIAL
DOLE
RUNNING MATES
DOLE - THURMOND
SUDDENLY, NO MORE AGE ISSUE
DOLE · BARKLEY
BLACK RUNNING MATE WHO IS ACCEPTABLE TO THE FAR RIGHT
DOLE · BONO
I GOT YOU, BOB...
DOLE · KING
INSTANT MEDIA ACCESS
DOLE · HAPPY
MOOD · BALANCED TICKET

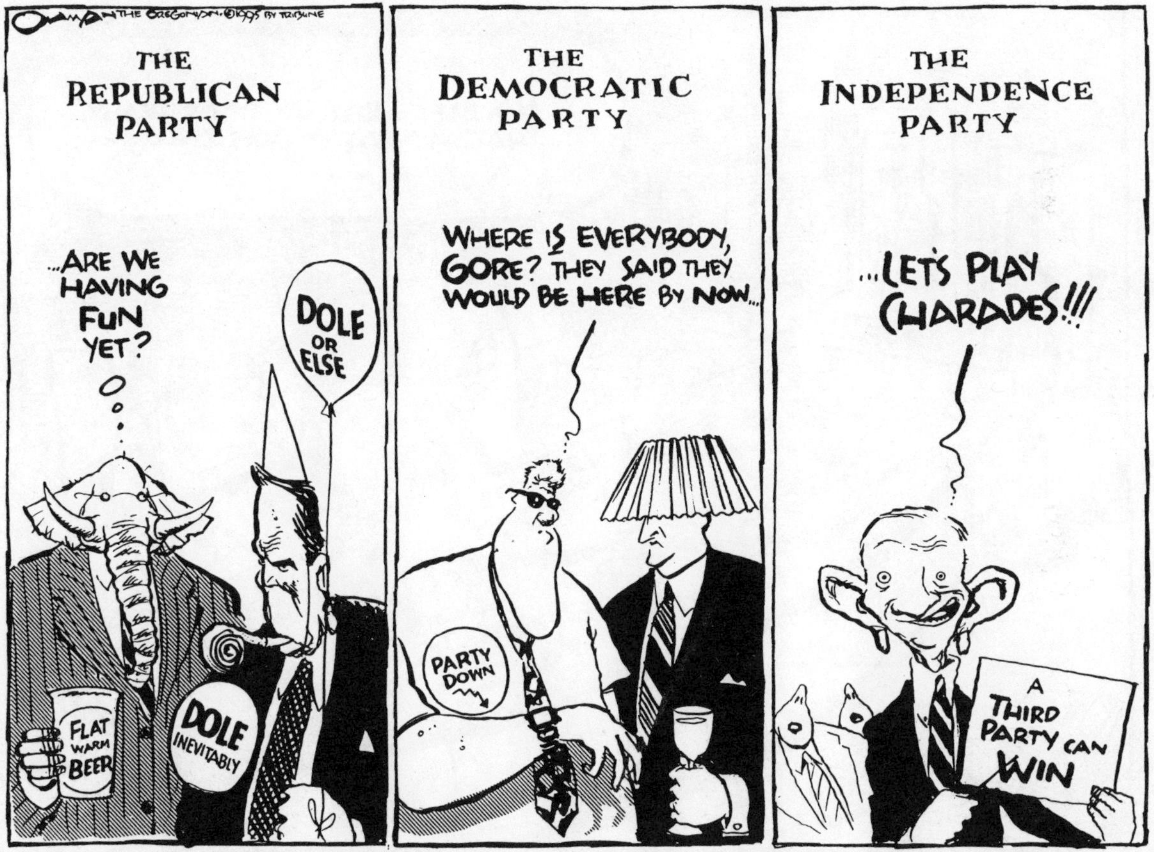
OHMAN THE OREGONIAN ©1995 BY TRIBUNE
THE REPUBLICAN PARTY
...ARE WE HAVING FUN YET?
DOLE OR ELSE
FLAT WARM BEER
DOLE INEVITABLY
THE DEMOCRATIC PARTY
WHERE IS EVERYBODY, GORE? THEY SAID THEY WOULD BE HERE BY NOW...
PARTY DOWN
THE INDEPENDENCE PARTY
...LET'S PLAY CHARADES!!!
A THIRD PARTY CAN WIN

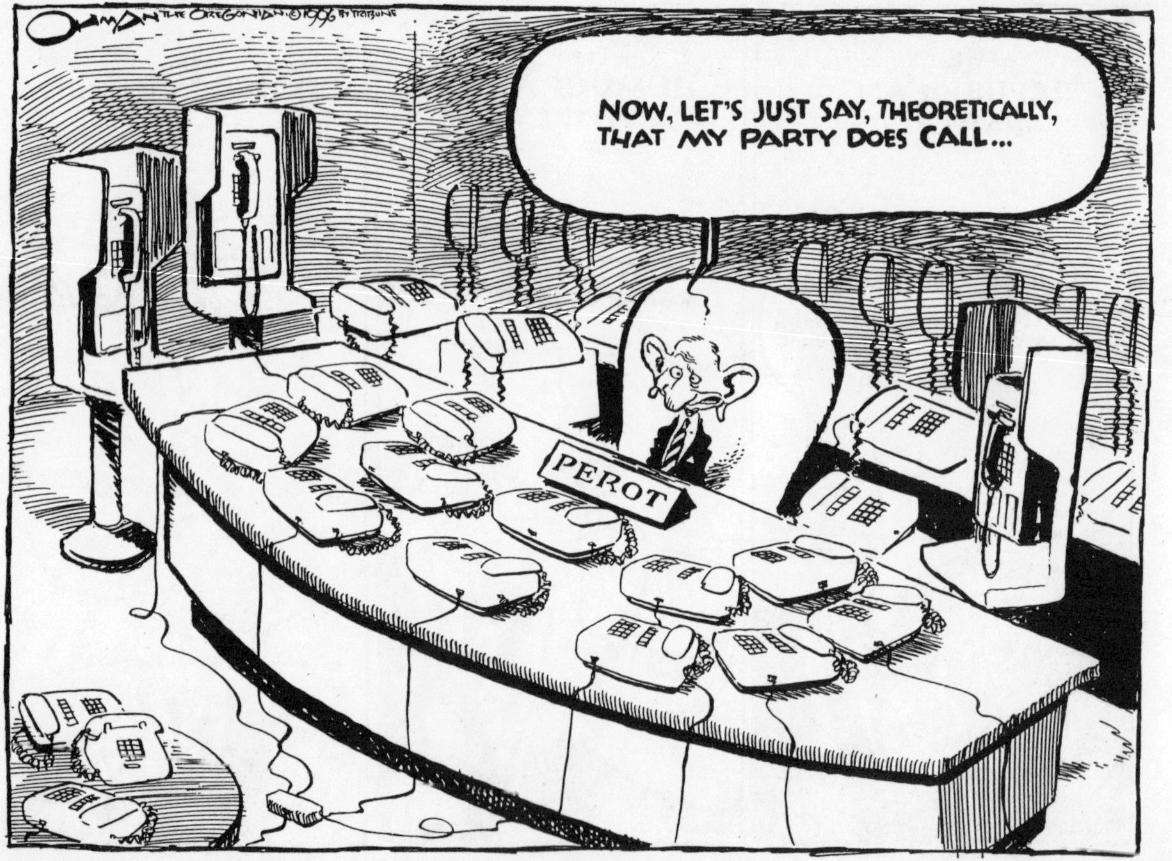
OHMAN THE OREGONIAN ©1996 BY TRIBUNE
NOW, LET'S JUST SAY, THEORETICALLY, THAT MY PARTY DOES CALL...
PEROT

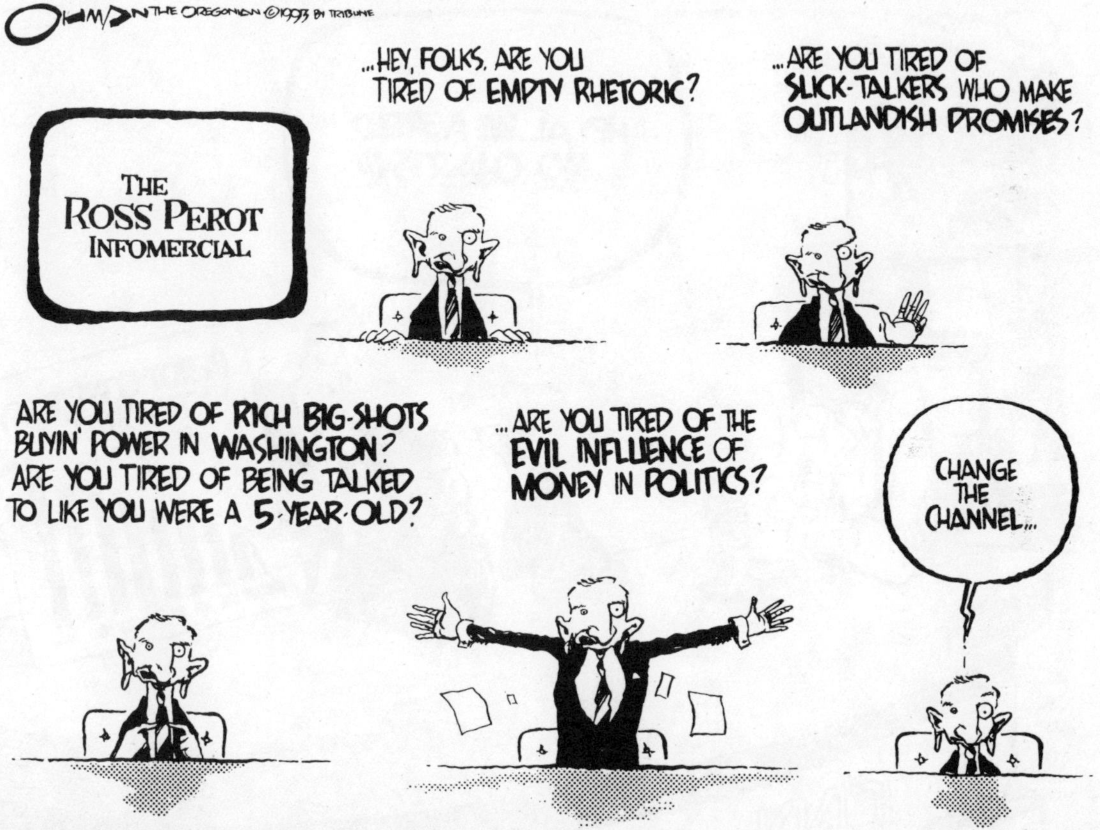
OHMAN THE OREGONIAN ©1993 BY TRIBUNE
THE ROSS PEROT INFOMERCIAL
...HEY, FOLKS, ARE YOU TIRED OF EMPTY RHETORIC?
...ARE YOU TIRED OF SLICK-TALKERS WHO MAKE OUTLANDISH PROMISES?
ARE YOU TIRED OF RICH BIG-SHOTS BUYIN' POWER IN WASHINGTON? ARE YOU TIRED OF BEING TALKED TO LIKE YOU WERE A 5-YEAR-OLD?
...ARE YOU TIRED OF THE EVIL INFLUENCE OF MONEY IN POLITICS?
CHANGE THE CHANNEL...

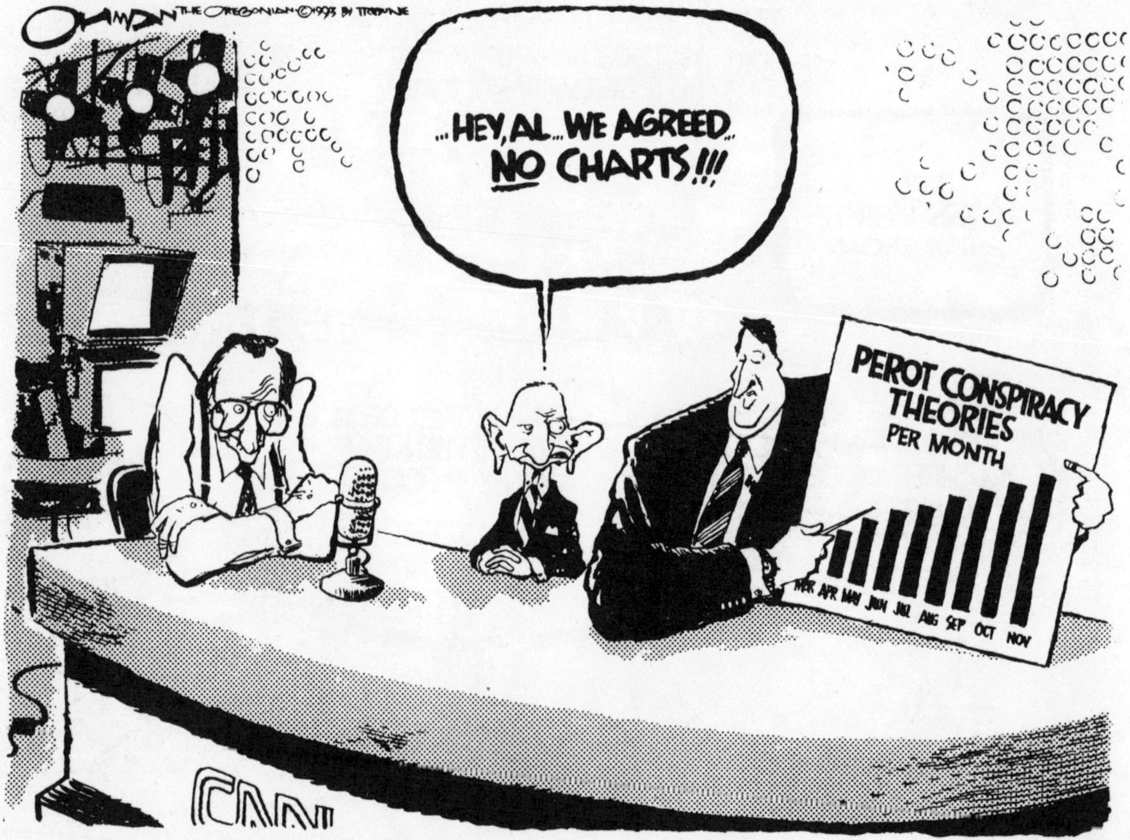
OHMAN THE OREGONIAN ©1993 BY TRIBUNE
...HEY, AL... WE AGREED... NO CHARTS!!!
PEROT CONSPIRACY THEORIES PER MONTH
MAR APR MAY JUN JUL AUG SEP OCT NOV
CNN

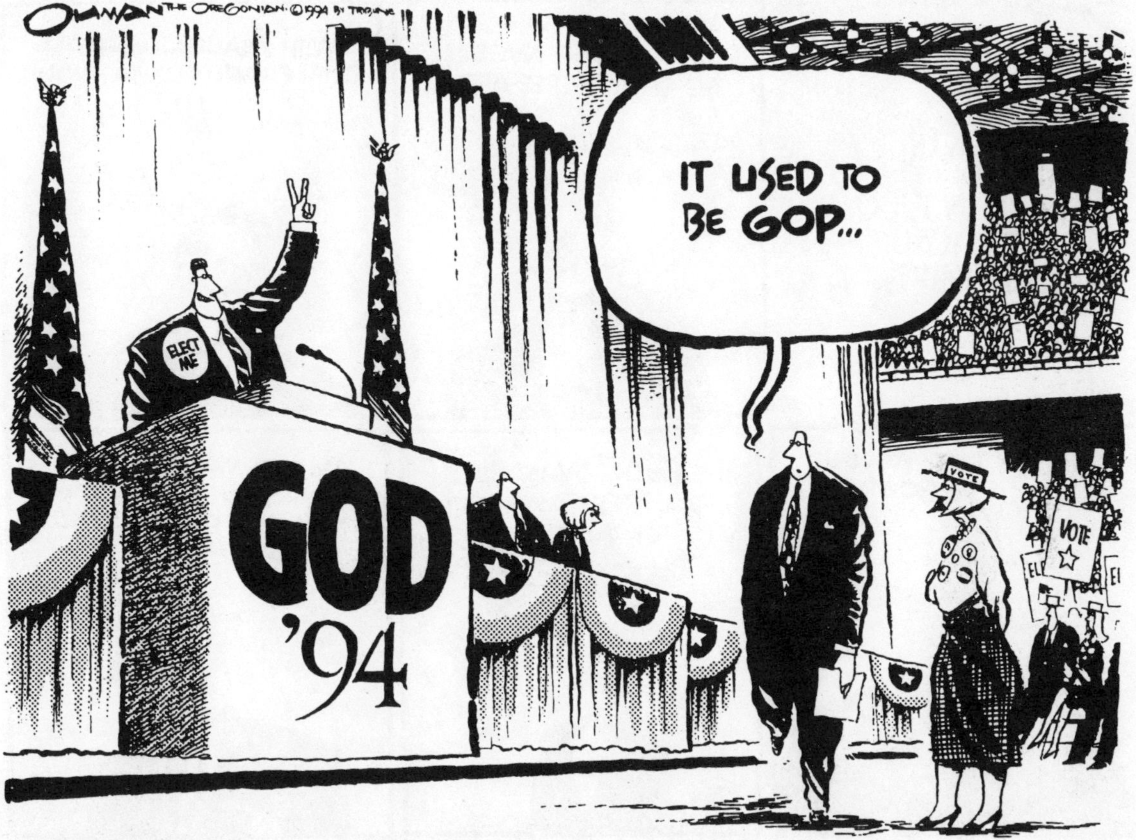
OLIPHANT THE OREGONIAN ©1994 BY TRIBUNE
IT USED TO BE GOP...
ELECT ME
GOD '94
VOTE
VOTE

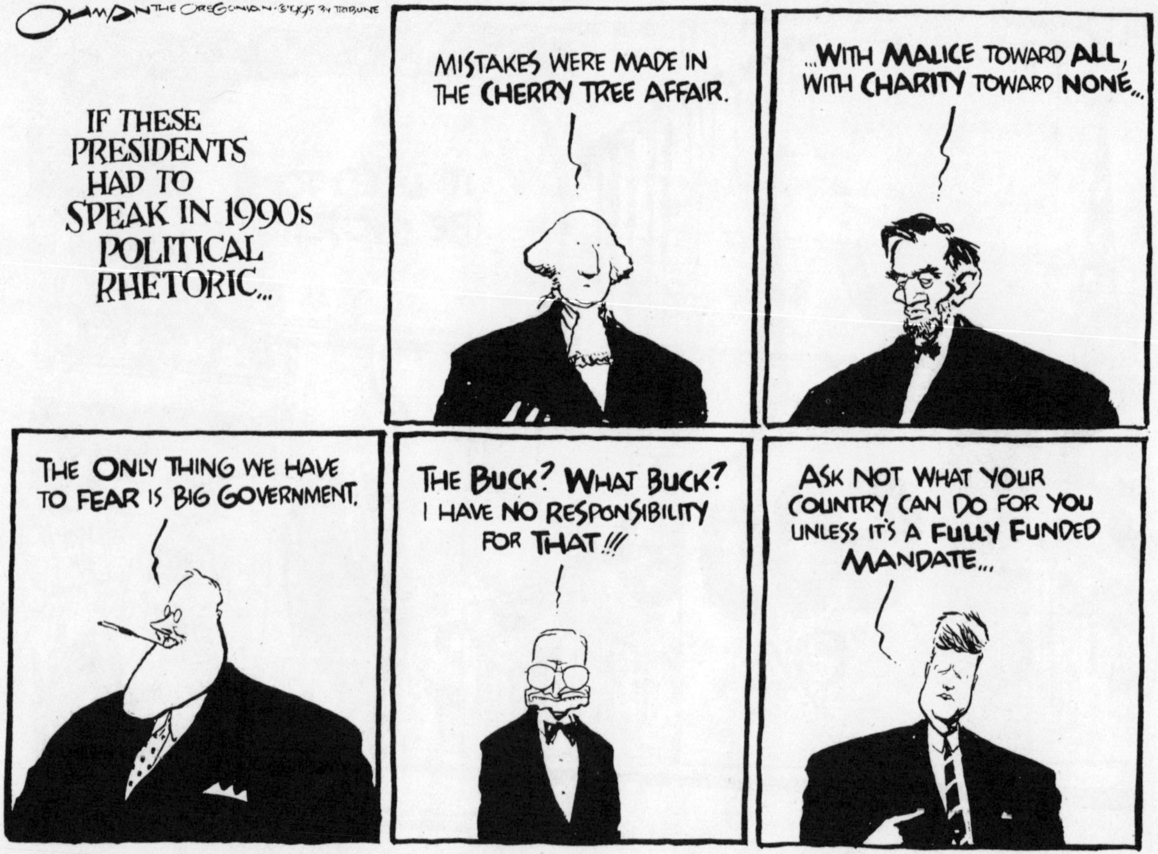
IF THESE PRESIDENTS HAD TO SPEAK IN 1990s POLITICAL RHETORIC...
MISTAKES WERE MADE IN THE CHERRY TREE AFFAIR.
...WITH MALICE TOWARD ALL, WITH CHARITY TOWARD NONE...
THE ONLY THING WE HAVE TO FEAR IS BIG GOVERNMENT.
THE BUCK? WHAT BUCK? I HAVE NO RESPONSIBILITY FOR THAT!!!
ASK NOT WHAT YOUR COUNTRY CAN DO FOR YOU UNLESS IT'S A FULLY FUNDED MANDATE...

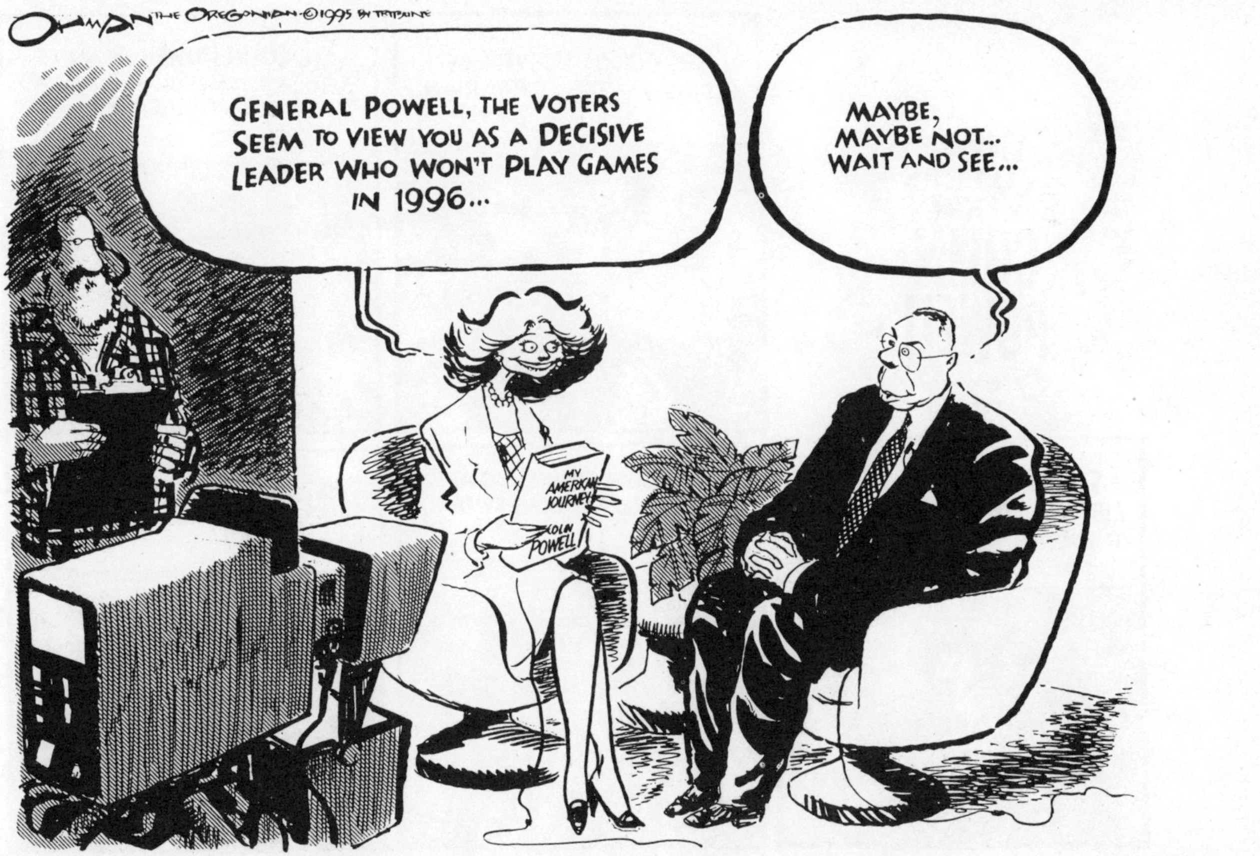
OHMAN THE OREGONIAN ©1995 BY TRIBUNE
GENERAL POWELL, THE VOTERS SEEM TO VIEW YOU AS A DECISIVE LEADER WHO WON'T PLAY GAMES IN 1996...
MAYBE, MAYBE NOT... WAIT AND SEE...
MY AMERICAN JOURNEY COLIN POWELL

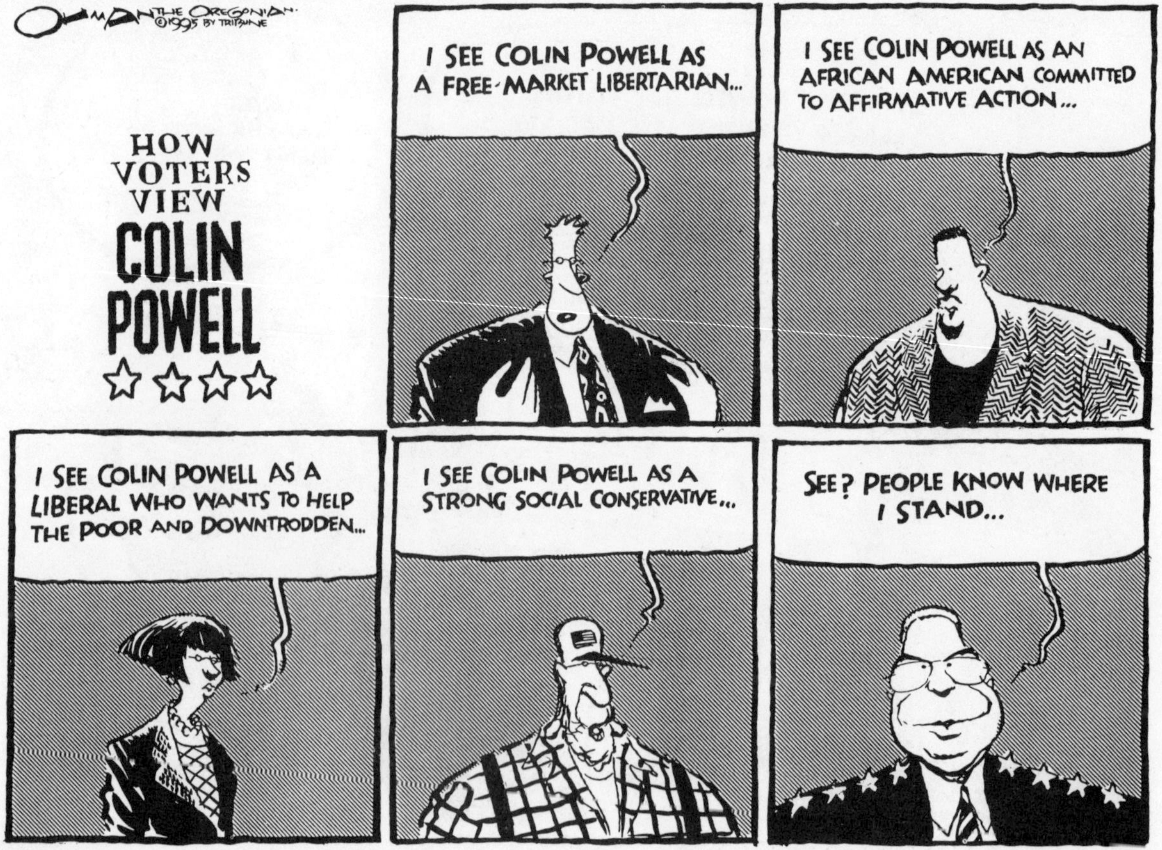
OLIPHANT THE OREGONIAN ©1995 BY TRIBUNE
HOW VOTERS VIEW COLIN POWELL
I SEE COLIN POWELL AS A FREE-MARKET LIBERTARIAN...
I SEE COLIN POWELL AS AN AFRICAN AMERICAN COMMITTED TO AFFIRMATIVE ACTION...
I SEE COLIN POWELL AS A LIBERAL WHO WANTS TO HELP THE POOR AND DOWNTRODDEN...
I SEE COLIN POWELL AS A STRONG SOCIAL CONSERVATIVE...
SEE? PEOPLE KNOW WHERE I STAND...

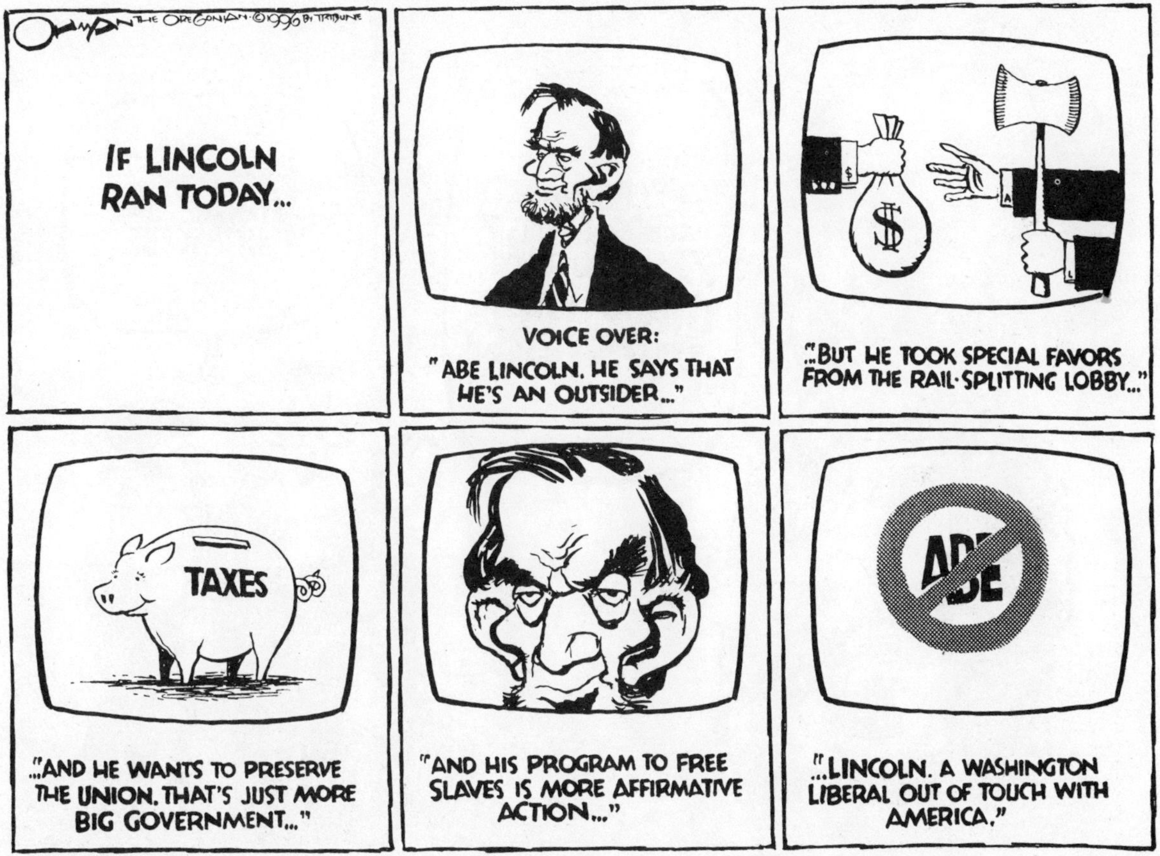

THE OREGONIAN ©1996 BY TRIBUNE
IF LINCOLN RAN TODAY...
VOICE OVER:
"ABE LINCOLN. HE SAYS THAT HE'S AN OUTSIDER..."
"...BUT HE TOOK SPECIAL FAVORS FROM THE RAIL-SPLITTING LOBBY..."
$
TAXES
"...AND HE WANTS TO PRESERVE THE UNION. THAT'S JUST MORE BIG GOVERNMENT..."
"AND HIS PROGRAM TO FREE SLAVES IS MORE AFFIRMATIVE ACTION..."
ABE
"...LINCOLN. A WASHINGTON LIBERAL OUT OF TOUCH WITH AMERICA."

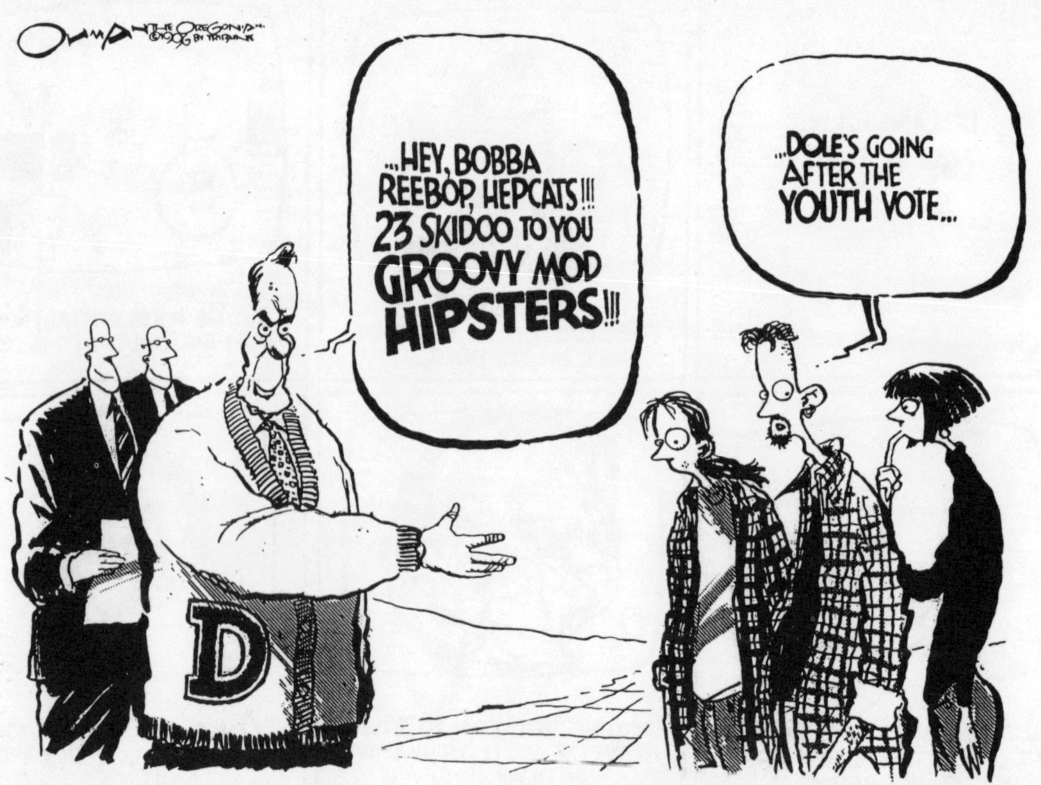
...HEY, BOBBA REEBOP, HEPCATS!!! 23 SKIDOO TO YOU GROOVY MOD HIPSTERS!!!
...DOLE'S GOING AFTER THE YOUTH VOTE...

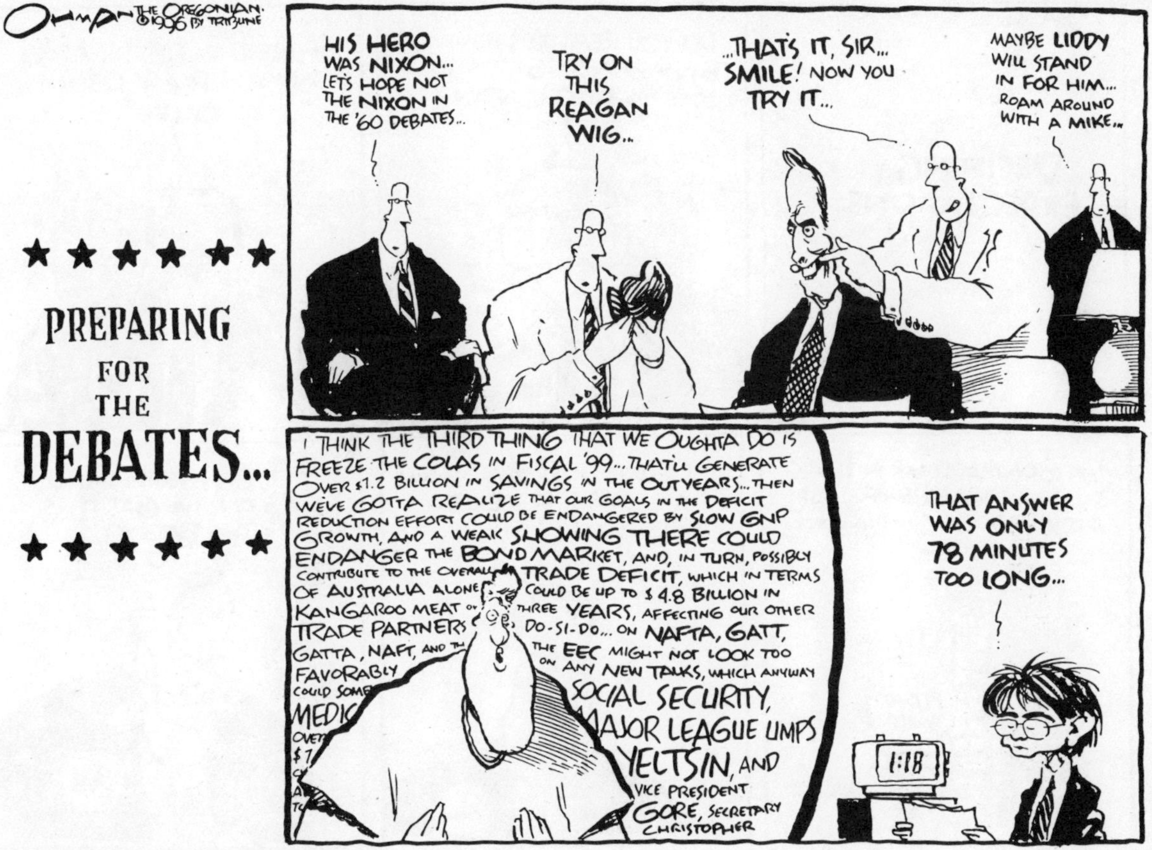
OHMAN THE OREGONIAN ©1996 BY TRIBUNE
PREPARING FOR THE DEBATES...
HIS HERO WAS NIXON... LET'S HOPE NOT THE NIXON IN THE '60 DEBATES...
TRY ON THIS REAGAN WIG...
...THAT'S IT, SIR... SMILE! NOW YOU TRY IT...
MAYBE LIDDY WILL STAND IN FOR HIM... ROAM AROUND WITH A MIKE...
I THINK THE THIRD THING THAT WE OUGHTA DO IS
FREEZE THE COLAS IN FISCAL '99... THAT'LL GENERATE
OVER $1.2 BILLION IN SAVINGS IN THE OUTYEARS... THEN
WE'VE GOTTA REALIZE THAT OUR GOALS IN THE DEFICIT
REDUCTION EFFORT COULD BE ENDANGERED BY SLOW GNP
GROWTH, AND A WEAK SHOWING THERE COULD
ENDANGER THE BOND MARKET, AND, IN TURN, POSSIBLY
CONTRIBUTE TO THE OVERALL TRADE DEFICIT, WHICH IN TERMS
OF AUSTRALIA ALONE COULD BE UP TO $4.8 BILLION IN
KANGAROO MEAT THREE YEARS, AFFECTING OUR OTHER
TRADE PARTNERS DO-SI-DO... ON NAFTA, GATT,
GATTA, NAFT, AND THE EEC MIGHT NOT LOOK TOO
FAVORABLY ON ANY NEW TALKS, WHICH ANYWAY
SOCIAL SECURITY,
MAJOR LEAGUE UMPS
YELTSIN, AND
VICE PRESIDENT
GORE, SECRETARY
CHRISTOPHER
THAT ANSWER WAS ONLY 78 MINUTES TOO LONG...
1:18

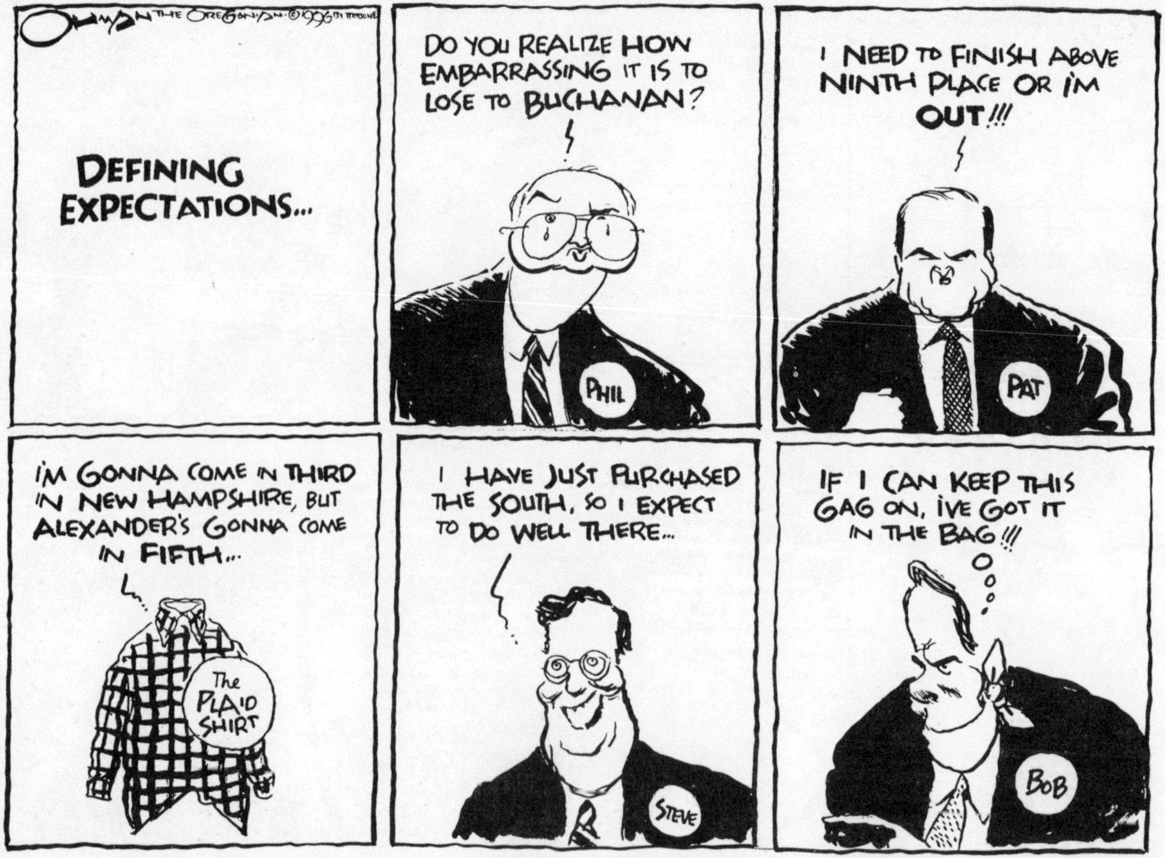

OHMAN THE OREGONIAN ©1996 BY TRIBUNE
DEFINING EXPECTATIONS...
DO YOU REALIZE HOW EMBARRASSING IT IS TO LOSE TO BUCHANAN?
PHIL
I NEED TO FINISH ABOVE NINTH PLACE OR I'M OUT!!!
PAT
I'M GONNA COME IN THIRD IN NEW HAMPSHIRE, BUT ALEXANDER'S GONNA COME IN FIFTH...
The PLAID SHIRT
I HAVE JUST PURCHASED THE SOUTH, SO I EXPECT TO DO WELL THERE...
STEVE
IF I CAN KEEP THIS GAG ON, I'VE GOT IT IN THE BAG!!!
BOB

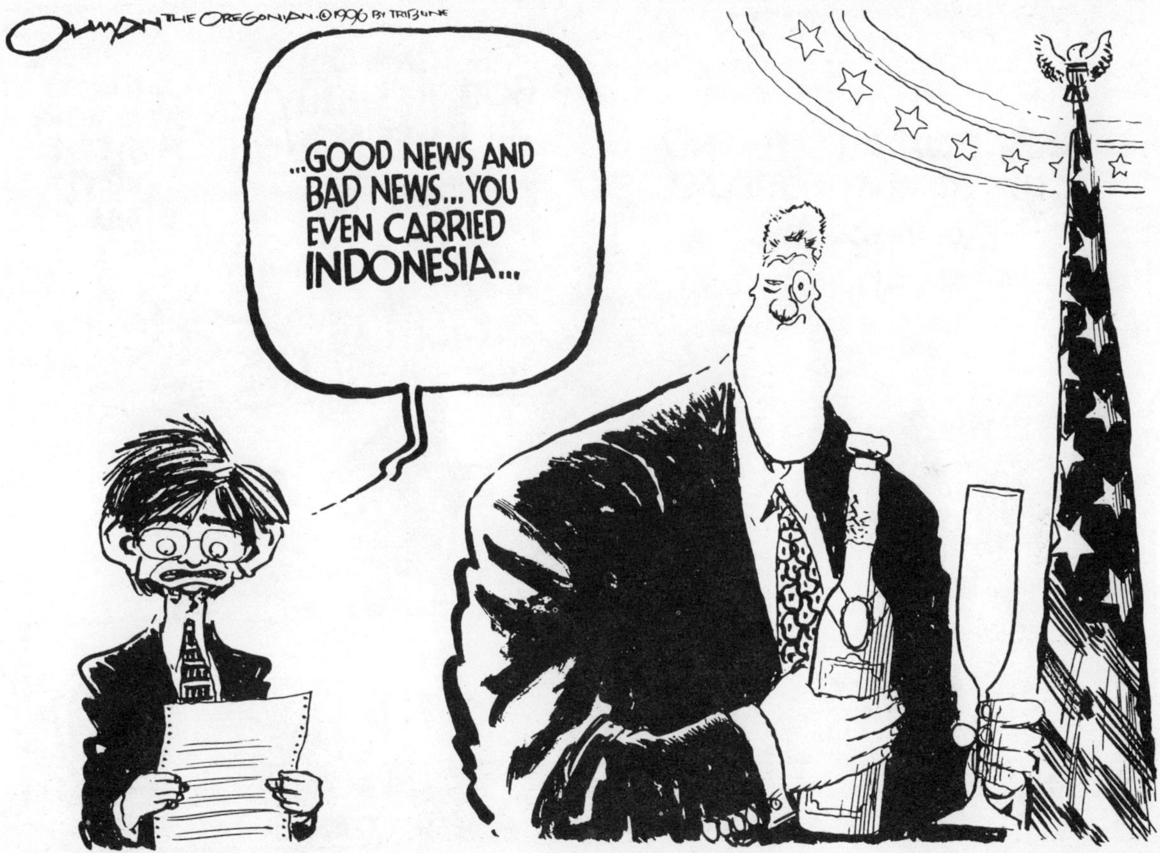
OLIPHANT THE OREGONIAN. ©1996 BY TRIBUNE
...GOOD NEWS AND BAD NEWS... YOU EVEN CARRIED INDONESIA...

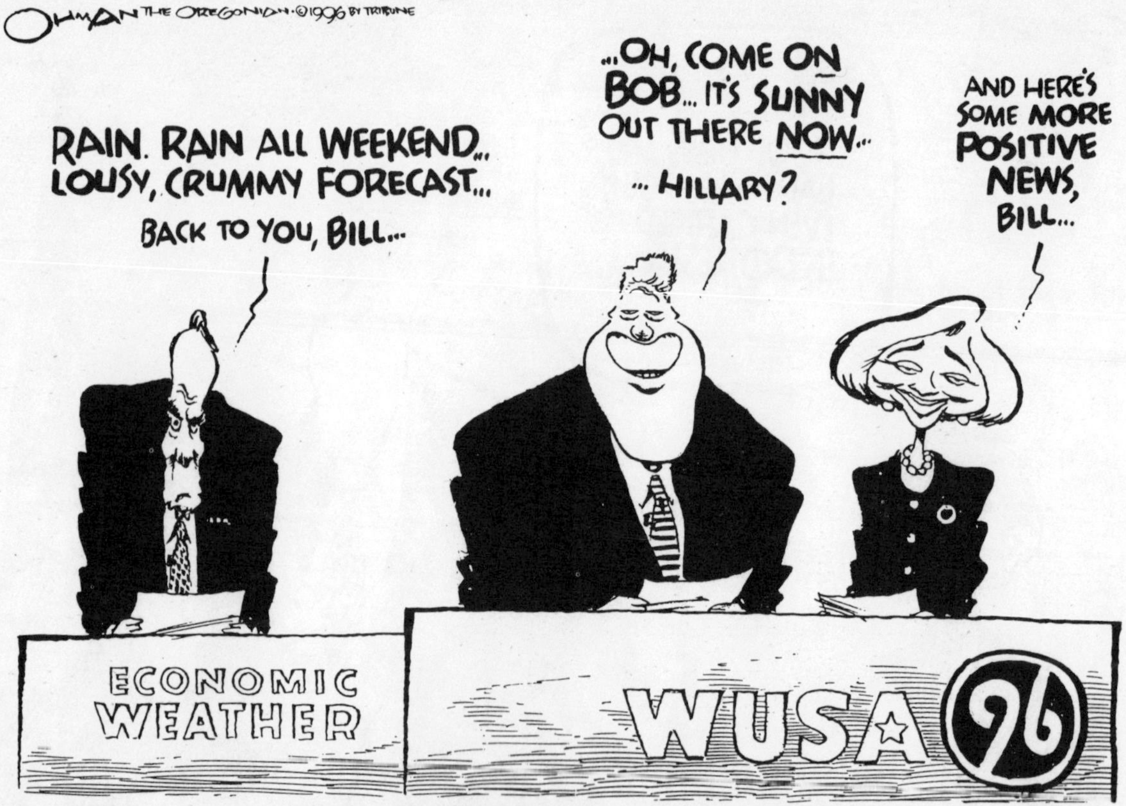
OHMAN THE OREGONIAN ©1996 BY TRIBUNE
RAIN. RAIN ALL WEEKEND... LOUSY, CRUMMY FORECAST...
BACK TO YOU, BILL...
...OH, COME ON BOB... IT'S SUNNY OUT THERE NOW...
... HILLARY?
AND HERE'S SOME MORE POSITIVE NEWS, BILL...
ECONOMIC WEATHER
WUSA 96

IF THE CAMPAIGN WERE A NEWS TEAM...

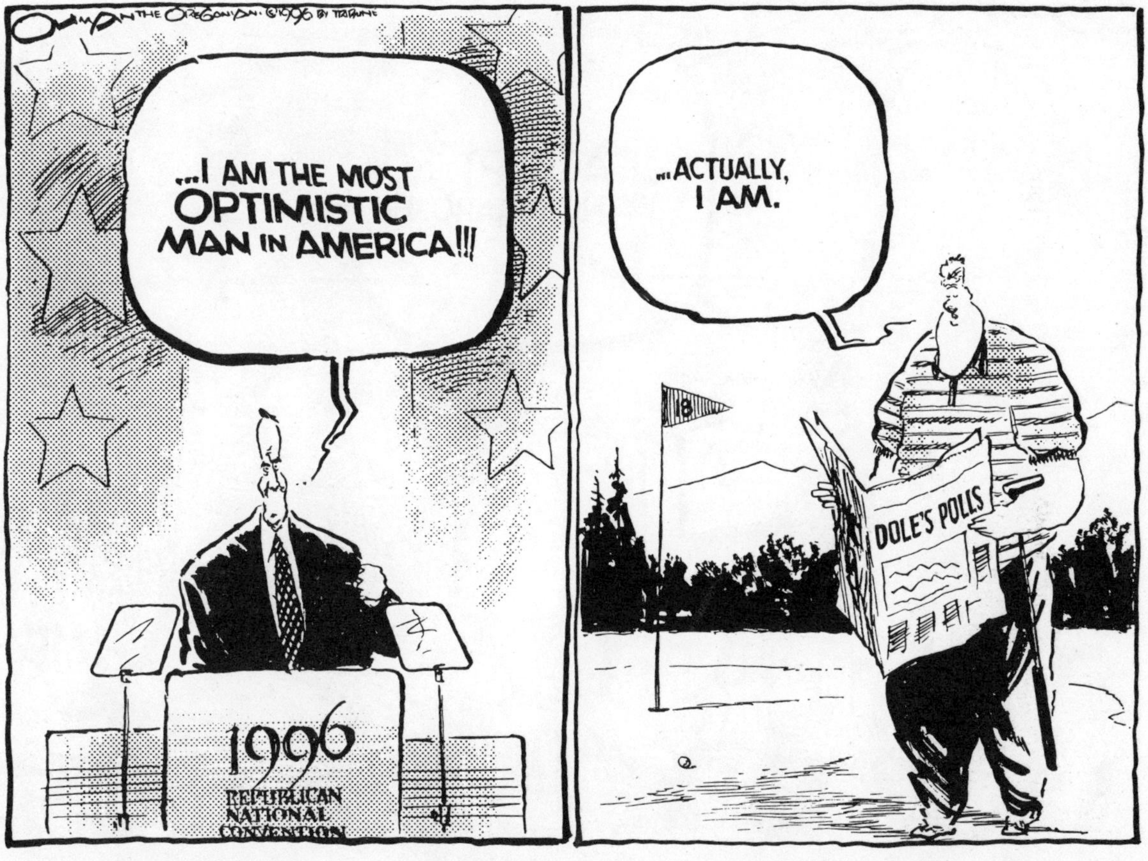
...I AM THE MOST OPTIMISTIC MAN IN AMERICA!!!
1996
REPUBLICAN NATIONAL CONVENTION
...ACTUALLY, I AM.
18
DOLE'S POLLS

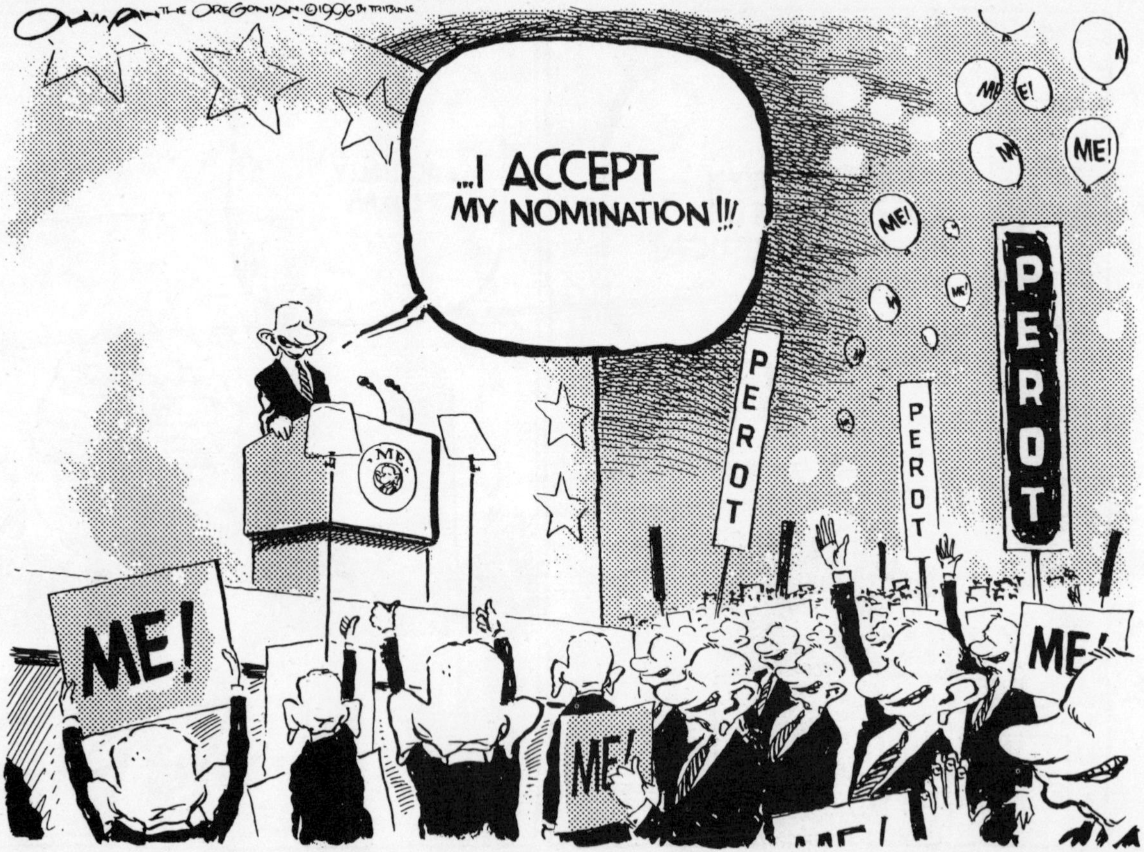
THE OREGONIAN ©1996
...I ACCEPT MY NOMINATION!!!
ME!
PEROT
PEROT
PEROT
ME!
ME!
ME!
ME!
ME!

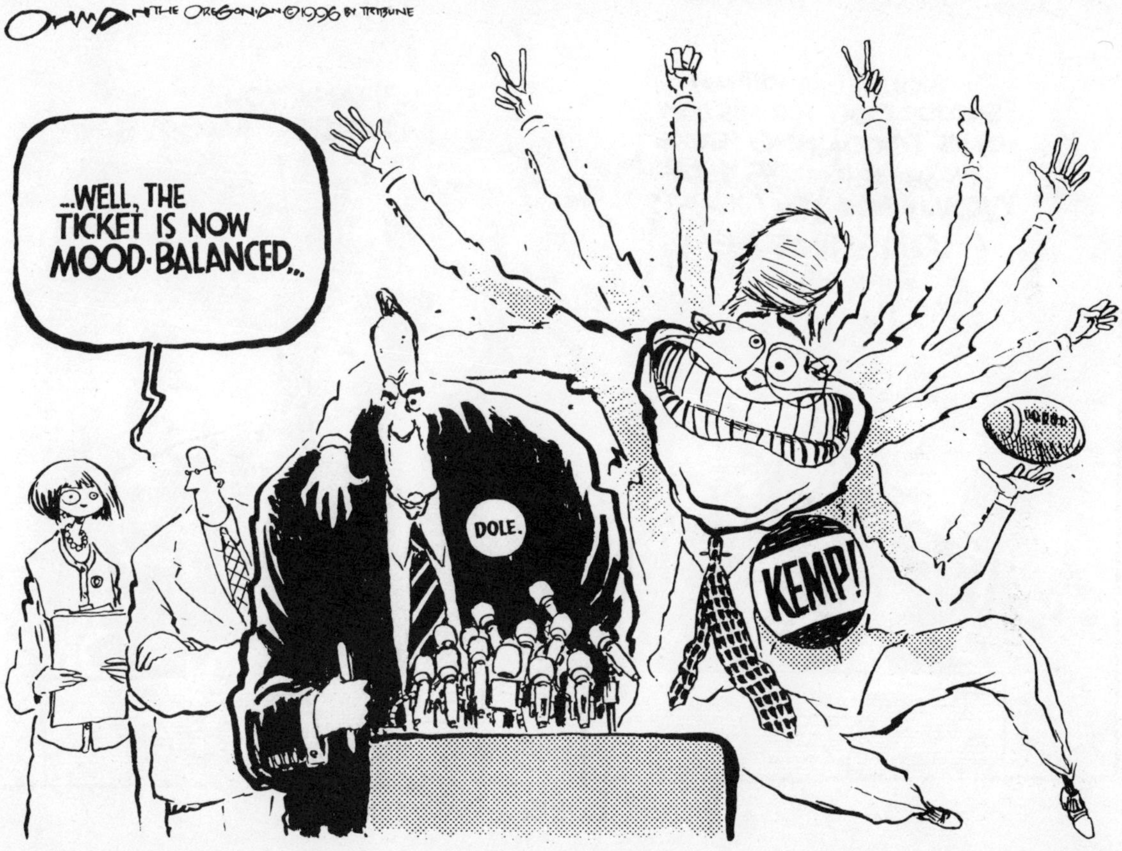
OHMAN THE OREGONIAN ©1996 BY TRIBUNE
...WELL, THE TICKET IS NOW MOOD-BALANCED...
DOLE.
KEMP!

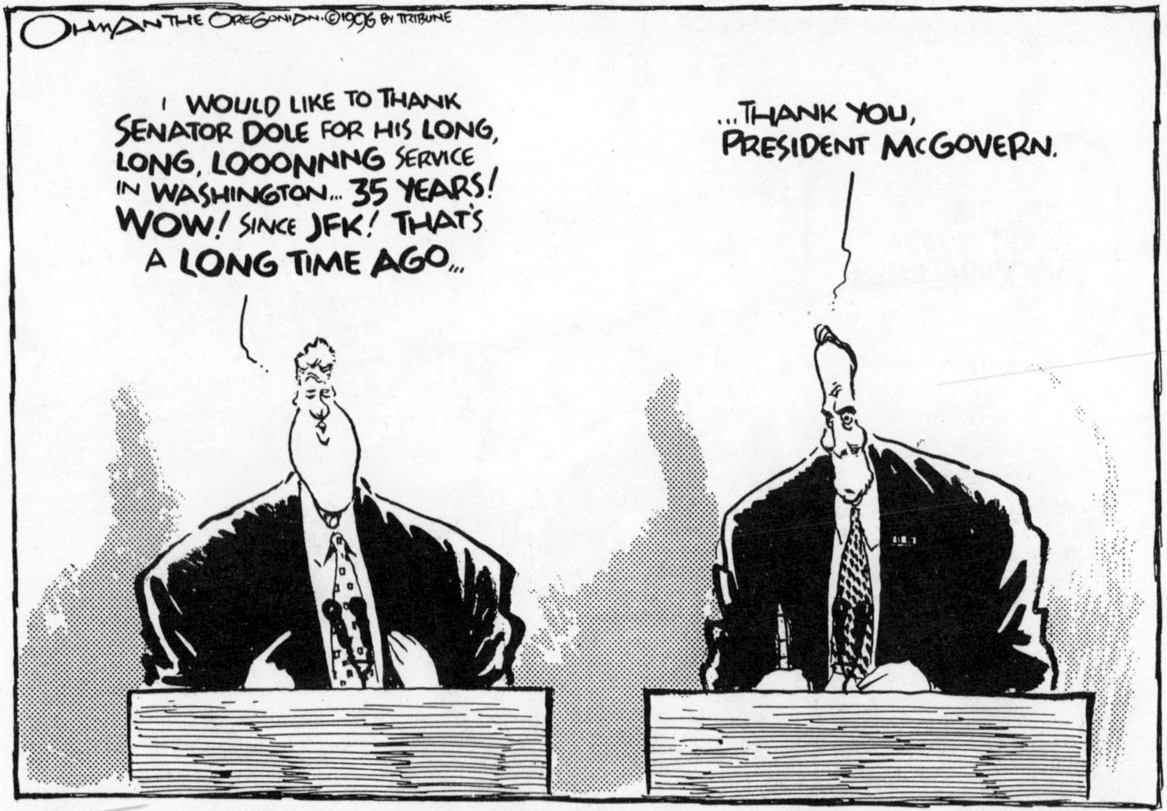
OHMAN THE OREGONIAN ©1996 BY TRIBUNE
I WOULD LIKE TO THANK SENATOR DOLE FOR HIS LONG, LONG, LOOOONNNG SERVICE IN WASHINGTON... 35 YEARS! WOW! SINCE JFK! THAT'S A LONG TIME AGO...
...THANK YOU, PRESIDENT McGOVERN.

THE CLOSING STATEMENTS.

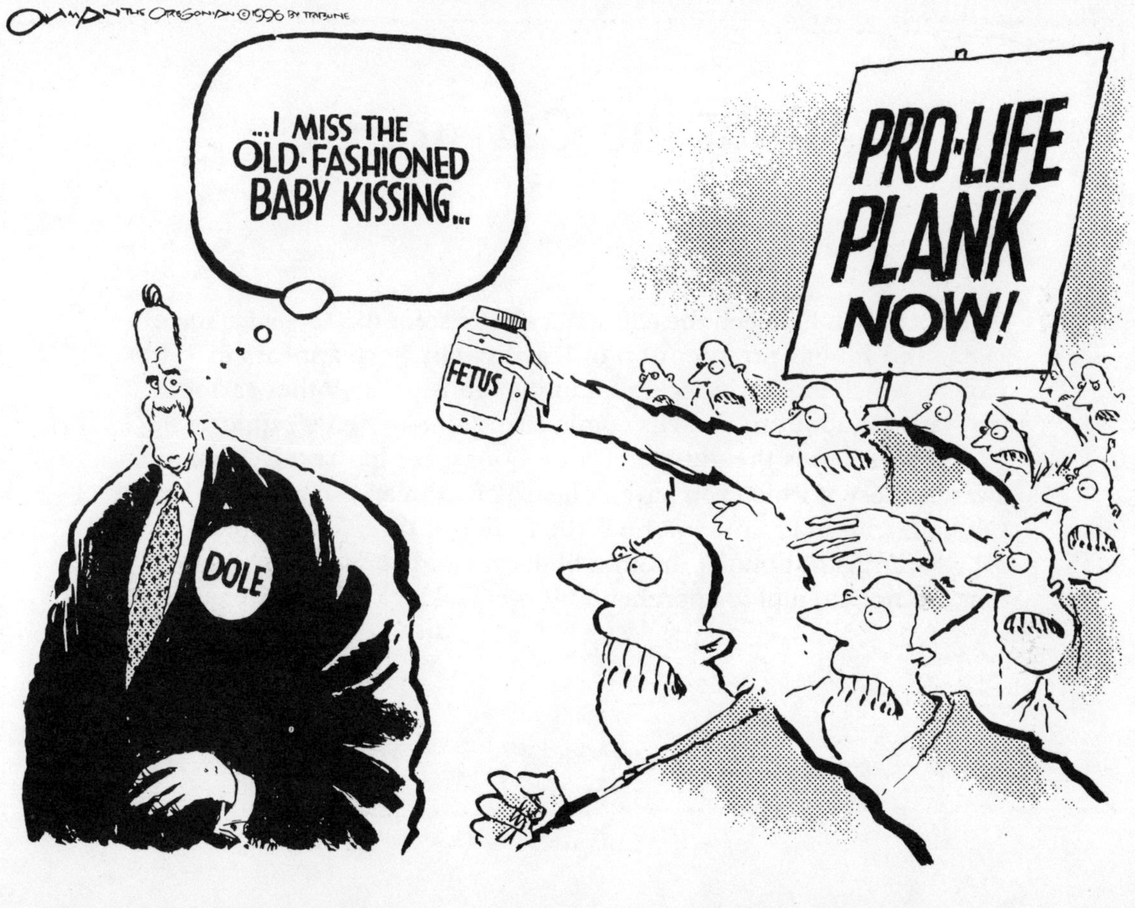
...I MISS THE OLD-FASHIONED BABY KISSING...
PRO-LIFE PLANK NOW!
FETUS
DOLE

# About the Cartoonist

Jack Ohman has been the editorial cartoonist for the *Oregonian* since 1983, and he has no intention of leaving. His work appears in 150 papers, which is a fairly accurate number considering other cartoonists flatly lie about theirs. His comic strip "Mixed Media" appears in 175 papers. He is the author of nine books. He has received many awards, most of which you haven't heard of. Ohman is married to Jan Ohman, who is a saint, and he is the father of three children. He is 5'11", weighs 170 pounds, and has blue eyes and comically overstated hair. Do not attempt to apprehend him yourself.